WOMEN EVOLVED

**Narratives of Love • Pain • Strength • Redemption
Of Single Women**

WOMEN EVOLVED

**Narratives of Love • Pain • Strength • Redemption
Of Single Women**

Kwaku Person-Lynn, PhD

Knowledge Power Books
Valencia, California 91355

Knowledge Power Books
A Division of Knowledge Power Communications, Inc.
25379 Wayne Mills Place, Suite 131
Valencia, California 91355
661-513-0308
www.knowledgepowerbooks.com

ISBN: 978-0-988864412
Library of Congress Control Number: 2013930813
Edited by: Michelle Otis
Cover Design: Rene Cross-Washington, rcwgrafx.com
Interior Design: John Sibley, Rock Solid Productions
Cover Art: Tina Allen

Printed in the United States of America

Tina Allen

Sculptor

1955 ~ 2008

CONTENTS

WOMEN EVOLVED

"If I never find a man in my life who is compatible with who I am, I'd like to think that I can make a very worthwhile, meaningful, and interesting life for myself as I have already done with or without a man."

"I want you to know that I know you really are interested in me, and that's good. It's very important for you to know, I do not believe in having a sexual relationship. The next time that is going to occur, I am going to be a married woman."

"He was sitting across from me and I kept noticing him. Actually, I approached him. There was just something about him. I felt I had to meet him. I didn't know what was going on; I just knew that I had to meet this man. I had to have an experience with him."

"Maybe part of me didn't feel that I was worthy of getting what I wanted. I had to come to the realization that I am a child of God. I am worthy and I am holding out for a real love."

Nadia - 97

"Her friendship alone was soothing to my whole being. Women share intimate relationships that could be classified as lesbian love. It's just that the physical is left out of it. At the time, she nurtured the part of me that he kept tormenting."

Cynthia Stanford - 123

"After marriage, I involved myself in other relationships immediately. I don't know why, but my whole life I've never been without a man. I've had boyfriends since I was 15. I didn't know how to be by myself. I didn't want to be by myself."

Margaret Richardson - 145

"I can say to him or anyone else, 'Hey, I really tried to make that work.' It wasn't until it was shattered completely that I say, 'Okay, this isn't going to work.'"

Yvette Mackeka - 169

"Men have abused their positions. They have abused their authority. Women are saying, 'No. You don't know how to behave. You don't know how to make the position you want the woman to be in worth her time.'"

Loretta Fuqua - 189

"I wanted a commitment. I wanted this person to stand before God, the world, and everything else and say, 'This is my wife,' as opposed to saying, 'This is my lady.'"

Makeda Shareem - 221

"I will not approach a lighter-complexioned Black guy for the simple fact that perhaps he doesn't feel that I am as attractive as a lighter-skinned Black woman."

Shanté Lewis - 239

"Men have to realize that women do not just automatically appear and not have a previous life. They've experienced different things that make them who they are today."

About the Author - 258

Acknowledgments

Eternal praise to the Creator of the Universe for all that has been given to us. Isidra, for being my great woman and partner, and our sons: Jaaye, Jarim, So, Ayo, and Ravim for making me smile every day. Thank you so much to the magnificent, wonderful, and beautiful ladies who allowed me to share their stories for the benefit of those who want to have a positive and fulfilling relationship or just an understanding. Thank you, Adrienne Lynn, my sister, for being so encouraging and helpful. Joanne Lynn Hollis, my sister, for helping me to understand. Terry McMillan, for laying such a huge foundation. The late Tina Allen, one of the world's most renowned sculptresses, for allowing me to use her creativity for the cover. Musical accompaniment: John Coltrane, it's still "A Love Supreme." And all the men and women who are growing and sharing, so that love and understanding are the most prevailing forces between them. René Cross-Washington for the beautiful cover design and Ravim O. Lynn for cover inspiration. Willa Robinson for seeing the vision and making it reality; you are beyond special. Lastly, for all men who take responsibility.

Introduction

Do I want a man?
Do I need a man?
Yes.
If he is a good man.

--- Universal Woman Code

Statement of Purpose

The best possible way for men to understand the intimate thoughts of women on relationships is to put some energy and focus into what women are about and what women have to say. Entering the soul essence of women, who are willing to bring forth their deepest inner feelings, thoughts, and experiences. It is a rare occasion when that happens. *WOMEN EVOLVED* makes every effort humanly possible to bring a new reality in the discussion of relationships. It contains the narratives of eleven single women, at the time of writing, who explain the myriad of circumstances they have gone through in their intimate relationships with men. It also embodies the human and spiritual transformations many of the women went through to arrive at a state of contentment with themselves. These are women of various backgrounds, ages, and geographical origins.

This is not a how-to book, but slices of real life that serve as a reflection of what the various women, along with their male partners, endured in their relationships. They expose their joys, pains, recovery, enlightenment, and in a few cases, their private sexual experiences. For some, it was a spiritual journey of women trying to get along with men in a healthy relationship, but failed. The amazing revelation is how they survived and evolved as whole women. Through time, healing, and spiritual nurturing, they were able to arrive at a state of personal peace and rediscovery of who they are.

The women involved weave human interest stories of relationships that reverberate in the memory long after the last page has been turned. Delores Naylor, a 52-year-old woman, is the epitome of how one can be happy and content being alone. Georgia Millet, a 34-year-old woman, demonstrates how she has made religion the central issue in her relationships with men. Rita Moore, a 47-year-old business owner, explains how shyness affected her, but she was determined to experience the love of a man. Kamla Johnson, a 39-year-old divorced mother of one teenager, shows all of us how an extreme personal tragedy cannot hold back the human spirit. Nadia, a 27-year-old mother of a young child, reveals how a different female lifestyle affected her life. Cynthia Stanford, a 34-year-old divorced mother of three young children, is an example of how one can evolve out of a negative gang environment and succeed. Margaret Richardson, a 52-year-old divorced mother of one young adult, exposes us to the influence that being raised by a dominant father can have on relationships. Yvette Maceka, a 41-year-old single mother of one young child, is an example of a woman who supposedly does not support marriage. Loretta Fuqua, a 47-year-old divorced mother of one young child, displays the result of being too emotionally needy. Makeda Shareem, a 21-year-old university student, demonstrates how the effects of colorism can influence relationships. Shanté Lewis, a 42-year-old single woman, suffered from early sexual abuse and perceives herself as "damaged goods."

Personal Statement

Thinking about the concept for this book, I knew I wanted to do something on women. This was a burning issue with me. Though the idea had been floating around my head for some time, I wasn't sure how to approach the subject. Most of my work is in the scholarly area. It had always concerned me when I heard women ask at conferences, talk radio shows, personal conversations, and so forth, "All of this knowledge you are giving us is good, and we certainly need it, but how does it help me with my relationship? I need help." Most of the scholars I have heard respond to that concern could not adequately reply.

While walking one day, when I do my clearest, solitary thinking, it dawned on me, "As men, we do not intimately know what is in the minds of our women." There is so much discussion about relationships, but we men do not actually know the inner soul of women and what they are really thinking. Other than movies and personal experiences, many of our impressions come from literary depictions.

Of course, we have such works as: *Black Macho and the Myth of the Super Woman, The Color Purple* and *Waiting to Exhale.* We even had *A Blackman's Guide to Understanding the Black Woman*, and the classic works of Toni Morrison, among several other brilliant works. We also have the great inspirational works of Iyanla Vanzant and the pioneering works of Riane Eisler. Valiant efforts, all of them, but their common thread: they were all written by women.

Realizing this, the task began to reveal itself. "What if there was a book that unveiled the unknown essence of several women: their growth, feelings, mistakes, influences, and the fierce battles they endured in relationships, but from the viewpoint and interest of a man?" A man guiding the discussion from his point of view, but the stories coming strictly from the hearts and souls of the women who participated; something that would broaden our awareness of why women and men have difficulty in relationships, from male interest and female insight.

Every now and then, when a few men get together and speculate on this very topic, all kinds of theories, thoughts, and presumptions surface. After a discussion on a bad experience with a woman, some men will characterize women as "Sapphires" – the brow-beating, controlling, emasculating woman of the 1950s TV program *Amos 'n' Andy*. Oftentimes, a broad conclusion is drawn, "All women are like that."

Watching a television program called *Boston Public*, about the goings-on in an urban high school, one episode focused on a student who carried a hidden gun into the classroom. Once the administration was alerted, the classrooms were put on lockdown, not allowing any students to leave. In one of the classrooms, as the teacher was trying to make the time meaningful, he asked his students to come up with a subject they wanted to learn something about. One wisecracking boy said he wanted to talk about women, stating, "I don't understand women and I don't know any guy that does." Though that was a Hollywood script, it emphasized the purpose for this exercise.

Thinking as a historian, and how much importance has been placed on great men of the past, it became apparent how little we know about great women who have practically been omitted from history. Someone like Auset (known as Isis by the Greeks), a goddess, was the first woman to have an Immaculate Conception, and was said to be the predecessor to Mary. In fact, she was venerated in such high regard that the city of Paris was named after her. We know nothing about Queen Hatshepsut the Great, the first absolute monarchy, and the first woman to challenge 3,000 years of male supremacy while ruling Kemet (Egypt, as named by the Greeks). How little we know of Queen Anna Nzinga, who led her armies against the Portuguese for 51 years in Angola, and held off slavery in her country during that time. Or Yaa Asantewa, the great general of the Ashanti Wars in Ghana, West Afrika, against the British. What may turn out to be even more significant is how we know almost nothing about how the practice of patriarchy began. This placed the male in a deceptive superior role, and the Church, rulership, and public policy sanctioned this behavior, practically eliminating the philosophy of an equal male/female partnership.

When reflecting on what Afrikan women had to go through during slavery for nearly three hundred years, no group of women anywhere on the face of the earth has had to endure such pain, degradation, and brutality for so long. The way those women were characterized and treated then has a direct relationship on how they are perceived today.

Black women were at the total mercy of their slave masters and were forced to become mistresses or concubines. Slavery legitimized and legalized sexual and physical abuse. Denial of a White male's sexual desires would result in the torturous pain of a whip, possible death, or suffering being traded to another plantation, being permanently separated from the children she had or the man she was allowed to be with. Worse yet, she could be confined to a breeding farm where her prime responsibility would be to produce slave babies from plantation-touring Black "studs."

Intuitively, some of these women knew what was ahead of them while crossing the Atlantic Ocean (The Middle Passage) on slave ships. They chose to throw their newborn babies overboard to the sharks rather than have them live their entire lives, and their descendants' lives as slaves under constant oppression, brutality, and worthlessness, never knowing the most cherished of all God's gifts: freedom and love.

Because of this legacy, these women had to constantly fight off the reputation of being perceived as nothing but a sexual slave, among other disparities. In 1895, thirty-two years after slavery, the National Organization of Colored Women was organized to erase the negative sexual images these women endured. Later in time, many women had to bear a manless home to survive due to the constraints of a modern welfare system.

Today, young women are almost portrayed as they were during the time of slavery, as sexual toys in far too many print ads, television commercials, songs, and music videos. It makes one sometimes question, "How could this happen and who established this pattern?" The answer is simple: those who institutionalized chattel slavery and the diminution of women. What is not so easy to answer is why this same pattern continues to this very day.

Sometimes when meditating on the plight of women who have been kept from respectful commentary in history, it brings one back to right now and why some men make the statement, "Man, I can't figure women out." I thought, "Well, maybe we haven't tried hard enough. Maybe we should stop trying to be mister macho and do some serious investigation into our women." It does not take a scientist to figure out that if men and women got it together, this thing we call "the struggle" would end yesterday. The business of building a solid and progressive nation together would be the order of the day, rather than succumbing to the lack of understanding causing man-woman stress and emotional turmoil.

Reflecting on the consciousness of the 1960s, the resurgence of a similar consciousness in present times, from my own observations, and some readings on the subject, there are many who are knowledgeable about their history and culture but still lack the insight to effectively deal with a relationship. Frankly, it seems hypocritical to be able to quote all kinds of historical facts, the latest research findings and philosophical trends, then go home and treat their mate with the highest level of disrespect.

Those of us who have worked exclusively in the fields of scholarship may have to pause from our specialties for a minute, diversify our interests, utilize our talents and skills, and attempt to work on a problem that we have. What use is it to talk about the great achievements of the Nile Valley, or the origin of this, that, or the other, when too many of our present day male/female relationships are falling apart?

The family is the foundation of civilizations, nations, and societies, but if men and women can't realize a unified harmony, there may not be any happiness to enjoy. Scholarship is useless unless its purpose is to provide the knowledge to assist us in understanding and making our lives better. If not, what is its purpose?

Realizing this, the next step was to see what I could do to help alleviate this condition. I wasn't going to save the world or anything like that, but just add one more link to maintain forward motion. I didn't want to write my individual views on the topic. That doesn't seem to be too effective and usually ends up personality-centered. Relying on my research skills, it came to me, "When you want to find the answer to something, you must collect data."

In the middle of my walk, it hit me like a bolt of lightning, "If I could get enough women to talk with me about their most intimate, painful, fulfilling, and intense stories of their relationships on tape, maybe we could acquire a sensitivity of understanding. Maybe this could allow us a window of opportunity on how to better understand the heart and soul of the female and begin developing a balance between the man and the woman."

Starting out with all the enthusiasm in the world, thinking it would be easy to find enough women to complete this task, turned out to be more complicated than originally planned. The first revelation was that there were women who were willing to do it, but only under anonymous conditions, except one. Convincing some to trust me, whether I knew them or not, and that I would maintain their confidentiality was the difficult part. I must have had four or five cancellations before I even got to the first interview.

Thinking about all the efforts there were to empower women, what good is that going to do if men have not made any efforts to grow in knowledge about this situation of the man and the woman? I dreamed once a sister said to a brother, "You have to read this before we can go any further."

It became clear to me that I had to take a different approach to address this very sensitive issue and how to conduct the work properly and humanly. I couldn't just charge in, do the interview, and split: "Wham, bam, thank ya', Ma'am," was not going to work. First, we had to establish a rapport. I had to slow down and talk about the issues and purpose without even mentioning the project. I knew in my head what I wanted to do and why, but I had to thoroughly communicate this to the various ladies. If not, the interviews would not have happened, or the entire endeavor would have ended up with just generic answers and a bland effort. Or worse, we would only have horror stories about men. And yes, there are some horror stories because they are real. Overall, however, they are not the root issues. I wanted to reach the center of the heart; the deepest parts of personal experiences that are sometimes hard to think about, not to mention talk about.

I wanted to see if there was a cause and effect without the simple cop-out of just laying blame. I wanted to look at the surrounding variables that may have had some influence on their relationships. This was going to be an experiment to determine if there were some universal issues that we tend to overlook but could easily be dealt with. Or were all the problems so personal that it would take a very complicated process to straighten them out? Whatever the result, it was going to be a sincere effort to investigate male/female relationships from a female perspective, but from the interest of a male. This was concluded to be an approach that would get us closer to answers.

Dealing with reality is one of the few things left for us to do, because so much of the information that is thrown our way is so diluted and distorted that we have become unnaturally attached to things that are not even real.

Going through the process, I had to ask the Creator for help. There were times when emotions were overwhelming with tears freely flowing. At different stages during the interviews, some of the ladies would exhibit such agonizing pain and deep-seated anger that it caused me to take a mental pause to maintain the focus of the interview, looking at the bigger picture, while at the same time dealing with some very sensitive situations.

Though I primarily started out with the vision that this work would help men to understand women a little better, after analyzing the breadth of the information, it became abundantly clear that attempting to broaden just the consciousness of men was a limiting enterprise. There were far too many women experiencing what the ladies in this book had gone through.

My sister told me when this idea was first mentioned to her, "You will find abuse very common among women." I didn't know that. You meet women in the course of life, but those things are rarely talked about, except in specific situations. That was just one of the revelations. There was also found a high level of spirituality and the various ways in which it is manifested. The tragic results of low self-esteem and other incredible experiences came forth. What was most enlightening is how many of the women "re-discovered" themselves and how that uplifted their lives. Some of the ladies stated, "I haven't talked about these things in years. This was really a cathartic experience for me."

One thing that is important in attempting to better one's character, behavior and habits is to realize that you are not alone with the same problems. This seems to be an extremely valuable asset in a healing process. What the ladies in this work reveal will eliminate that loneliness of relationship experiences.

Something of enormous value are the lessons young girls can pick up as they evolve into womanhood. When Afrikan women were brought to America during the era of the slave trade, old traditions were forbidden and faded during the passing of time. One of those traditions was the process of initiating (coming of age) an adolescent girl into womanhood.

The common practice was to take the girls out of the community for a specified amount of time while the elder women taught the young girls about being a woman, a wife, a mother, and survival, among other things. This was generally the rule before a girl could get married, the belief being that the girl could enter womanhood and married life with an experienced body of knowledge from which to pull.

Today, particularly in the West, it seems that young girls gather their female knowledge primarily from their peers, soap operas, music videos, and the media-at-large. If the number of unmarried teenage girls having babies is any indication of this, then this society is seriously projecting the wrong message.

If the experiences of the ladies in this book, their triumphs and their mistakes, can somewhat serve as a substitute for an old tradition, maybe we can see more informed young girls approach the complexities of a relationship in a more mature manner, rather than allowing raw emotions to rule the day.

One is constantly taught that living experience is the best teacher and that the greatest wisdom comes from that. If that is the case, then the ladies in this book have to collectively be classified as crucial teachers. Not only was it educational for me, but also transforming. My respect for women, which was always high, skyrocketed after going through this experience.

The same goes for young men. Since they basically have no training in understanding the perplexity of womanhood other than what they observe in their own families and peer groups, maybe the experiences of the ladies in this book can serve as a reservoir of knowledge for their efforts to be involved in a positive relationship. Knowing what a woman will accept and not accept, and what is expected, seems to qualify as a head start in understanding a relationship.

The possibility of men and women, gender collectively or not, sitting around discussing the situations of the various ladies in this book, debating their various circumstances with all kinds of ideas coming forth could become very therapeutic. Or maybe just a couple who are going through a difficult period but do not want to personally address the problems with each other, or lack the knowledge on how to effectively do so, may see a similar situation with one of the ladies in the book and be able to discuss her situation vicariously, gaining some insight for themselves.

Imagine a class of young students analyzing the behaviors of each person in this book. What would their mindset and opinions about a relationship be afterwards? Would they approach it with a greater level of maturity and understanding? That sure would help in increasing our chances for a more positive future. An interesting long-term study could be developed to determine if that holds up. There is one point I want to make crystal clear: Just because I had the privilege of putting this book together in no way makes me a relationship expert. Sure, I have my own wealth of knowledge based on my own experience, readings on the subject, and what I have learned or observed from others. There are those who are specialists in this area of human behavior, people who have trained and worked in this field for years. They are individuals who can serve as very valuable mediators in trying to figure out how to have a smooth-running relationship, most of the time. There are also family members and friends who have special insight in helping through some difficult situations. This topic was approached purely from a sincere concern, curiosity, and the idealistic hope that it can do some good.

There may be some men who are going to look at this entire work as another male-bashing effort and that the author has basically betrayed all men. I remember seeing *Waiting To Exhale.* After getting over the jubilation of seeing a quality Black film, I recall talking with a couple of men who virtually dismissed the whole experience as just another "male-bashing extravaganza." When I quietly analyzed these men to myself, based on further conversation and other observations, I concluded they were basically insecure men who were having their own problems with women and couldn't deal with maybe seeing a part of themselves on the big screen. I remember when Shaharazad Ali's book came out, *The Blackman's Guide To Understanding the Black Woman.* I have never seen so many women, and some men, attack a book like that in my life. It was the topic of conversation wherever people of Afrikan descent gathered. After the storm subsided, I began my own investigation and found that many of the women who were vehemently complaining about the book had not even read it, and that some of them were the main practitioners of the negativisms that were portrayed in the book. This is not a wholesale endorsement, just a mention of the surrounding circumstances.

It was learned that during the controversy surrounding the film *The Color Purple*, there were a few men who doubted that there could possibly be a man like Mr._____. Going through the investigation of this book demonstrated that there are all kinds of similar individuals.

To those men who may want to condemn this work, and possibly the author, read the book first. Then ask the questions, "Did you learn anything that could maybe help you understand what your woman could be thinking or her concerns? Was there something that could maybe aid in preventing you from hurting your woman?" It is certain that if a little introspection is utilized, there may be some other issues this book may help one to consider.

On the other hand, it is expected to garner hardly any complaints from women. It is surmised that most women will see some part of themselves in the various experiences these special ladies impart to us.

The only concern heard from a couple of women was, "I think a woman could do it better." That is probably true, but it would defeat the purpose of looking at this issue from a male point of interest. That is the implicit goal of this book. Opposites attract, and sometimes a lot of good things can come from an opposite point of view.

It is my ultimate hope and desire that somewhere in these pages a woman will read something that will prevent her from beginning to fall in a pit of pain, observing what someone went through. If one woman decides, "No, I am not going that way. I saw what the sister went through doing that," that will make this work worthy.

If a man reads this book and says, "I am not going to do that. I understand now, that will make her unhappy," that will be the beginning of a single human revolution. It is this kind of consciousness that allowed the following poem to be created:

Woman of Woman

As I write
Re-interpreting
Words, God, nature
Investigating my environment
Attempting to translate beauty
Associating its purest form
With you
You who acts
Reacts
Feels
Loves
Insecure male men
Stood over you
Labeled you
A socially acceptable deviate
A benevolent slave
Overcoming obstacles
Purposely put before you
Justifying their actions
By your beautiful color
Attitudes
Physical differences
Given you by God
Making you
A woman

Double jeopardy you live
Socially inferior
And Black
Great woman of earth/universe
Great woman of history
Great woman of yourself
I choose to love you
I choose to rid my mind
Of evil manifestations
Considered normal
I choose to see you
My way
Skin like mine
Blood like mine
Hair beautiful
Eyes meaningful
You contradict scientific proof
You feel
You are intelligent
You adapt
To the spirit of love
Nature provides me
All that man has destroyed
You give me that
Which man cannot
Find in himself
Which I cannot interpret
By word-symbols
Only by being with you
Filling the air with meaning
Creating non-dictionary sounds
Doing what almost seems

Humanly impossible
Making
Love

Kwaku Person-Lynn

Delores Naylor

Ms. Naylor is 52 years old and single. She is very independent and enjoys her solitude. She has been gainfully employed in the social services field for a number of years and earns a comfortable living. Prior to that, she spent twenty years working for a major airline. Her spiritual belief is a guiding force in her life and the center of her thought. Her willingness to work with those who would be considered less fortunate may have opened her human consciousness to a higher level than those of us who are accustomed to a so-called "normal" life. Her desire to be with a man is not all-pervasive. At this point in her life, where things are basically as she would like them to be, a man would have to fit into the world that she has developed for herself, and allow her to enjoy the independence that seems to be a non-negotiable part of her existence. She is very committed to the plight of young people and may be a hope for those who do not receive that needed caring at home.

I was born in Washington, D.C. I came to Southern California because of my job. I also had a romantic interest here at the time. My childhood had its ups and downs. I had happy times, but I remember being alone a lot of the time and often feeling lonely, even when there were others around. I never lacked for anything material. In fact, as a child I thought we were rich (we weren't), because with two working parents, we could afford a few things that others could not. I suppose I had an average childhood, living in a working-class neighborhood full of good neighbors and neighborhood kids.

My parents did not offer a good model to me for male/female relationships. Their disagreements centered almost exclusively around money. At the time I was growing up, I recall thinking to myself, 'I don't want that kind of relationship they have. I'll never get married.' Their behavior between each other most definitely had an influence on my dealing with relationships. Some of the reaction I had to their relationship was positive. I think I have turned their negatives into positives. I was able to look at some of the things they did, things I felt that were wrong and not do those things. Not make those kinds of mistakes. There are other ways they influenced me. I believe in a monogamous relationship. Essentially, they did too. I took that example. In all other respects they provided wonderful role models, but not with regard to their interactions with one another. Specifically, my mother often openly disrespected my father. For example, she would cut him off when he was speaking, introduce him to friends with a demeaning tone in her voice, she made disparaging remarks about him, or ignored him altogether.

My father disrespected my mother in less obvious ways. When I was born he was a confirmed bachelor of 35. He was reluctant to marry my mother. They were eventually wed, but not before he purchased our home in his name only. My mother never forgave him for the apparent lack of trust he showed her when he excluded her from this most important transaction. Also, she always seemed to feel she was bearing an unfair share of the financial burden.

My parents were exemplary in many ways. They believed in God, hard work, discipline, deference to elders, and the bonds of family. But they lacked the ability to build trust through verbally communicating with one another in a meaningful way.

Looking back on their relationship with the maturity of 52 years, I have come to believe that my mother's behavior was a misguided and destructive attempt to equalize the balance of power between her and my father by lowering his self-esteem. She was ten years his junior and I have often wondered if a woman closer to his age might have dealt with her hurt by handling things a little different.

My father didn't seem to understand the unarticulated source of the hurt underlining his wife's passive-aggressive behavior, nor the role his refusal to include her in financial decision-making played in the deterioration of their marriage. Nevertheless, he was very loving, committed, and always a patient father to whom I credit my compassion and independence. My parents divorced when I was 15. My mother was granted custody of my brother and me.

I was about 13 when I met my first boyfriend. My father gave free music lessons to the neighborhood youth and this young man, a friend of my brother, wanted to learn to play the drums. He was a nice boy and quite handsome. When he produced a plain little ring and asked me to be his girlfriend, I said, "Yes." After two or three weeks, however, I had become increasingly unsure of what to say to him or how to behave around my new beau. I was so uncomfortable that I returned his ring and told him I was just not ready for a close relationship. Through no fault of his own, I was somehow intimidated by the label "girlfriend," mostly because I was so unsure of what was expected of me in that role. Throughout my high school years, my interaction with members of the opposite sex consisted of classroom flirtations and casual dates at home listening to records or watching TV.

Following my freshman year in college, I became involved in my first intimate affair. I was 19 and he was 35 years old and married. At the time, I was attracted to the sophistication of more mature men. The affair was a brief one, ended by him when it became clear that I would not settle for a part-time liaison despite my deep infatuation with him. It was several months getting over the hurt, but I finally understood the moral lesson – married men are off limits. And they have been ever since.

I have come to believe that if a marriage has become truly unworkable, then one owes it to oneself and one's partner to summon the strength and courage to separate and seek a better life, if at all possible. Although the transition may be difficult (transitions often are), I think even children benefit in the long run, as long as responsibilities are appropriately dealt with. I think personal sacrifices are in service to the highest good. The trick is to determine what that is.

Clearly, I am not in favor of remaining in a stagnant relationship for the sake of emotional or material security. That sort of arrangement tends to thwart personal growth and I don't think anyone is well served by that. If a man tells me he is unhappily married, I tend to think he either lacks the commitment to make it work or lacks the courage to leave. In either case, he is not the man for me.

I had my first serious relationship, one involving some degree of commitment, with someone I met through mutual friends. I was 22, he was 24. He was handsome, had a college education, a promising career, and lived in a smartly decorated apartment in one of the trendiest parts of town. I admired his ambition, his independence, and found his tendency to non-conformity exciting. It wasn't long before I was very much in love with him and felt he loved me too, at least on most days. But things often did not go smoothly between us. We went together for a number of years, then he went overseas. In the meantime, I began to see somebody else. In fact, I was seeing two other guys. They were not serious relationships. I was very young and didn't want to sit home. I liked these other guys so I went out with them.

When my first serious boyfriend came back, we sort of resumed the relationship. We got back up to speed. We became as close as we were before he left. Then he moved to Hawaii. I was there with him for about three weeks. When he moved to California, I went back to Washington, D.C. Later, I moved to California and stayed at his place for a few weeks while he was in New York on business. When he returned, I had already acquired my own apartment and transportation.

When we first met, I had already become disenchanted with school and had left college to work full-time at a job in which I had little interest. Not only did I have an empty work life, I also found nothing to occupy my non-working hours. My boyfriend became my sole reason for being. He wasn't a part of my life, he was my life. I was constantly preoccupied with thoughts of him. I wanted to spend every spare moment in his presence.

Like the emotionally immature lyrics of many love songs suggest, I wanted him to be, "my everything," filling every void in my life. What an unfair and unrealistic expectation to lay on anyone. My life was so narrow focused and so lacking in balance that I couldn't have been a very interesting companion.

Certainly, there was this core of love, but it was wrapped in a blanket of my own neediness for self-esteem and a sense of purpose. I was as much "in need" as I was "in love." Making someone else the center of my universe made it easier to avoid, at least for a while, the responsibility of dealing with the issue of my own personal growth and development.

I think it is important to have your own interests, your own goals and dreams. Part of the joy of being 50% of a relationship is what you have to share in terms of your own uniqueness and abilities. But understanding your own special gifts and how to cultivate and actualize them involves a lot of self-discovery, and that takes time. Clearly, I wasn't there yet. I don't mean to imply that love and self-actualization are opposing forces. To the contrary, real love is the greatest catalyst of all to self-discovery, and ultimately it made a better person of me.

This is true in part because the act of loving exposed my vulnerabilities and weaknesses, and once I understood, that exposure helped me to develop my strengths. Ironically, in a sense, the man in my life had nothing to do with my identity crisis. He was often simply a mirror in which I saw my own reflected image, sometimes true, sometimes warped.

My boyfriend had a rewarding job in the field of computers that engaged both his intellect and his creative energies. In that area of his life, he had accomplished a lot. But he had his shortcomings. He was an only child and he tended to be rather self-centered. I often wished he had a sibling, preferably a sister. Maybe then he would have had a clue about what women are really like. He also tended to sleep with other women, at least twice that I knew of, even though we had agreed that our relationship would be exclusive.

He once shared his apartment with a woman he said was his cousin. In her presence, he explained to me that she was from out of town and would be staying with him for a couple of weeks until she could find her own place. Well, it later came to light that she was not his cousin, but she assumed that role for two weeks whenever I was around.

Apparently, he had made it clear to this woman that he wanted her to leave, but she had not done so. Finally, he and I returned to his place after a dinner date one evening and found her there. I thought nothing of it, but he became quite angry and began putting her clothing outside and telling her to get out. She turned to me and said tearfully, but emphatically, "I am not his cousin."

I think they both expected me to be angry with her, "the other woman." Not so. When she told my boyfriend that she had no money and no place to go, it became obvious to me that no woman would put herself in such a vulnerable position unless she had been grossly misled. I felt a sense of kinship with her. After all, the promise of faithfulness was not between me and her, but between me and my boyfriend.

From my purse I took out $40 and gave it to her, silently resolving to get it back from my boyfriend, not because I needed it, but because I wanted him to take some responsibility for the damage he had done. The woman accepted the money and left. It occurred to me to leave right behind her. But I did not.

About two years into this relationship, I decided that the feminists were absolutely right, that "what's good for the goose is good for the gander." At a party, I encountered a man I had met casually on one or two occasions who was visiting from out of town. He was a good friend of the host and was spending the weekend at his home. He had a quiet strength about him, an active intellect, and a genuine interest in people. The party was at a small, newly renovated wood-framed roll house. It wasn't a get down dancing party, but sort of a laid back conversation gathering with some great jazz in the background. Not a lot of people were there.

This guy and I started talking and kind [of] connected with each other. He let it be known that he was attracted to me and I was to him, but I didn't let him know it, not right then anyway. He sat down in a chair and I sat on the arm. He pulled me over in his lap and I kind of kissed him. After we had established that we were attracted to one another, he said, "Let's go in here." We went into the room where he was staying. When we got in the room, we didn't say much. We kind of both knew what we were about to do. We sat down on the bed, embraced, and had one of the most passionate kisses I can ever recall. The next thing I know we were taking each others' clothes off. I grabbed his most private part, gently laid back on the bed, and pulled him inside me. Our rhythms were in sync from the first stroke.

Just as we were finishing, another guy started to open the door, saw us on the bed totally nude and said, "Oh," and backed out the door. We didn't jump or anything. It was almost like we didn't care if someone saw us.

We spent the night together. I never imagined that one of the people also attending the party was a co-worker and casual friend of my boyfriend, or that this acquaintance would correctly piece together and report to him the events of that evening.

Days later, when my boyfriend unexpectedly revealed to me what he had been told, I simply could not contain the deep chuckle that spontaneously arose. I felt compelled not to deny the truth, although I loved this man and did not want to lose the relationship. But I had come to believe that when a man feels within himself that he cannot commit to a relationship, he ought to have enough integrity to say so, and enough of a sense of fairness to realize that he must forfeit any expectation of exclusivity.

We were not living together. I've never lived with anyone. I never wanted to do that. I love having my own space. I've always been that way. What's the point? You can have it all without living together. If a couple decides to marry, that's something different. It's different because it speaks to commitment. If either or both are not ready for that commitment, then I don't see the point of living together. I've always been fortunate enough in being able to support myself so it was never a matter of saving money by doing that. As long as he wants his freedom, I think I should have mine. I feel very strongly about that.

I dated this man, on and off equally, for nearly fifteen years. He sometimes spoke of marriage, and I thought nothing could have made me happier – that is until over drinks at a restaurant one evening, I casually mentioned that I was seriously thinking of returning to school. Despite the enormous expense, I wanted to make a chance to have a more satisfying career. His immediate response was, "I need a wife who's an asset, not a liability." I made no reply, but it was at this point that I realized I had no desire to spend my life with a man who couldn't understand and support my need to seek a higher degree of meaning in my life. I wanted to prepare myself for the work that would be satisfying and fulfilling to me.

Shortly after this conversation, I ended our relationship. Ironically, after an absence of perhaps a dozen years, he has recently begun calling me again. He never married. I guess we are all "a work in progress." Perhaps he has progressed.

But prior to his calling again, I had sort of a dating type of relationship with another man, someone who I thought very highly of. We spent about a year-and-a-half together. He wanted to get married. As much as I thought of him, I wasn't in love with him. I didn't want to marry him. Eventually, that relationship ceased because it was too difficult to maintain a relationship when one person was really very serious about the goal of marriage and the other person wasn't. I just stopped seeing him over a period of time.

Following that, I got involved in another relationship; someone I was seeing. He wanted to live together. I didn't. This relationship stands out in my mind because of its uniqueness. He happened to be extraordinarily good looking. It slowly dawned on me that although I liked this person, I knew the relationship was not going to go anywhere beyond what it already was. I realized that I was seeing him because it was just a kick to be out with someone who was that devastatingly good looking. I really thought that was immoral. That was not a good thing for me to do, so I closed that relationship. We stopped going out on dates. Actually, if he had been able to maintain the status quo, without wanting any more than that, I would have seen him longer. But because he was pushing for more, I knew that the only way to handle that was to stop seeing him.

For several years after that, I really didn't date very much at all. I became involved in a relationship (laughs) with a guy who was really a lot of fun. That too was a unique relationship, because it was all about fun. Just having fun. And we did just that. We knew exactly what we wanted from one another. It was a very lovely relationship. I didn't want to marry him. He didn't want to marry me. We just had a great time together for a couple of years.

He eventually moved out of state and married. If he had stayed, I don't think we would have gotten any closer. I actually did not think he was capable of making a serious marital commitment to me, or anyone else. But that was fine. I was not in love with him and did not want to marry him anyway. Although I was very fond of him, I knew I would never be in love with him. It was a very nice relationship while it lasted. That was my last.

I haven't necessarily chosen to be alone; I simply have not met anyone that I wanted to have a relationship with.

℘

I had my first sexual experience when I was 19 years old. I was away from home visiting another city at my cousin's house and no one was home but me. He was at work. I had sort of decided I didn't want to be a virgin anymore. It had become burdensome. Often times, I went out with guys and they would push for sex, or whatever. There were times when I wanted it, but was afraid because I wouldn't appear experienced, for good reason. I was afraid of being embarrassed by having no clue what I was doing. And yet, I was afraid to say that I never had sex. It had become burdensome, so I decided I was going to do something about this. The next really attractive offer I would get, I was going to take him up on it.

It happened to be a man who was 35 at the time, and I was 19. That was kind of good because he knew what he was doing, or I thought he did. In retrospect, I don't think he did. It was over so quickly. My first reaction was, "That's it? That's what everybody's been raving about?"

I was so preoccupied with the mechanics of what was happening that I really wasn't that into it. It was kind of like getting a shot. You're half afraid and you're waiting to flinch, I just wasn't that into it. It was over very quickly.

Later that day, another man that I was really interested in also came over; he was closer to my age. This was actually a friend of the cousin I was staying with. This guy had come to visit him. I had not seen this guy in several years. The last time he saw me, I think I was about 13. I just had the most incredible crush on him, and still had it at 19. But of course, when I was 13, he treated me totally like a kid sister. At 19, I had gone through a few physical changes. I flirted with him just outrageously with my voice and body language. I let him know just exactly how I felt about him. He got the message. I think he found me very attractive. To make a long story short, I ended up sleeping with him. This time, I really enjoyed it. You could say I warmed to it.

He was a good lover. He knew that I was very new at this. He didn't know how new. After he left, even in the glow of romance, I began to be just mortified that I had turned into some kind of absolute slut. I couldn't believe that I had sex twice in the same day. I thought, "What if there is no end to this? What if now that I have opened Pandora's box, I can't put the lid back on?" that I would just go on and on sleeping with all of these men.

Your parents tell you things that make you feel that this is such a God-awful thing in the world. "You must not sleep with anyone before you get married." I thought, "Well, this is my punishment. I'm getting my just rewards. I am out of control. I can't control it. I'm just going to go on sleeping with one man after another." Of course, that did not happen. I had what I'm sure, for my age, a normal sex life. But it sure was scary, honestly scary.

I was sure that the next time I saw my parents they would be able to look at me immediately and go, "I knew it! You've done it haven't you?" I just felt that I looked different. Of course, I didn't. But you think your parents know everything. It wasn't rational. This is not a rational process.

Now that I broke the ice, so to speak, my fear was unfounded. It didn't become a regular habit. When I returned to the town that I lived in, I left both of those men there. I did not see them and there wasn't anyone in the town that I lived in that I cared to be sexually with for quite a while. When there was, then I did that. I have always been rather restrained in that way, despite the beginning.

My sexual life did not come without consequences: I got pregnant three times; I had an abortion each time. I couldn't believe I was pregnant. When you're young you think that certain things will not happen to you. I was absolutely in denial for a while. Abortion at that time was illegal. As soon as I came to my senses, I went to a doctor and he did confirm that I was pregnant.

My girlfriends had been telling me anyway, "I think you're pregnant." They could just look and tell. Your body changes a little bit. So, I had an abortion. It was a very difficult thing to arrange because it was illegal, and there were all these connections to be made. It was just an anxiety-provoking experience before the fact.

The actual abortion was not horrible. That's never fun, but it wasn't horrible. A medical doctor did it, an under-the-table kind of thing. He knew what he was doing; it worked out. I did get some kind of infection. It wasn't done in a hospital; it was done in a private home. I didn't know the people who lived there. We went upstairs in the front bedroom. I got undressed from the waist down and he put a sheet over me. When he asked me to spread my legs and went inside me with some instrument, I knew it was too late to change my mind then.

It wasn't done under sterile conditions. In case anything happened afterwards, he had given me the name of another doctor who was in a hospital. I didn't feel that normal, so to speak. Indeed, I had a blood infection. I did go to this other doctor. The irony was, it was the hospital I was born in. They kept me for a couple of days.

I tried to tell my mother what happened. We never talked about anything like that before. This was a first. Here I am, in the hospital, and she comes to see me. She had guessed that I was pregnant. She sort of hinted at it and I knew she knew. She knew why I was in there. But I had not said it and I felt an obligation to say it to her. I was 21 or 22, I think. I said, "There's something I want to tell you." She looked at me and she knew what I was going to say. She just said, "No, no, no." So I never did tell her. I knew right then that she knew, but she just didn't want to hear it from me. I didn't have to tell her, so I didn't. Even now, after all these years, and we are very close, we have never spoken of it again.

I did discuss it with my boyfriend. He knew I was pregnant. Honestly, I don't remember if I told him I was going to have an abortion or not. Actually, no, I didn't tell him. I told him that I had a spontaneous abortion. I knew what I wanted to do. I was pretty sure that he would not be in favor of that. But it was my decision, that's the way I looked at it. It was my decision, not his. Had our relationship been on steadier ground, his opinion would have carried more weight with me. But because it wasn't, in my opinion, he had forfeited the right to have a whole lot to say about it.

Regarding the other two abortions, I never told my male partners that I was pregnant at all. To this day they don't know. I had an abortion extremely early on in those pregnancies. By then, abortion was legal, so it wasn't a problem. You didn't have to spend time trying to find somebody or be afraid or anything like that. It was a very quick, easy, simple procedure.

Knowing that I was terminating a life the first time, I actually prayed for forgiveness for having done that. I don't know how to explain this, but I got a very clear message right at the time that I asked for forgiveness. I am not sure, but I think I asked, "How long would it be before I am forgiven for this?" And so clearly, the message came back, "Three days." I don't have any clue what even made me say how long or where that voice came from. I was surprised just to hear an answer.

It was a voice that I heard very clearly in my head. On very, very, very rare occasions, in my lifetime, I have heard this voice and it was never wrong. Never. It said three days. I didn't worry about it after that. I knew that it was okay. Why three days? Why not right away? Why not three years? I don't know. I can't understand that. But I knew it was absolutely right. I knew it didn't come from me, at least not any me that I was in touch with.

The other two, I didn't mourn them. I was barely pregnant, if there is such a thing. I was newly pregnant. It wasn't something I thought much about. But the first one, even years later, I mourn it. It made me feel as though I was not a good woman. Not to say a good person, but a good woman. Women are supposed to be all about being nurturing and that sort of thing. If I wasn't doing that, then I must not be a good woman. I felt a sense of lost potential with the relationship I might have had with that child

Looking back over that now, there are times when I would have liked to have a child. As any good parent knows, there are a lot of pleasures, a lot of joys to be reaped from child-rearing. On the other hand, there are a lot of sacrifices. In retrospect, I was not willing to make those sacrifices as I could see them at the time. It was the best thing to do at the time, I thought. And looking back on it, you never know for sure, right? There's just no way to know. I think of the economic hardship, the lack of freedom, perhaps being unable to go to school the way I wanted to, to work in the kind of job situation that I wanted to have, all of the freedoms I would have missed. I've seen that happen. I just didn't want to be put into that predicament. I just could not deal with the idea.

If a young girl approached me who was pregnant, and was seeking my advice whether to have the child or get an abortion, I would probably tell her to let abortion be her very last option. I would tell her that when I had an abortion, I did not think it was sinful to do that. Somehow, after the fact, I felt it was. It's difficult to explain. As the experience faded, because it was many, many years between the first abortion and the others, I began to think it was all right. It was a woman's choice. It was all right to have that.

Now, I have come full circle. I'm thinking, at this point in my life, maybe it is a sin. If you think it might be one, then you have to err on the side of caution. I'm not absolutely sure that it is. For that reason, I would tell her to let that be her very last option. I would have to tell her that it may be a sinful thing to do.

℘

I have a metaphysical orientation. It has affected my personal life in this way. It has given me a deeper insight into myself that has allowed me to understand others. It has made me more tolerant of the shortcomings of others. I really seek to understand where others are coming from. It has opened me up on a spiritual level so that I'm able to connect with people in ways that I wouldn't have been able to otherwise.

With the age that I am, and my mental growth, the availability of men has diminished in a yes and no fashion. Everyone says that there are not many available men at this age. I have not found that to be true in the last couple of years. It seems that men who were not available, due to marriage, are now divorced and looking for another marriage. Men that were confirmed bachelors are having a second thought about that. Those two things primarily have brought more available men to the fore, in my experience.

Because I have taken great pains to grow mentally and spiritually beyond the norm, I do agree that there are less available men for me. My standards are pretty high. That eliminates and excludes a lot of men. That's a difficulty.

My standards are, I enjoy men who are purposeful, who have a mission in life, have something to give to the world and who are about doing that. That makes them more interesting to me. It usually means they travel in a more interesting circle of friends, which helps. I enjoy men who are financially secure. Men who are seekers themselves. Men who value spirituality, who, first of all, understand it. It's difficult to express. It's perhaps something that is more felt. A more feeling thing than cognitive in many ways. There has to be sort of a chemistry that people talk about. That has to be there. Without that, who needs it?

I honestly don't know if I can be content without a man for the rest of my life. As I get older, I think I would like an exclusive relationship. On the other hand, getting older, I feel that would be such a very different thing for me, to share my physical space with someone else, to share decisions with someone else. In the best of all worlds, I would like to be with someone who would not be intrusive in my space, someone who would enhance my space. I think that's the way it's supposed to work. I would like to have someone who is independent, who would respect my independence. We could be together but still have our own personal independence. That's it, absolutely. Someone who is very much about his own thing, and yet can include me in that. For example, I can envision someone coming home from work, really being glad to share what has occurred during their day, their accomplishments. Maybe their disappointments, if there were any. That sort of thing.

I had a girlfriend once say to me, "I wish I could have a man that I could share the kind of things with that I share with my girlfriends." I totally understood what she meant by that, a communality of interests, not those stale roles that men have been traditionally expected to fulfill.

I was with a girlfriend last evening for dinner. She doesn't come home and cook dinner for her husband; he gets his own dinner most of the time. When she has the time, she enjoys cooking for him, but that actually is not something that occurs a lot. Those kinds of things are important, if it works for that particular relationship. It may not for someone else. As they say, "The devil is in the details." Even after you find someone that you feel you would like to share your life with, in the most meaningful ways, there are still all those little things to be worked out.

If I found the so-called "right" man, and we clicked, but later he settled into old habits and wanted to definitely be the head of the household, making the major decisions without us discussing them, it wouldn't wash. I would not be able to tolerate that. I'm simply too independent. I don't envision being attracted to someone who would have that mindset. I think that would reveal itself in other ways that would send up a red flag. I can't imagine why one adult would want to make decisions for another adult. That is alien, foreign to me.

When I am with a group of my single girlfriends and the discussion is about men, we talk about our various experiences with them. And yes, there are times when we do a little male bashing, but not a lot, actually. We just don't feel like that is the proper thing to do, a proper use of our time and energies.

When there is male bashing, one of us will tell of an experience we've had or something that a man said to us. But very often, it is not a man that we know. It's someone we've encountered in a shopping situation or a work setting or something like that. It's not someone we are having a one-on-one relationship with. We will simply share that incident and look at one another and say, "Can you believe he said that?" or, "Can you believe he did that?" or, "What could he have been thinking?"

I know that some men think that when women get together,

when they are talking about men, all that they do is male bash. Not at all. Not at all. When I'm together with my women friends, we spend, I'm sure, 85% of our time talking about our own issues in terms of personal growth, in terms of our ambitions for ourselves. We talk about school. We talk about the job, a lot about the job.

I travel in circles that do some kind of social work, most of us. Those are the things we talk about. We talk about politics a lot. We all still have that vision of Prince Charming. All of my girlfriends would like to find that special person who will be what they dream of. At the same time, we drive a hard bargain. I think we all do.

There are times when a woman who wants a man, and is approached by a man in a respectful manner, through her body language or something she says will turn a man off. Personally, I have not really seen or experienced that. I can only think that perhaps without realizing it, the man has done something to communicate to that woman, something that's displeased her. I have not had that happen to me, nor heard of it happening to my girlfriends except in a way that I previously cited. Someone while you're out shopping, or someone in the work place will say or do something that's totally beyond the pale, you get turned off by it. I suppose it's possible the man doesn't know what he's done.

As far as a woman telling the man what he did wrong, if it is the initial encounter, the space hasn't been created for that kind of dialog to take place. She's almost forced to just let it go with him, to just pass that one up. If the relationship has begun, and that happens, then certainly it's something you can talk about.

If I was to paint a scenario for meeting a man and developing a relationship, I would imagine that any man that I would become involved with I would meet through my work. We would get to know one another on a professional basis first, and from there, perhaps, evolve into something deeper.

In all of the relationships that I have mentioned, there was sexual involvement, and they were satisfying to me. That could happen with the new person I would meet, if the situation was right.

One of the elements I mentioned that was very important to me was spirituality. The way that I would identify spirituality in a man is the way he treats others, the way he speaks about others, the way he treats his family.

Spirituality pervades everything for a spiritual person. I would imagine seeing it in every aspect of his life, from the art he enjoys, to the music he enjoys, to the kind of people he chooses as his friends, all of that.

If the man has children, that would not affect me. I would welcome that. There are certainly some challenges inherited in that situation. It would not scare me away. I wouldn't find it off-putting at all. That, of course, is something that would have to be handled rather delicately for the sake of the children involved. It would not put me off.

If that relationship evolved into a marriage, I absolutely could become their mother, or love and treat them in a motherly way. I would have no qualms about that at all, despite the fact that I have never had children. But I've been a child and that helps. I have spent time around the children in my own family. I have an interest in young people. I wouldn't foresee any major problems.

When I was very young, in my 20s and even as a teenager, I had an ambition of having children. I thought I wanted to have children. Relatively speaking, that did not last very long. As soon as I was out on my own, as soon as I left the umbrella of my parents' care, I began to think of having children as second thoughts. I had pretty much decided, "No, that is not something I have wanted for myself." Not that there haven't been times when I thought, perhaps upon seeing someone with an infant, a darling little infant, "Oh, I wish that could be me. I would really enjoy that." But I think I have made the right decision for myself to not have children.

I would consider adopting. I've thought about it. Because now, I feel better situated to raise a child. I am less distracted by other things. I feel more like devoting myself to the raising of a child than I have previously.

When I was younger, I was always chasing the next adventure. Whether it was travel, a job, a relationship, or whatever. I think that now, I feel more settled.

If I was to adopt, I would prefer a child of about five or perhaps older. I really don't know. It doesn't matter that much to me. I suppose I would want a child who is not older than maybe eight or nine, because of where they are at developmentally. So many patterns have already been set by that time that it might be difficult to try to influence the life of someone who's not been yours and has not been with you after that long period of time. So for that reason, I would want a younger child, but certainly not a child in diapers.

℘

I work with the developmentally delayed. Specifically, those who are learning disabled, those who are mentally retarded. I teach independent living skills. Independent living skills are those skills that an individual would need to acquire in order to live as independently of others as possible, meaning: how to balance a check book, how to count money, how to count change, how to do grocery shopping, what kind of a diet would be considered a balanced diet, how to interact with other people, what is appropriate social behavior, those sorts of things.

Many of my clients are able to involve themselves in a relationship. Unfortunately, it is often the case that men who are perhaps not developmentally delayed especially take advantage of women for purposes of financial gain. Many of the men that my clients tend to be involved with take their money. Often times, the person who has the disability is either unaware of how much money they are giving their love interest, or if they are aware of it, they do it anyway because they feel that they will lose that love interest if they don't. It's very common that people with disabilities feel they will lose their love interest if they do not give them money. In essence, they are trying to buy love.

In advising my clients of this, who can be very sensitive and touchy, while I don't try to hold them to the same standards that I would hold myself to, I do try to have them understand that you cannot buy love. To try to do so is to act in a way that is against their own self- interest. Those kinds of discussions usually take place over many sessions with them. This is not something that I sort of lay on them all at once. Certain things become self-evident. If they've given their love interest money, and they don't see that person until they're going to get another check, then it becomes evident that the only thing that person wants is money, and perhaps sex.

I use the term self-evident, but it is not always as evident to the client as it is to me. So, it is just a matter of trying to very delicately point that out. The ways in which it is pointed out vary with the client, what they are able to understand.

Some of them could make very good parents. Others, no, not at all. Again, it varies with the client. I have seen clients who have very good parenting skills, usually because they themselves were very well parented. I have seen other clients who are a nightmare as parents. I believe because they were not parented well.

℘

I am a very independent woman, and do not have to deal with loneliness too much. I am very blessed. I am never lonely. I knew loneliness as a child growing up, but since I've left home, I've had only one lonely moment. That was immediately after my father passed away. Other than that, never lonely. There's always something to do, there's always friends. I am very blessed in that respect. I have many very good friends, very close friends. I am just busy all of the time.

I don't feel that staying busy is a way of avoiding the issue of loneliness. There is no issue of loneliness to avoid. When I say I'm busy all the time, I mean I am as busy as I want to be. It doesn't mean that I don't allow myself to just veg out. I do that, and I do that well. I do it as often as I can. Being alone and being lonely are two very different things. I am busy because life has a way of just sweeping you along. I don't make busy for myself at all. In fact, I am only too glad to come home, close the door, and be with myself to watch a good old movie, to read a book I've wanted to read. There's always something to do.

Very rarely do I think, "It would be nice to share this with a man." Very, very rarely. Almost never. I can't think of a time when I've thought that. I appreciate being by myself so much. I can get so into something. Just be so full of that which I am appreciating that I don't feel any lack of another presence at all.

I have not been involved in a serious relationship for about five years. I don't know if I want to say that I don't need a man in my life. I'm real close to saying that. There are times when I feel that I don't need a man. I just want a man in my life? It's like I don't need a new car, I just want one. It would be nice to experience the smell of a new car again. They sure ride nice. But I don't need one. The one I've got runs just fine. It comes and goes, let me say that.

Certainly, there are times when I envision myself in the future of being with someone. Right now, I don't feel the need for that, not at this time. It's like right now, I don't have the psychological space for that. It's as though I can see the time coming when I will have the psychological space for that. And there's a consequence of that, to feel the need for a man.

Chronologically, I am not getting any younger, but maybe I am getting younger from the neck up, inside in some ways. I think what age is allowing me to acquire is a loosening up. Maybe that is actually a youthful thing, to be able to accommodate the needs of another on an ongoing basis. It's one thing to accommodate the needs of another on a weekend, but in a permanent-type situation, that is quite another thing. In the way of loosening up on that, maybe I am becoming more youthful.

During this day and age in relationships, I think young girls are missing role models. I don't think they've had before them models of good relationships in any realistic sense. I think they ask much too little of themselves and the men they become involved with.

There is an important way in which I feel they ask too much. Young people tend to ask of one another that the sun rise and set right where their beloved stands. That's an awful lot to ask. I think young women ask of the men they're involved with, "Be my world. Be my everything." That's what the songs say. That's what the songs promise. I think that's a grave mistake. I think you need to find yourself and bring a more evolved self to the relationship. So many young women, men too, seem to be very empty inside. I think they are attempting to fill that void with another person. They are empty of self-esteem more than anything else. Empty of the notion that they can achieve. Empty of a dream that they feel they can live out.

Some of the remedies for this lack of self-esteem could be better unions between people. In a very, very important way, a woman starts being a good mother long before a child is conceived. She starts being a good mother when she chooses the man she is going to date, and perhaps sleep with. That's the time to be very considerate, to consider long and hard what you're doing. More stable relationships would lead to more stable children. But after the fact, now that these unstable people are here, what do I think the remedy would be? To say education sounds so trite. Honestly, education geared toward raising self-esteem and enlightening of young people to help them to understand what makes them tick, where they're coming from, what their motivations are.

In the future, for those children having children, as a nation, we may go through a very difficult time. I don't regard myself as a pessimist, and yet, the more I see the more pessimistic I become. What indeed is to become of the many fatherless children? I don't know that this country has the will to care for those children. And yet, if we don't, we're going to see big time fireworks down the road.

In the course of my work, I see children who are pretty often times unparented. Just simply unparented. Adrift. Sometimes they have almost predatory instincts. I mean they are opportunists. They are looking for an opportunity to get their needs met. I don't know that they act different than the rest of us in an overt way most of the time. Of course, it depends upon the age. I have always had the feeling that they are alert for any opportunity to be loved, or on a more negative side, swipe whatever they can to get their needs met.

Young boys need the same thing that young women need in order to evolve into good young men. They need positive self-image. Again, it goes back to self-esteem – to how adequately their inner needs are being met or not.

Knowing who they are as a people and as a race and what they have accomplished in the world certainly would help. I feel that is a little abstract for most youngsters at this time. When I talk about elevating self-esteem, I'm talking on a more immediate level. I'm talking about someone in the home who is interested in them. In whatever difficulties they are having in school. In whether they're getting their homework done. In whether they're even attending school. In who their friends are. In what they think about the things they encounter day to day. Someone who is in the home all the time, if that is possible.

℮

If that right man comes along and he wants me to give up my place to go to his place, or get another place, that would be fine. Whether he comes with me, I go with him, we get another place, it really wouldn't matter. It is important to me that my space is set up in a way that works for me. In a way that I can enjoy it. In a way that gives me energy. I like to think that anyone I would be attracted to would feel the same way and that we would have enough common ground to work that out.

Throughout my life, I have never seen myself as being beautiful. Attractive is a different issue. It means so much. It's a loaded term, because when we speak of someone being attractive, we are not necessarily speaking of physical beauty. We may be talking about something inner that is attractive. I won't say that I am not at all attractive, but certainly not pretty – I never have been – or not beautiful. Sometimes that can have an effect on my own self-esteem, depending on what day I am asked that question. Sometimes yes. Sometimes no. I don't think, in any significant way, that has impacted my self-esteem. It has been my experience that I have attracted to myself, for whatever reasons, enough men to keep life interesting.

I disagree with the premise that being to one's self make a person self-centered. Other things make one self-centered. Being alone has not made me that way. I am not sure that being self-centered is a bad thing. It has not made me selfish. I am accustomed to having things my way when I walk in and close my door. One has to deal with the world once one is outside. One spends eight hours a day at work, has to, at that time, engage in the give and take. That's life.

Having my way in a relationship depends on the hierarchy of the needs involved. If we are talking about what we are going to have for dinner tonight, that's not so God-awful important. If we're talking about how much we are going to pay for a new house, then that gets to be very important. It simply would depend on what the subject was.

In any case, I don't think I am a person who has to have things my way all of the time. I'm very fluid. If the right man comes along, I envision being very flexible. When we're talking about the right man – and so far this is a fantasy, meaning it has not yet happened – but when that happens, I will do all that I can to please him, if he is doing the same for me.

I do a considerable amount of reading. Some has influenced my outlook on life. Things that I read tend to be on the metaphysical side. I read then for that purpose, to influence my outlook on life. By this time and at this age, perhaps it's not so much to set a new direction, as to reinforce, broaden, and deepen the understandings that I have already acquired.

My initiation into a metaphysical way of life goes back to what I now realize has always been my way of thinking. Where that came from I don't exactly know. However, when I became actively involved in the pursuit of metaphysical studies, I came to California and at that time there was a proliferation of groups studying Eastern religions. I became involved in one of those groups. It was from that wellspring that my metaphysical interests flourished.

The most primary tenet of metaphysics is that the point of power is in the present moment. That an individual can determine his own fate. That in fact, we do determine our own fate. We simply do not realize that we are doing it. We do it on a subconscious level. Metaphysics simply teaches awareness. It's all about awareness. If I were to talk to a novice about metaphysics, I suppose I would have to stop there. It gets very deep.

I could not define awareness, to begin with, in any precise form. Yogis have been trying to do that for centuries and have written many, many books on what awareness is. I would not try to encapsulate it. I don't know if I would be able to do that. It involves a self-consciousness. Desire plays such a role in obtaining awareness. One has to have a profound desire to wake up, to become awake, to become cognizant. I am simply restating the problem, not getting at what awareness is or how you obtain it.

If I was to meet a man and we had mutual interests, I with my metaphysical perspective, he with an old traditional Christian perspective, I don't know if that would work. I would need to introduce him to some of my notions about Christianity. Perhaps where I would have the advantage is that while I am familiar with Christianity, because in this country it is omnipresent, he would not perhaps be familiar with metaphysical thought. I would hope to be able to show him how very much metaphysical thought is a part of Christianity. It simply is, but many Christians overlook it or perhaps take it for granted. Jesus was tremendously metaphysical. I believe that. I don't think I have known anyone who was more metaphysical than Jesus.

If I met someone who was not into metaphysics, I feel I could still connect with that person, if there was an openness. It is such an integral part of who I am. If he is unyielding or unwilling to at least explore who I am, I don't think we could connect in the ways that I would need us to connect, to form a permanent bond.

Who I am is: I am spirit; I am metaphysical; I am woman; I am black, in that order.

If I never find a man in my life who is compatible with who I am, I'd like to think that I can make a very worthwhile, very meaningful interesting life for myself, almost as I have already done. But because now, being older, I have greater wisdom and more tools to work with. So, I'd like to think that I'll be able to live a fulfilling life, with or without a man.

Georgia Millet

Ms. Millet is 34 years old and single. She is an executive in the corporate world and volunteers in various activities to help others. She is so full of energy she almost gives the impression that she works in her sleep. She is dedicated and committed to what she perceives is her vocation in life, bringing others closer to her religious belief. It is the central thread in her life. The human urge is to wonder about when her husband is going to materialize. This is done in a non-compromising fashion. Based on the experiences she has gone through in various relationships, she has grown to know what she wants and what she will not accept. She reflects a life direction that is almost fading in American society today. The lessons in her story are almost an individual formula for those who believe as she does, and takes us back to a time when an intimate relationship seemed to allude more integrity than what is typical of present times.

I was born in Maryland. I had a wonderful childhood. Fantastic parents. My parents are very loving, very kind. I grew up knowing that my parents loved me. I feel that I was brought up with a lot of good traditional values. I knew that my father loved my mother. I knew that my mother loved my father. They got along very, very well. My parents are professionals in the computer industry.

I lived in a household where there were very few male/female roles. When my father had the time, he cooked. He was the one who did the grocery shopping. He was the one who went to the cleaners. He picked me up from school, all of those kinds of things. When I go back and look at the pictures of my father with me, I can see how much he really cares. You can just see it in his eyes how much he loves us.

My mother is just as significant. I don't have the greatest vision in the world. I had those thick ugly glasses. I now wear contacts. My mother said to me when I was an early teen, "If there is an operation where I can give you one of my eyes so that you could have perfect vision, then I would do it." I said, "Ma, I would never ask you to do that." She was very serious about that. This was an example of the love she had for her child; wanting to do that. Parent-wise, and all of the loving I got from them, I think I grew up very, very well.

My parents were excellent role models for me on how a man and woman can love and treat each other. The most important things they taught me to look for in a mate were his belief in God, his character, how he treats his family, how he treats a woman, and is he consistent and dependable.

My parents did not place importance on a man having a lot of material possessions when choosing a husband. But of course, like most parents, they wanted the best for me, not someone who can't even take care of himself. My paternal grandfather had a saying, "You can do bad all by yourself." My maternal great-grandmother, she had a saying, "You need two things to survive in this world: God and money." I think they made fantastic role models for me.

My aunts, my uncles, and my grandparents, put a lot of emphasis on making sure that as a woman, I was treated well and that I respected myself. This was really important to my aunts. "You make sure to act like a lady." A lot of it was by example, in terms of how they lived their lives, how they were treated. My father has never hit my mother or anything like that. I've never been in a relationship that was physically abusive. I think that is kind of interesting. I have never chosen a man who had that inclination. I've been very fortunate not to have that occur. I've never had to address it. You know, there is a theory that says, "We can subconsciously attract and be attracted to a particular negative behavior, so we continue to repeat the same relationship over and over again with new people."

I am the type of woman that if a man hit me, he might as well take me out, because I am going to go down trying to take him out. I'm one of those kinds of women (laughs).

On the other hand, I believe that in some ways how I was brought up backfired on me. My wonderful parents instilled in me the traditional values of being responsible and being productive. So, I did all of the supposedly right things. I went to college, worked very hard for different positions, volunteered, was involved in church and most of all, did not get pregnant. Sometimes I run into men who resent me, or they are intimidated because I either have a higher position or make more money. Some did not go to or finish college. Because the above is not necessarily a measure of success, I would venture into dating these gentlemen. Unfortunately, even though these things weren't important to me, it reflected in those men who had problems with themselves, and thus it created a problem in the relationship.

I first started getting interested in boys about the third or fourth grade, you know, a little crush on somebody. "He's cute," or something like that. I remember an incident in the fifth grade. There was this little boy who thought he was all that. His big thing was, he would go around and take things from different girls' lunch boxes. I don't know what he expected, but one day he came around to my lunch box (Spiderman) and wanted my Ding Dongs. He just took it and started unwrapping the paper. I reeled back and with all of my force, lunch box in my hand, knocked him out cold. The ambulance came for him. Needless to say, he never bothered my lunch again.

My first serious relationship was in college. I was a freshman and 18 years old. He was three years older than I. He went to another college down the road. The Lord blessed me the first time with a very good man. He was very smart. I love brilliant men. He treated me well. He respected me. We were together for four-and-a-half years.

My initiation into the sensual realm occurred during my sophomore year of college with this man. He had cooked dinner, albeit in his dorm room, but the thought was sweet. The romantic atmosphere was encouraged with soft lights and tranquil music. He didn't know it was going to happen that evening . . . but I did. When I told him I was ready to *go there*, he was speechless after waiting for more than a year. I mostly remember that the experience brought me closer to him. Well, let's just say that I enjoyed it so much, that we kept getting "closer" for the rest of our four-and-a-half year relationship. Looking back, I know that I disappointed God because I was not married, but it is never too late to make a change. Thank God for the forgiveness of sins.

I didn't know this until a couple of years into the relationship, but he always saw me as his little "Georgie." He just thought I was so sweet and innocent. Over time, I guess I grew up. I wanted us to talk about more things. He just wanted me to stay his little woman. At first, he was resentful over the breakup. He wanted to talk about only three things: the relationship, sports, and how to make money. Years after, he agrees that we probably would have gotten a divorce. We've stayed good friends. You grow. He's still a very good man, but I just have so many varied interests. What can he do to make more money, is still his number one conversation. He never really wanted to talk about anything else. And I must admit, he now owns two homes, a boat, and is close to being a millionaire. He is still single, after having several other relationships, telling me I messed it up for all women to follow. I was his first love. Maybe I should call... Naw. We would still be targeted for divorce court since God is not a priority in his life.

I feel very fortunate about the relationships I've had. I don't regret breaking up with any of them. I don't look back and say, "Oh, he was the one." Thank God none of them headed towards a marriage because I have grown so much. I now feel prepared and well-equipped for a lasting relationship.

In my twenties, there were a few friends. A date here, a date there, nothing of any lasting nature that makes an impression on my brain. I did meet one gentleman, a good man. I met him after I received my first job after graduation. He didn't press for a sexual relationship. He believed it was a sin against biblical beliefs. That was refreshing and endeared him to me. I thought this might work out, because he was wealthy for his age, even though I had been to school and he hadn't. The fact that he made much more money than I did, I thought that would help him in his feelings to not be intimidated. I was wrong. He felt insecure. I would talk about something and he would look at me and say, "I should have gone to school." That was a problem. I guess it has to do with the fact of him not feeling secure in himself. I wasn't too pleased about that at all. The relationship did not last because he felt "less than."

My parents really did raise me not to focus on those kinds of things with people. Yes, I've been very fortunate going to school and what-not, but if someone hasn't gone to college, I don't look down on that. There are lots of ways to be smart, lots of ways to be intelligent. And yes, having a college education helps pave a path for you in a particular direction. But there are a lot of people who are extremely successful who have not gone to college.

My parents never said to me, "Your husband should be of equal college education." I think I would miss out on a lot of good men that way. I never thought that. But when men have those problems themselves, it can be difficult. I've never been the type of woman to make a man feel less. Someone might ask, "How do you know you're not?" Because of my personality. It is not in my psyche to treat people poorly. If that were a problem for me, I wouldn't have gotten into the relationship.

A few years later, I had another relationship. This was a mistake. I met this gentleman and I knew on first seeing him, "That's my husband." A lot of my background started coming out. We were together for about four-and-a-half years. This gentleman was legally separated when we met. That was fine. (Repeat, warning sign that this was a mistake.) They were in the process of divorce. Things were fine for a year, two years, or something like that. Then he started to pull the old disappearing act. In hindsight, I should have ended it right there, but I think I was a little obsessed at that time. I stayed with him. Family was telling me, "Leave this man alone. Get away from him." I just wanted this man and thought things would work out.

I remember one time, I don't know if I was going to look for him or what. I was in my twenties. I got a straight razor. I went to his house with evil intent. Nothing came of it because God is good. There's a saying, "God takes care of fools and babies." Sometimes I don't know which category I fall into, depending on the particular situation. I got a hold of my mind and left before I caused havoc.

He was telling me that he loved me and everything was fine. He got the divorce. I started feeling that I was being followed. I saw cars behind me longer than they would normally be there. Things got a little strange. I was thinking that the ex-wife was trying to find me to do some harm to me. I felt this way for a while. It was a horrible experience. I'm thinking there might be a contract out on me. This was really going that deep. I've had a colorful life. You hear clicks in your phone that weren't there before, all kinds of things.

I recall discussing this with him and he said, "I think that might be true. There might be that possibility." He had noticed people following him. I knew it had something to do with the settlement. There was a big settlement, one of those kinds of situations. But still, I was there. I was right there. It just so happened that I got a new job and moved to another city in Mississippi. Once again, it's just how God works things out; how he's looking out for you when you're not even looking out for yourself. He just realized that this wasn't a good situation. "Nothing is going to come of it. She needs to be out of this. She's not going to do it herself. Let me help her here."

I kept hanging in there though, like a nut. Then I called one day and spoke to his sister. She was over his mother's house. She mentioned something like, "Well yes, he got the divorce, but he's thinking about maybe going back. Then there's something about a woman over in this city. There might be one over here." You know my head was reeling, "I don't believe this." Then I got the courage to make the break to just end this. That's a story within itself. That's a book.

℘

Let me tell you about some things I went through that greatly affected me as a young girl. Something happened to me growing up. I had a great childhood in terms of my parents. But unfortunately, growing up for myself, there were some other things that occurred in there.

In my preteen years, some physical things took precedence with me. You already know about the glasses. Well, I was also very short and brown-skinned. Unfortunately, black children still made fun of each other for the shades of their skin back then. I hope black children no longer do this. Isn't it a shame how slavery still affects us?

As time went on, I went through that whole acne stage. I was one of those unfortunate young ladies who had a very bad case of it. I'd say that did a number on my self-esteem and my self-confidence.

Remember the movie *The Elephant Man*? I associated with him so closely. I was sitting in the movies. I was about 11, 12, or 13. Those years are so important in a girl's life. That's when she develops her self-concept about what she looks like to the world. Tears came flowing down my eyes. I really understood what he felt.

When it came to boys, I wasn't considered attractive to them. It wasn't even a thought. I was always the one that was made fun of, always. I used my strengths. That's how come now my personality is the way it is. I think there are very few people I know who do not like me. Personality had to take over. My mind had to take over. I wasn't going to get anywhere based on what I looked like. That wasn't going to open any kind of door for me. I never even thought that. I never even grew up with the concept of that even being possible.

But little girls, even now when you watch a movie or you watch television, the girls are treated by young men in terms of being pretty, or having a choice to be able to say, "No, I don't want to go out with you." I never had those kinds of choices as a preteen growing up. That affected me a great deal.

A lot of times people, even social scientists, will look at a person and how they're raised in their family. People should also study some other things that may happen. The thing now is, "How did your father treat you when you were little?" Those kinds of things. Yes, that has a lot to do with it, but for some people there may be some outside factor that occurred. "As long as the child knows that she's loved at home," that's supposed to be the answer. For me, it was more than that. I guess it is taken for granted what you have. My parents gave me unconditional love. I knew that. But maybe I was also trying to see if someone else would love me.

I remember praying nightly, "God, when I grow up, please let me be beautiful on the outside. Please let others think that I am." God answers prayer. Most of the people I know count me as one of the most beautiful or physically attractive women they have ever met. Of course, I don't ask. It just comes out in some conversation here and there. Now, don't I sound conceited or like I think "I'm all that (laughs)." But the truth is the truth! Obviously, I am no longer lacking in self-esteem. Thank God, childhood is a just a stage.

In the last relationship that I mentioned, my childhood demons plagued me. I am so glad this is in the past. I don't exhibit any of these behaviors anymore. If he would call me, I'd immediately call him back. If he didn't call for two or three days or something, I'm now beginning to wonder if something happened to him. Was he in an accident? All of those kinds of thoughts. Of course, you do the exact opposite of what you want. Trying to pull the person closer to you, you drive them away. You're sitting by the phone wondering what is wrong. What did you do? Not realizing at the time or not thinking clearly, "I'm not being treated correctly. This isn't right. This isn't the kind of man I need in my life." I know this now, but I guess you have to go through those things. The stuff that I went through in my childhood has affected my relationships. I've learned. I've come out of it.

My last significant relationship was several years ago. He was a good man. He was a hard-working gentleman. Everything was going fine. He treated me well. He was just a serious workaholic though. He began to take me for granted. That's one of those leftover behaviors from when I was little. I allowed myself to be taken for granted then. He thought that I was always going to be there. The field of business that he was in is not a salaried field. He has to be constantly working all the time to make money. His money was made on commission. He can do really well at it, but he has to be there to make the money. I could call him at his office any time of day or night, on weekends, and he'd be there.

I kind of made it clear to him, "Remember me?" I'm the type of woman who understands if you have to work really hard. If we're married, you're coming home to me, eventually. But if you are single and since I don't believe in living together, I will never see you. He just thought that I would always be there. He didn't provide time for me. He didn't take what I was saying to him seriously. He would cancel on me or get to me really late when he was trying to get something done. I looked into the future and said to myself, "You can't change anyone. This is him. This is what he loves to do." I'm so happy for him. But I had to look into the future and see that this would always be this way. Then I started thinking about myself that I would one day like to have the option when I'm married and pregnant that I could be able to stay home for the first year or so to raise the baby. This was not the type of relationship that was going to help with that. I couldn't count on a certain amount of money being there. His money was very unstable for a family life.

I know this is the life of an entrepreneur. I would accept this lifestyle if he was working towards owning or running a business, but he is working for someone else on a commission. It just said to me, "It's always going to be this way." I ended it. Then the love just started to also leave.

A lot of times you should know when to end it. Sometimes you go a little beyond when you shouldn't. Fortunately, I ended it at the right time. Some of the signs that led me to that conclusion were all those things in the beginning of the relationship that I ignored like, "Isn't that cute. He does this. He does that." Those things began to disturb me. Little habits like going to the refrigerator and leaving the milk carton open. Leaving the juice carton open. Those kinds of petty things would never have bothered me before, but they were now. "Why is he doing this? He's going to come over to my place, open the refrigerator and..." Little simple things like that. It just let me know that the love in the relationship was leaving. He was not pleased at all. He didn't want it to end, but I thought it was best.

I would say right now, currently, I have two proposals on the table. He's one of them. I'm not going to take either one of them. I've learned what's right for me. These men are not right for me. I've been out of a relationship for four years. Even though I am not in a relationship now, I have full faith in God that my husband is coming really soon. I keep hope alive. There have been people I've gone out with. Something may start off but then I come to realize this isn't right.

I've come up with a lot of theories during this time. For one thing, I believe there was a time when getting married in your twenties was extremely common. Couples decided they would grow together, build careers and financial goals together. Nowadays people, especially men, want to have all of this before they get married.

All of my theories come out of my experiences and things I've seen from other friends and what they've gone through in relationships. A lot of brothers don't feel that they're ready until their late thirties. It seems to me, it takes black men longer to jump-start their careers. They want to have everything set up before they get married. I understand that racism plays a big part in our brothers taking a longer time in believing that they are a success, or even getting that opportunity to move up the ranks to be successful.

I think the past has held fewer options for our black men. Positions weren't that important. Twenty years ago, there were fewer upwardly mobile positions to even shoot for. So, maybe men didn't really have that as a focus because the "powers that be" weren't going to let him achieve anyway. Of course, these are all my interpretations. Things have changed. A career position is much more important now since it can be achieved by some of us. It's also like they are looking for a particular salary that they want to have before they get married. I think a lot of men do not want the responsibility of having a wife because it is a responsibility.

I've discussed with some friends that we sometimes feel this "no man thing" is a conspiracy of keeping black people who can actually contribute something to society down and away from each other. Then of course, we won't have any black marriages. You destroy black families. There would just be a majority of fatherless homes because there would always be women willing to get pregnant without a commitment from a man. That takes us out of society right there.

I don't see myself as desperate. If I were desperate I would be married. Like I mentioned earlier, I have two proposals on the table right now. One of them, I am not going to consider. The other one, once again, is a very well-meaning gentleman who also took me for granted. Did one of those seven whole days' things. You know, Toni Braxton had that song, "Seven Whole Days." Well, that's what he did, seven days without calling me. The first time that happened, it's interesting because that was maybe one of the relationships where I was at a turning point. I think I had my brain together then. I really had everything together. I was able to tell him the following,

"This is your first time doing this. I just want to let you know a couple of things about me. I don't appreciate that. I like people to communicate with me and be consistent. That's one of the things I really feel strongly about. I've never been a woman that feels a man has to take me out all of the time, or we have to go to dinner every other night or we have to go to the movies every single weekend. I was never like that, but I do like to hear from you. You go so many days without talking to me and I just don't appreciate it. I like that communication. You go seven whole days without talking to me, I'm thinking something's wrong. I appreciate it if you wouldn't do it again."

"This time we're having the discussion. If it happens a second time, I'll remind and warn you because, hey, you could have forgotten. But if it happens a third time, I am not even going to speak to you anymore. It's over. It's done with. I say that because that shows me that you obviously don't care how I feel. You don't care about me."

That was one of those relationships where I don't know if it was a challenge to him or maybe he didn't take me seriously. I also told him when we started the relationship I had this little rule for myself. After a man takes me out on the first date, okay. The second or the third date, depending on what kind of connection I'm feeling between us, I will sit down and give him "my speech."

In this speech, I tell him, "I want you to know that I know you really are interested in me, and that's good. It's very important for you to know I do not believe in having a sexual relationship. The next time that is going to occur, I am going to be a married woman. If you have a problem with that I understand. If you decide not to call me anymore, not to see me anymore because of that, I will understand. I'm not telling you this because it's a joke. It's not a challenge. I don't want you to continue to pursue thinking that this is going to happen, or for you to think that you have something to conquer, BECAUSE IT'S NOT GOING TO HAPPEN (her emphasis). I just wanted to let you know that. I made a decision many, many years ago that the next time I'm intimate with a man, I will be his wife."

I made that change after realizing that my life was not going where I wanted it to go. I felt like I was hitting a brick wall and not achieving any major happiness in my life. So, one day, I took some time to examine all of the aspects of my life and realized that I was not being obedient to God in this area. It hit me, "How do I expect to be blessed if I am not completely living as He would want me to?" So from that day, I made a decision that the next time I explored that joyous pleasure with another man, he would be my husband. So, eons of years later, I know that I am forgiven and that my husband is just around the corner.

Yes, I keep knocking myself off with different men because of all of these things. Like the whole sex issue, that's a big thing right there. "Well, you know, I have to," a guy told me, "Of course, I can't think of having a relationship without that being involved." I said, "But yeah, you don't even know my middle name, so how can we even talk about that yet?"

I've had men whose phones would fall out of their hands when I told them this, or guys who would just sit and stare at me like I'm crazy. There was one guy I was riding with; he stopped the car in the middle of the street, just put on the brakes and said, "What? What did you say?" I repeated it and we moved on to another conversation. He went back and said, "I guess it's easier for women to be...," I said, "What are you talking about?" He said, "Celibate." "Oh. You're still on that? Okay, let's talk about this because obviously you need to discuss it some more."

Men still have that good girl, bad girl thing. They have the woman that they're just going to see, mostly for sex. Then they have the woman that they want to marry. A lot of times some women will say, "Oh, that's not true. That kind of thinking went out with the 50s. Women's liberation changed that." No, some things never change.

A man's going to think something different of you if you decide to sleep with him on the first, second, or third date. Yes, he's going to accept it, but his thought is, "If she does this with me, she'll do this with someone else." I think men look for what differentiates a particular woman to him, depending on what he's looking for, "What makes her special to me?" Most men will not choose a woman just for the sake of choosing, but see something that is special or unique about her that appeals to him.

Too many women are disrespecting themselves. We are treasures. We are to be treated as queens, our whole persona, our physical being, from the top of our heads, to the tender tips of our toes, because we're precious. Someone has to prove to me that I am loved, I am cared for and provided for before we develop an intimate relationship. The only way to guarantee that is to be married.

You can break up any old time. When you hear people talking about breaking up, it's easier for them to break up with someone when they haven't had an intimate relationship. For women, we take it harder because that is a very personal thing. She feels that she's given away a very personal part of herself.

That particular gentleman, the one who did the seven whole day scenario, I had this discussion with him. We were doing fine and everything, but he did it again. Just took me for granted. I have a habit of being, I don't know if you would call it overly nice or what, but I have learned since then that men have to do a lot for me before I do things for them. Just that whole concept of earning my love; that's a concept I don't think I really grew up with when I was younger. I have realized now in terms of getting my head together, about how I should be treated by someone. So, I left him alone. And guess what? He steadily leaves messages professing his eternal love. Well, I can't dip back into the past.

Once again, going back to that whole childhood thing, I think I had the tendency to do too much for men. I was never one to go and buy people things. That's not my style. My problem was I was too dependable. I never learned to play the game. Sometimes you hear that men and women shouldn't play games. But maybe we should as women be taught a mating ritual. They say, "Women who know how to do this well, know how to go with the ritual," in terms of being courted. So, I've learned that. It's very, very sad but this is true. If I consistently do what I say I'm going to do, I'm taken for granted. Your kind actions are taken for weakness. If she is where she says she's going to be, and is good and kind and loving to you, then some men, not all, take that for granted. They begin to think that the challenge isn't there for them. It's like they always have to be in constant pursuit. They realize that, "She's there for me. She cares about me." When you don't call, they begin to think, "Where is she? She didn't call me. Oh wow, have I done anything wrong?" You're on their minds now and they can't help but to think about you and vie for your attention.

It's very interesting, but I'm just beginning to realize how this works. It really does work. When you're just not so dependable, I don't know if that's something that happens maybe as the relationship develops, or maybe it's in the love stage or something. It's definitely past the courting stage when you can now give without being taken for granted, but not too much in the beginning. I guess that's just one of those things I didn't catch on to in my twenties or early on because I wanted to be loved so badly. I think it's that whole thing of, "You want what you can't have." Men will go after that and women also do the same thing. I've learned that.

The thought that a husband may not find me, and that I may not have children has run through my mind. Literally run through it. I don't take that seriously. 2 Timothy 1:7 says, "For God has not given us a spirit of fear, but of power, love, and a sound mind." There's another scripture, Matthew 6:33 that says, "Seek ye first the kingdom of God and His righteousness, and all these things shall be added unto you."

I truly seek Him, as a matter of fact. I know that my spiritual purpose for being on this earth is to bring others to the saving knowledge of Jesus Christ. So, every day I pray, "Lord, I thank you for working through me to bring someone to a closer walk with you today." And guess what, somehow God makes a way for me to proclaim His love to someone every day. I am so blessed. God is so good. So, I know that "thing" will be added unto me because I am seeking Him first and doing His Will.

I'm a Christian. I believe in God. He's first in my life. He knows the desires of my heart and a husband is the desire of my heart.

When it comes to a relationship, my spiritual belief is extremely important. That's what guides everything. That's what guides everything now. When I was in my early years, my early twenties, even though I was a Christian, I didn't put all those godly principles into place. Then I started realizing that His Word really is the foundation for a fruitful relationship, at least how I would want it to go. That has guided the relationships. That is also another reason why maybe some of them have not worked out. A lot of men weren't willing to go with that program.

The first thing I look for in a man, of course, is the fact that he is a Christian. And not just a Christian, but a growing Christian. "Yeah, I'm a Christian. Yeah, I believe in God. Believe in Jesus Christ." But if he is not doing anything in his life to show that growth, or to want his spirituality to increase, to have that closer connection, that relationship with Him; if he is not doing that, then we could never grow together and the relationship wouldn't work. It's so beautiful. It's so wonderful to walk with Him, to know His Word, to be a child of God. Those things are so important. That's the first thing I look for.

I can meet a man who is really nice, really spiritual. If he's not a Christian we won't be seeing each other. We will not be equally yoked. In the Bible, equally yoked talks about how if you're not going in the same way together, that you're going to be apart. Things just won't go well. I know that the Bible talks about more than just being a Christian in terms of being equally yoked. Two people can be Christians and not be equally yoked. They will have different goals and what-not.

I know some Christians who have made the mistake thinking,

"Oh, he's a Christian. Everything's all right." A couple of years down the road they are divorced. We have to have Christ as the head of our home. If we don't have Christ as the head of our home and we both are not serving Him, we're going to have problems.

I had a situation a couple of months ago where I was talking with this brother. He claims to be a Christian, but says he is unhappy with how the Church is. He says, "Church isn't everything these days. One of the problems I have with the Black Church, they believe in worshipping Christ." I'm just listening. He says, "That's sacrilege. There's only one true God." I brought up, "There's God the Father, God the Son, God the Holy Spirit, the three in one; The Trinity." He says, "Yeah, I know all about that. It's blasphemous. Christ is only supposed to be seen as our brother. We're not supposed to be worshipping him." Now, he calls himself a Christian. He doesn't even know when the last time he's been to church. But he has his own views. He's also going through some kind of metaphysical, half New Age, half something, scientific whatever.

I could not submit to him as the head of my house because our views on the most important aspect of my life go in two separate directions. Jesus Christ is the foundation of my life. I believe I am to submit to my husband's leadership of the home.

This may surprise you. People look at my career, all of the great volunteer activities I am involved in, my independence, but I truly do believe in the biblical belief of submission to the husband. He's the head. He's the head of the house. I think a lot of times when some women hear that word, hands go on hips, fingers go out, heads go from side to side, "Uh, uh. I am not...," you know. Even a lot of Christian women are like that. I think it might have to do with whom you choose as a mate. If you respect someone and his opinions on things, and if you admire him, then you're going to want to follow his leadership. You're going to accept his leadership. You believe in him and what he's saying.

I think some women hook up with fellows they don't even respect. They end up talking about them in public or in front of them to other people. "Oh, he doesn't know what he's talking about. He doesn't know anything." I would not do that to the man I love in public or even in private. There's a certain type of respect that has to be there.

The whole thought of submission has been taken out of context. Submission is saying, hopefully, that the two will walk with each other, that the woman was put here as a helpmate to the man. So, as a helpmate, she would be there to help him. They would walk, especially in today's terms, as a partnership, doing things together in one accord. He, of course, because he cherishes his wife, respects and loves her, he will usually, always, hopefully, seek her opinion and views on certain things about how should we do this and that. But if it came down to a point where a decision had to be made, then I believe we would go with what my husband said, especially if we have varying views and we can't compromise. I would respect that and believe that he would know what he was doing and pray that God would give him insight to that knowledge.

℮

Most of the Black women I know, including myself, are single by choice. Meaning we are not desperate to take just anybody, but we are selective. We are not running into what we would like to meet. Yes, I could get a date just to go to the movies or dinner, or just to say I have someone. But why waste my time? I believe in holding out for what I really want. Yes, this means that I am alone a lot, most of the time. I do believe that when love finds me, the wait will be worth it.

I remember a young lady saying to me she would rather be unhappy than alone. I'll never forget that. She was in an abusive relationship. The guy was beating her off and on. He was dealing drugs, all that kind of stuff. She would come home and see him being intimate with other women. She would just continue to go on with him. That's something I don't believe in. I'd rather be alone than unhappy. At least being alone, there's always that opportunity for God to bless me with that special person.

I realize, and I've discussed this with a lot of my friends, there are couples who are together all the time, here and there. It doesn't mean they're happy. There are a lot of people who just can't do things by themselves. They have to have someone with them, just to be there. I'm sure this has happened to so many people. Scenario: They are with a person walking down the street together, holding hands, sitting in the movies just to be there with someone, and they see THAT person. THAT person sees them. They can't do a thing about it because they have an appendage connected to them at the time.

I had someone to tell me, "Well, you know you're not going to find someone perfect." That's not what I'm looking for. I'm not perfect. I'm an imperfect being. The choice you make is so important because some other people can say, "Yes, that's a good man. You should accept him. He's good enough or he's okay." I'm going to be the person to roll over, hopefully, for forty or fifty years and have to look at that face every morning. You're the one who is going to be involved in a relationship with that person. If you make a poor choice, you're going to have to deal with that. A lot of people are dealing with that. We all know people who are in those kinds of relationships. If they look back, they would do it differently.

When I'm with my girlfriends and we talk about relationships, we are really defining what we are looking for in someone in terms of inner qualities. We're coming to that place of honing in on what's really important. We hold each other up a lot. There are those times when being alone does get to you. Like, "What's wrong with me? What in the world is going on here?" I quickly remind myself that God has a plan and He has not forgotten about me. I must live by faith because Hebrews 11:1 says, "Now faith is the assurance of things hoped for and the evidence of things not seen." Well, I have to have faith because I don't see a thing (laughs).

One of the things that we talk about now is how Black people do not introduce people to each other the way they used to, the way I believe other cultures continue to do so. Most of us are no longer living in the cities where we were born, where our parents are or where most of our family is located. When you move to other places and meet other people, you're making friends with people you basically have no roots with. We're so concerned with what we have to do to get through the day, your career and your family. People do not think about, "Well, you know, I think Raymond should meet your sister Rebecca." People don't think in those terms. They don't think about, "So-and-so's been single for so long, I think these two might do well together." That's something we talk about. So much so to the point that we came up with an idea. The idea was to get three single women, three single men and just give a friends sort of get together, maybe a dinner at a restaurant, not a party. Parties have their own dynamics. You're the person who invites and you see what comes of it. If one couple comes out of it, that's wonderful. It's not even about me getting a relationship. If I can help someone else do this, then the next time someone else takes one of their friends, and then maybe they will introduce two friends that I have together or something like that.

Someone had thought about it as a business. We said, "No, no. We want this to be free for everybody. Just do it. Take the idea and run with it. Tell your friends. Tell everybody and get more people together."

The major problems I see with teenagers and young adults is that the young women are really having a hard time being grounded on how they should conduct themselves. For example, things are so twisted girls are now calling guys for a first date. They're calling them all of the time. Guys don't even have to do anything.

The younger women complain that there is no solidarity among the sisters of today. I've been told that the friendliness of the past is not really there. I don't know if this has anything to do with men or if this is a competitive thing between the women. I think for one thing, the women may be ready to be a little more serious than the brothers. Some of the young brothers are at that stage where they want to "play" women, enjoy the "player" life. You have some of that going on because there are more females than males. Young people who are going on to college sometimes run into this as a problem. Things have changed in terms of how young people conduct themselves around each other. They are really, really trying to feel their way in how to conduct themselves in a relationship in the first place. They might be getting to know each other intimately a little too soon, before they even build a friendship with each other.

When it comes to sex, some of the young brothers I have talked with say the women are worse than the guys. Of course, that's from their perspective. I don't know if that has to do with this whole video culture. The tops are too short. The shorts are too high. Cleavages are too low, just my opinion. Those things may attract, but they don't hold. He's just going to go off to something with a deeper cleavage and higher shorts. The girls are still feeling their way with that. I see that in high school students. It's a whole different time for them. Some of the concepts that we have may be seen as old fashioned.

I think the music videos, peer pressure, and other things that young people have to face are having an affect. You see it in just the way they dress. The emphasis, I don't think right now, is on anything real. It's on what he's wearing. It's not even about what kind of car because he may not even have one. It's based on what he's wearing. The name brands are featured.

It's kind of sad, but when I do have a chance to talk with young people about relationships and what to look out for, I tell the young ladies to respect themselves. You do not have to sleep with someone just because he wants you to. Choices like that can just derail your future. Still, in these times, we have too many high school students getting pregnant.

I tell the guys the same thing: "You're also responsible. If you want to have the future that you desire, you better 'suit up." I can discuss the whole abstinence thing and, depending on the situation, I do. But you have to go where they are. If this is what they're doing, I emphasize to them to be really careful. One of the things that I try to make really real is, "You may not want a future with this person. This may be something you want to do right now. But something you want to do right now can turn into a baby, turn into a disease, turn into something you can't get rid of. That's going to be a life-altering decision. When it comes in terms of a baby, if you do not want a baby with this person, or this is not someone you can see yourself having a baby with, you may want to leave that person alone. When you lie down with someone for a fling, it could turn into a lifetime of regret and responsibility."

I had a conversation with some young people about self-control, "Just because your body may be telling you something, you may have this urge, doesn't mean that you have to act on it. It will pass. That's what self-control is about. It's not about, 'You have to do this.'" For one young lady, that made a big difference to her. She told me, "You know, I just never thought about it like that." It's self-control, Whatever the situation is, then and there, I try to address it. I try to make it as real to them as possible.

If I was having a conversation with myself, relationship-wise, and I was saying, "Look, this is what happened in the past, and nothing is going on in the present." I focus and meditate on the following: "I am truly content. I need to be content. I have everything. I have been extremely blessed. There's nothing wrong in my life. I have everything but a husband and I have to really look at that. That is extremely important to me, but I have to realize that as Philippians 4:11-13 says, to paraphrase, because Paul was talking about being content: No matter what type of situation I find myself in, I have learned to be content. Whether I have or whether I have not. Whether I am full or whether I am hungry. Whether I am in pain or not. I have learned to be content. I picked that up in my spirit. I have come to the place of realizing, "Okay, I am not married at this time for a reason. God has something really wonderful out there for me. It's coming and I just have to be patient and wait on Him. He's working all this out. Maybe that particular person isn't ready yet. He's preparing him. Maybe there are some things He is working on in me, like preparing me not to be frustrated, not to be angry. To live in this moment of the goodness that He's given me. To enjoy this time right now. Be content and be happy with what I have and realize that if God wanted me to be married right now, I would be married right now.

"Everything's okay. You've done this. You've done that. You do see the years going along. You just have to realize that God is so powerful. He's so almighty that the years won't matter. All of that won't matter. It's just what you have now."

I think a lot of us live in fear, which translates into being bitter, being frustrated, and being angry. That's not helping you. That's hurting you. That's not doing anything for you. I still have those moments of complete distress about being alone. A lot of times I think that married people, and people who either have never been alone, or have not been alone for a long, long, time, can't really understand what it's like.

Let's say I coordinate a computer expo event. It was a great fantastic success, got all kinds of applause and accolades. "Oh wow, great show." It went so well. Perfect. I could make all the money I wanted in the world, be involved in so many volunteer and church activities. Being able to say, "I have a fulfilling life." All of those kinds of things I've done. But when you come home and there's no one to say, "How was your day? How did things go? Tell me about it. Let me share my success with you. Let me tell you about my project." Or someone to rub my shoulders or lean my head on and say, "Oh what a day," or to exchange or to give, they don't know what that's like. It's a different experience, especially if you live alone. So, instead of mulling over that, I just focus on everything that God has given me. I try to just be content.

Rita Moore

Ms. Moore is 47 years old and single. She owns a very successful business. The problem that it poses: she is involved in the business at such a level it does not provide enough time or opportunities for her to be involved in enough social activities towards meeting a mate. She started late in life before involving herself in a serious relationship, which turned out to be a major challenge for her. She has found comfort in her spirituality, which is a primary aspect of her life. Meditation and prayer are probably the elements that allow her to maintain some measure of inner peace and fight the loneliness that sometimes enters her consciousness. She is eternally hopeful that the right man will come around, but she also realizes that things happen in their own time. She gives such a powerful lesson in faith and positive attitude that it makes one wonder what this world would be like if most of us could share her demeanor. She is particularly committed to helping and advising young girls as they travel through the difficulties of their lives.

My childhood was very good. I was a kid who didn't know what was going on in her house. Didn't know anything about money issues. I used to think we were rich because we lived in a big house. My father worked six days a week and my mother went back to work when we finished grade school. I was a dizzy kid until I was ten. I had a young sister who was born with Down syndrome.

My father sat us down one day and said, "We all have to get out of ourselves and get into raising Tammy." My life changed when that happened. She's deceased now.

When I was young, my parents provided a great role model for me. My father was definitely the head of the household. He was a very responsible person. He paid the bills and checked everything. He was very fair. If he went to the bank and they gave him too much money, Daddy would take it back. When he was shortchanged, he would go back and let them know. He taught us to share what we had. Mother, the same way. When my father would come in he was affectionate. He would always kiss my mother when he left and kiss her when he came home. He would do the same thing with my sisters and me. I knew early on that a man could be tender. I had a warm and loving environment to grow up in. My parents were home every night. My mother was home when we returned from school each day.

My father was not a talkative person. When he did talk, he was giving instructions. For him to just sit down, talk and laugh, he very seldom did that. He was real serious. He didn't do a lot of that.

I was real shy as a child. Boys were coming around I guess when I was about 13 or 14 years old. I have a sister who is 14 months older. She would go out and visit them. I would sit in my room and paint or read and not go out and talk.

My first boyfriend, or he called himself my boyfriend, was when I was about 13 or 14. That was a strange relationship (laughs). It was not really a relationship at all. We didn't really communicate well. A group of us would go to the movie and we'd sit by each other. We'd talk on the phone. He'd come by, that's about it. We really didn't have much to say. We would just sit like kids do. We did communicate some, but most of our communication was non-verbal. We just didn't have a lot to say, didn't know what to say. I realize now that I wasn't the easiest person to communicate with. I would give "yes, no," kind of answers. That was it. I wasn't very open, just shy and I still am.

I was in my 40s when I had my first serious relationship with a person who I trusted. Before that, I never trusted. That was the first time I allowed someone to get close to me. I loved that man unconditionally and trusted him. I think I was about 41 when that happened.

We met at a meditation that I had gone to. There was a group that would meet on a monthly basis for meditation and prayer. He was sitting across from me and I kept noticing him. He was tall, bald, Black and had just wonderful eyes. He wore an ethnic top with exotic designs and jeans. He wore no jewelry, earrings, or rings. What he did have was a magnetic personality. He was very charismatic. I felt drawn to him. Actually, I approached him. There was just something about him. I felt I had to meet him. I didn't know what was going on. I just knew that I had to meet this man. I had to have an experience with him.

After meeting him and having several conversations, I took a giant step towards a relationship. I was very direct, very honest. I said to him, "If you're in a relationship, then we shouldn't talk." He told me that he was. I said, "If for any reason it doesn't work out, whether it's a month or a year, give me a call if you feel like it." He called me two weeks later when it didn't work out. I had no inhibition at all about a woman being the initiator of a relationship, not at all. I think that if it hits you, you have to move on it. If there's something you need to say or it's an experience you need to have, you have to move on it. There was no fear of rejection. There was a possibility that he could have said, "No, I am not interested in you in that way." That would have been okay. I just needed to say what I needed to say at the time.

That relationship lasted about three years. For me, it was a turning point. From my perspective, it opened me to life because I was very shut down, not trusting, not knowing how to trust, not being able to trust. Here comes this person and I didn't know what his status was, what he had, what he didn't have. It didn't matter. There was something about his spirit. I had to just have an experience with him. I grew a lot. We both did. It was a great learning experience. I got great lessons. We lived together for about three years and we're still very, very close. We're good friends. He's in another relationship now. We've been friends for years.

Some of the key lessons I learned in that relationship was most of all, being able to express myself, saying what I wanted to say when I wanted to say it. Being able to say, even if it sounds critical, like I'm being critical of you, "Know that everything I say is out of love, not out of malice or one-upmanship." We didn't have that kind of relationship; it was just straight ahead, where you could just communicate. That was the best thing.

I would come in from work some days in tears because of something that had happened. When I'm like that, I don't want to talk. He understood and would say, "You need to be alone?" "Yeah." He would just leave the room and let me have my space. When I was ready to talk, I could talk. He would not take it personally, the same with me. If he needed space, take the space, and not take it personally like something's wrong with him or something's wrong with me. It was great, really good.

Our sexual relationship was good from the beginning. I think that our spirits just meshed. It wasn't a struggle. The relationship wasn't a struggle. I will say that when we just dated, about two months into it, another woman approached him. He wanted to see her and see me. I couldn't do that. He really wanted to experience this other person, so he did.

I was really hurt. He came back later and said, "I really made a mistake. It was glitter." The woman was glitter. At first, if it had been five years ago, maybe three years before that, I would have said, "No way." When I thought about it, when a person is being honest with you, how can you dislike that person? We split during that time for about three weeks. We came back together and it was stronger than ever.

During those three weeks, I was shattered. I felt that I had opened my heart, everything, and somebody didn't want me. I didn't feel like there was something wrong with me, or maybe I did feel there was something wrong with me. "How could somebody not want me? I'm a nice person." That's all I could think, "How could this happen?"

Then I saw the woman and more than ever, "How could this happen?" Not that she wasn't an attractive woman. She was glitter and I'm not. I'm thinking, "I'm a good person." I really had to look at myself and what I thought about myself. I realized out of that three weeks, it wasn't about me, not at all. It was what he was going through. It was about him. After thinking about that, it was fine. But for the first two weeks, I was just out of it. I would like to say that it did not affect my work performance, business is business. I try and leave my personal life outside the door.

The difficulty was, he was calling me during that whole three week period, so I decided that we're just going to be friends and it was okay. He was very honest. He called and said, "I don't understand why I even did this. You probably won't even consider dating me again, but if you would, I would appreciate it." It took me a minute, more than a minute, to think about it. I knew I cared about him so I said, "Why not? Let me try it again."

I felt we were friends. I felt that if it came up again, he would say it to me. If it came up again, I couldn't deal with it a second time. I felt that he really made a mistake. People do that. People are allowed to make mistakes.

When he came back the second time, I felt secure because we really talked about it. We talked about why men go for the glitter. This woman was a very assertive woman. He said it was her body. She was very aggressive and that's why he went that way.

For me, the time that I had with him, I had done something that I had never done in life. I had always been chosen. I chose him. It's like I wanted to follow through. I wanted to see how I would grow, what it would do for me having a relationship with him. It was worth going forward; I felt different. I was being assertive for maybe the first time in my life in a relationship, saying what I wanted, doing what I wanted, and being able to say anything.

My father was very strict, you wouldn't ask him questions. If he said, "I want you to go. I want you to do this," you had to go and do it and you couldn't ask why. I use to say "why" all the time. Every time I'd say why, it was like, "Are you being smart?" I'd say, "No. I just need to understand." He would say, "You don't have to understand anything. Because I said it, you just do it."

When I was ten years old, being told that, "you have to get

out of yourself and get into raising your sister," I stopped saying what I felt. It was all about raising my sister, not with resentment, but I just stopped expressing myself. I realized as I was growing up that I didn't say what I felt in a lot of situations. I would just allow things to happen, allow people to choose me to be their friend or they want to be my friend. I would never say, "No." I would never pull away. I would allow men to choose me, so I'd say, "He likes me, so all right. If he likes me, then I should be really nice to him."

This last situation I was talking about, that was the first time for me that I chose. I was aware that I chose. That was pretty powerful, so I wanted to follow it through. I talked about that. I told him that was the first time that I chose, so we just went on with it.

The second time was stronger because he really trusted me. I really trusted him. We did a lot of things together. We had a lot in common. He was very spiritual and so am I. I just think that communicating made it stronger. We talked about things that we felt. I talked about things that I felt, and that was a first time for me. I felt free enough to express myself.

When I realized that he was not a very responsible person, which was the beginning of the demise of the relationship. He's a political activist, a writer. He has children. When I met the children, he didn't do anything for them. That kind of shook my belief of who I thought he was. There were two boys who were absolutely wonderful. I could not understand why he wouldn't do everything for his boys. He did nothing.

His income would fluctuate, but I would say, "Why don't you take a percentage of everything you make and if you want, I'll put it in an account? We'll just give it to the boys." "I can't do that," he would say. I'd say, "Why not?" "Because I've got to pay my portion of the rent and everything." I said, "That's fine too, but if you just take a percentage and put it aside, that would work." He said, "I can't commit to that because I'm not sure if I'm going to have money."

It started out with the boys, and then it started with him not paying his portion. I made more money than he did, that was okay. When we decided to live together I said, "Tell me what you can do. What you can do easy." He told me and I said, "Okay. That's what I expect you to do without fail."

He told me a month in advance because he didn't have a lot of business, "You know, I don't think I'm going to be able to do this next month," meaning meet his financial obligations. I'm not used to that. I didn't know how to deal with that. I said, "How can you predict?" I feel like my needs are always met. Even if it's down to the wire, they've always been met. I couldn't understand how somebody could verbalize a month in advance that I'm not going to be able to because that was not a part of my reality, not being able to. Because I loved him I said, "Okay, let me try to work with this." But it came up repeatedly. I just couldn't deal with it. I loved him dearly, but I knew that I would be unhappy if I continued. I can't be unhappy like that.

I didn't feel he was trying to live off me, but I understood that his pattern had been like that. He had been with women who allowed that to happen. He had been with women he ended up owing a lot of money to. I have never been the type of woman that would give up money. I'll help you, but I won't just give you money. I'll help you if you help yourself, but I can't take care of you.

When we got involved, I didn't know that he had a track record like that. It wasn't about him. It was about me. It wasn't like I was going to pay to have him in my life. I wasn't going to do that. We talked about things. He started out very responsible, taking care of everything. He admitted to me that it was the first time in his life, since he had quit working a regular job and decided to do what he wanted to do, like the political activism and writing.

He said that since he had pursued that, his biggest fear was that he would not be able to take care of himself. He didn't say that he had always been with women who could help him, but as our relationship grew, I realized that he had been. I also realized that he hadn't been with many Black women. That kind of surprised me. I feel like I am about as Black as you can get. I asked him about it and we talked about it. It turned out that was a subject we couldn't talk about. I have feelings about that. He did too. They weren't the same. As I look at him today, I do know that he makes it a point to get with women who can help him. I remember my sister said that to me, but it didn't matter. I was doing what I wanted to do. I wasn't giving him money so it was all right.

Presently, he's with a White woman who is basically taking care of him. When we did get around to talking about this subject, it centered on Black men and White women. When I found out that he had been with only White women, like from the age of 20-something on, and he is in his 40s, I wanted to know why.

I understood that he really had problems with his mother. He said to me, "Who would you rather be with, somebody who thinks they can have anything in this world, and the world is theirs, somebody who tells you that you can do and have and be anything you want, or would you prefer to be with someone who says to you, 'We can't go over there. We don't belong there. You can't do that because that's not for us?'" He said that's what he ran into when he had been married and that he didn't want that in his life anymore. That was why he had been with them.

I disagreed. I said, "Well, it's got to be more than that. There are Black women, or women of color, who feel good about themselves." He said, "Yeah, you do. That's why I'm with you. But it's hard to find." I disagreed. I said, "I think it's more to it than that. Did you love your mother? Did you have problems with your mother? Are you trying to get away from who you are? Are you trying to get away from who we are?" I said, "We don't operate the same. Black women and White women don't deal the same. I would not allow you to get away with as much as maybe they do."

We got into this real heated argument about it, so we just decided that we would not discuss that anymore, and we didn't. We thought we'd split. I'm not a screamer, and I never scream, but it got to the point that we disagreed so that we couldn't agree to disagree.

It was heated, very heated.

I asked him why he was with me. He said, "Well, at first because you were assertive. I like that. I don't always like having to approach somebody. I like the way that you approached me. I liked our conversations, our honesty. And I have to admit, you didn't allow me to do some of the things that other women would allow me to do." I think that was like borrowing money. I didn't ask him what, but I think it was giving up money and that I loved him unconditionally. I didn't say that he had to do anything. I did say up front, "Tell me what you can do financially." I expected that to happen. He said, "I kind of forced him to take care of business." For those reasons, he said he loved me.

The day that we decided to split up, it was right after New Year's. I remember on New Year's Day, I woke up and said, "What do you see for this year?" He said, "I don't know. What do you see?" I said, "I see creating a fund for fun, and working on getting some property. Do you want to do that?" He said, "Yeah, but I can't commit to putting money into that. My income fluctuates so that I can't commit to doing that." In my head, if he had said, "Listen, I'll give you $5.00 a month on this account," it would have been fine, anything. You don't have to give up everything. But when he said, "I can't commit to that," I just said, "Okay."

Part of my prayer and meditation is that God and the universe will always show me the truth, and then give me the strength to act on the truth. That was the truth, and all I could say was, "You're giving it to me. I do hear it. Now, Rita, what are you going to do?" He had to go out of town in January. I took that time and really thought about it, really meditated and prayed on it for a while. It kept coming up that, "It's over." I didn't want it to be. Every time I'd get ready to ask the question, it just kept coming up, "It's over."

When he came back, we talked. We agreed that we would split. We agreed also that we really loved each other, but we have to be happy. I couldn't be happy. I wasn't happy anymore.

The main reason was not economics, just being responsible.

Money has a lot to do with it; it wasn't the issue. Being responsible for what you said you were going to do. If you tell me you're going to do something, I just want you to do it. I'm going to take care of my part. I want you to do the same. It was the issue of not being responsible.

For me, if I know that I have to do something in a month, and it doesn't look like it's happening, I'm going to get out there and do what I have to do to make it happen, so when that deadline hits, I'm going to be as close to the goal as possible. I'm not going to sit today and say, "Well, next month, I don't think I can make payroll." And do nothing about it? I'm going to get on the phone. I'm going to get clients. I'm going to go and work overtime. That's me. My father was like that. He took care of business. I come from a responsible background, so it's very difficult to deal with people who are not.

That was the key, not being responsible. It started when I saw that he wasn't being responsible with his children. That kind of tore something.

Before, we were having a great time, then I met the kids. It was like a reality check. I don't have children. I hadn't thought about it. When I met them and they were so great, it was like, "How could you not do everything to take care of the kids?" I asked. He said, "It was either do that, or really pursue what I wanted to do in life." I said, "Why can't you do both?" "I can't do it. I can't do my research and my work and have a job." So, I said, "Okay."

I'm not saying, "You got to do it," and I never said, "You got to do it." I loved him just the way he was. I feel like people have to do what they want to do. I can't think of anybody on this earth that will say to me, "You made me do something."

I was devastated when he left, wiped out. I could sit and do my work, but tears would be streaming down my face. My clients never knew it, but I was just wiped out. I really loved him, really cared about him. At the same time, all I could say was, "Thank you, Father, for giving me the strength to act on the truth, and to do what I needed to do. Thank you for bringing him into my life." It was a joy to fall in love and I didn't think I could do that cause I never trusted. I didn't think I had it in me to be in love and to love someone unconditionally, and it turned out that the man had nothing, absolutely nothing. It didn't matter to me and that felt good. I want that again. Now that I've had it, I know that I can fall in love.

"I'm real, real grateful for the experience," I had to keep saying as tears were running down my face, "This will pass. It will be okay. I know that letting this go, a door for something else is going to open. I can't stay, knowing the truth, and living a lie." It was okay. It takes time, but it was okay.

It took me a couple of months of tears, maybe six months or so to reach some level of normalcy. The thing is, when we split, he didn't move immediately. We split like about the 16th of January, and he was still here. I would come home from work every day and he was still there.

Finally, one day I said, "You got to go." He said, "I don't have any place to go. I have no money." I said, "I'll help you find a place. You just hold on to your money." I went and helped him find an apartment. His credit was so bad that you would think he couldn't find a place.

I really meditated and really called on God and the universe to help this man get on with his life so I could get on with my life. I wasn't bitter. He was my friend. He's still my friend. When I realized he wasn't going anywhere, then the tears were gone. I used to come home and cry and look at him. I would say to him that, "These are not tears of 'I wish we could be together.' It's just tears because there's been a death. When there's a death you grieve and I'm grieving for the death of our relationship." He understood that. When I realized he wasn't going, it was like, "Let's get this man moving. Let's get him out of here. Help him find a place. Help him move on." So, I did.

After that relationship, I really got into my work. I haven't been in a real relationship since. Just dated and that's it. Haven't had those feelings since. Looking forward to having them because I know I will again. Next time though, in a relationship, I know it's important to have somebody that you're equal with.

You don't necessarily have to have the same goals, but be together spiritually. If you have a poverty mentality, that's not a part of my reality. Thinking that I can't have, and I won't have. I can't have a roof over my head.

I forgot to mention that this was a guy that once lived out of his car. That was okay with him until after we had gotten together. Then it wasn't okay with him anymore. That didn't bother me. It's like "You're still a good person. It's not a big deal," but I understand that it is. It is important to have someone that, spiritually, you're along the same lines. You know that your needs are being met. You know that you have a roof over your head. You just know. You know that it is not a part of your reality to be on the streets.

I do understand that if the earth shakes and everything falls down, we all may be on the streets. I know that I go to work every day. There's no reason for me to be on the street or even think about the possibility of, "What if?" I just don't do it.

I know that in my next relationship, I would have to have a person who at least believes along those lines, that their needs will be met. Their needs are being met. The next person would have to have some kind of financial stability, but I'm not opposed to someone who is trying to make their way. I can't say that money would be the basis of a relationship, or whom I would allow myself to get involved with. It's not based on money. My business could close today and that means I got to start all over again. Being 47 and starting all over again, I could have nothing.

Before I moved here, before I started the business, I was in a house. I gave up the house, moved to a little tiny apartment. Paid $500 per month and it was fine with me. Money and material items, those are not the most important things.

Now that I am very involved in my business, without a man, loneliness can be an issue. It's funny. I had surgery last month. I've got wonderful friends. People were here and I had everything that I needed. A girlfriend that I grew up with came and stayed for 15 days. When she left, all of a sudden I was faced with loneliness.

I was changing bandages and stuff and said, "Where's my man? Where's this person in my life that should be here? This is the kind of stuff that you do for each other." I had to sit and realize that it's just not time. I don't deal with being the age that I am. I just feel that it's not time.

I tell a lot of people that he was killed in Viet Nam. When I'm sitting around a bunch of women and talking, they'll say, "Where are the men?" I'll say, "They were killed in Viet Nam. That's where my first husband was killed." Sometimes I really think that's true. I've always believed that the person for me I just haven't met yet. I will meet him in this lifetime.

I deal with loneliness by thinking, "Oh, he's coming." It's just not that time and I'm patient. There are so many of us and I work with so many women who are talented, attractive, who are nice women and they're without men. A lot of them are in that age group between 40 and 50 or a little older. I just think that the men were wiped out in Viet Nam.

When I am around women and we talk, a lot of it is one-on-one. For some reason it seems like there's so much anger with people today. Women are telling me what they don't want. "I'm not having a man come in that is not making x amount of dollars. I'm not having anybody who drinks. I'm not having anybody who, whatever."

I find myself saying, "So what do you want?" They can't say what they want. One will say, "God knows what I want. He'll give me what I want. He knows." I'll say, "How can He give you if you don't know?" I hear a lot of what they don't want and a lot of distrust.

Sometimes I think that is why there are so many women without men because we have so many conditions. Instead of just looking at people and looking at the good and going with that it's like, "His hair's too long. Tell him he looks better with his hair cut." If he doesn't dress right it doesn't matter. We've got all these conditions that people have to go through. We're not perfect, so why do we expect him to be perfect? I think we are looking for this false something. A lot of women are looking for someone to take care of them.

I'm glad I'm at that point in life, I think it comes with late 30s, early 40s, you've taken care of yourself most of your life, that's not what you're looking for. I think that is why, for me, the money thing is not that important. It's not like I have money, but I know that I can take care of myself. It's more like wanting a companion, someone you take care of myself. It's more like wanting a companion, someone you can share things with, someone you can communicate with, someone you can talk to, someone you can trust. Trust is a real issue with me, someone who is responsible. If they say they're going to do something, it's a done deal.

There's a lot of anger and distrust. It's because most of us have been through something in our lives. If it hasn't been incest, it's rape, or some kind of abuse. If we don't work on whatever happened, facing it, dealing with it and work through it, then I think it's always there.

There was a time in my life if Mister (so-called) Right had come along, I couldn't have recognized him. I was so angry and not trusting that I wouldn't have seen him. I hate to think of it, but he may have come and gone during that time that I was angry and not trusting. I think that is the reason a lot of us are by ourselves.

We need to deal with where the anger comes from. A lot of times we say, "Our parents should have done... If they would have done..." It's not about that. My parents did the very best with the information that they had. They raised me the way they thought that they should.

My first sexual experience, I was raped. I was only sixteen. I didn't realize it until I was around 38 or 40 that the reason I never trusted any man was because I had been raped. I never thought about that. I was raped and I never told anybody, just kept it a secret until my 30s. I didn't even tell my girlfriend who I was staying with that her boyfriend's best friend raped me. I just got my stuff and went home. Didn't tell my mother. Didn't say a word to anybody, just went within.

At that point I had never done drugs. I started getting high. None of my friends got high. They used to say, "Where is this coming from? Why are you doing drugs?" "Cause I like it." "Why? You never did it before." "Because I want to. If you got a problem, then you don't have to come around."

I moved away from home, getting high. Did everything, all the drugs that I could find. I never understood what I was trying to get away from. Finally, I went through the thing of drugs and let that go. I moved to California. When my sister died, I was so devastated. She had Down syndrome and at the age of ten my father said we need to get out of ourselves. My mother's biggest fear was that she would die before my sister. My older sister, who is 14 months older, we made a pact that no matter what, we would always take care of our sister.

Neither of us is married. Neither of us is in relationships. Neither of us have children. When my sister died, I guess it was subconscious, I knew that I would always take care of her. My other sister and I shared a home out here for years. We would get involved. Men would ask us to marry them. If they were the kind of guys who made fun of anybody, we'd cancel them. We said that they couldn't love our sister like we loved her. Most people make fun of people's shortcomings. We didn't do that. We grew up not only with my sister, but a girl across the street who was mentally and physically handicapped.

There was a guy next to us who was an adult. He played with us when we were children. He was mentally challenged. We had people in our neighborhood we grew up with who were like that. We all helped. We didn't grow up making fun of people. We could never do that. If we did and my father caught us doing that, what he would do to us was worse than anything that could happen.

I said all that to say that the anger and not trusting came from the rape. Part of the reason that I didn't get married was because I didn't think anybody could deal with my sister the way we would deal with her.

When she died, I went into therapy. That's when the rape came up. It was like, "Oh, wow! I totally forgot about that." Once I remembered the rape, everything else started to click. Within the last seven years so much has clicked. I've had all these revelations about why I did what I did, who I am today. It's really about facing the truth about yourself, really doing work to try and understand why we are what we are, why we do what we do. In doing that I know that is how I got to the point I am today. I'm really comfortable and at peace. It doesn't mean I don't get stressed, but I can always come back, pull myself back.

I think there are a lot of women who have gone through abusive situations who may not have faced them or dealt with them, who have that anger. With me it was like if a man says, "Boy, you're pretty." The one who raped me said, "Oh, you're really pretty." I smiled. After he raped me, anytime somebody would say that to me, in my head it was like, "What the fuck do you want? Why are you saying this to me? What do you want from me?" I would almost frown. It would just turn me off for somebody to say that. Later, I realized why. That's what the guy who raped me said. I understand all that now. That was the cause of the anger in me. Asking to deal with the anger was just a revelation for me (sigh). That really took me through. It was good.

I think some women in their 40s and 50s have given up. They say they've given up but they're hoping that someone comes along. I'll never give up. When I reach fifty, if I am still by myself, I will still tell you, "He's coming in this lifetime." I can't imagine feeling that the person for me is not out there and that I won't meet him. I've never thought that. I've never put an age limit on it. That didn't matter. I feel like I'm more ready now than I've ever been in my life. I feel like it's going to happen soon.

I think that because of the knowledge and experience I have, and knowing what I want, the percentage of men that would be attracted to me has decreased, unfortunately. I don't deal with that. I only need one man. However, I don't feel that I attract many men at all. It's okay as long as I attract that one person that I say is coming. I don't know why I do not attract, it's interesting.

I had a conversation with a very good girlfriend of mine. We had lunch and she was saying, "I just looked at you when you were getting out of the car and putting money in the meter. I said, 'Boy, girlfriend, you are so pretty.'" I said, "Really?" She said, "Yeah." "Are you serious?" "Yeah." She asked me, "Don't you think so?" "No. I don't think I'm unattractive, but I never look at myself and say, 'You look good.'"

I said, "As we were walking across the street, and you were a couple of steps in front of me, I said, 'Look at this woman, walking just leisurely, head up, straight body and walking like she is just royalty.'" I was telling her that I thought the same thing about her. She said, "I looked trashed walking next to you." I said, "Why is it that we can see the beauty in each other, and we're not looking and seeing it in ourselves?" I do love myself. I really do. That came like in my late 30s, early 40s. I realize that I am lovable. That came with the relationship.

My friend said, "You do attract men, but you just don't see it." I don't understand that. Not that when I go out I'm looking for anything, you know. I speak to everybody. I can't let people walk by and I not acknowledge their presence or they acknowledge mine. I noticed a lot of times if I speak to men, "Do I know you?" "No. I don't know you." "Okay, hi." And we move on. I don't speak in a flirtatious way. I just acknowledge people's presence. I think part of that has to do with my work. We have this policy; we speak to everybody. I just think that's a human thing to do. Doesn't matter who you are.

I can't say why I don't attract. It obviously has something to do with my spirit, with what I put out. I feel like I put out that I'm approachable; from what I get back, obviously not. So, I don't know what it is.

Sometimes I get so caught up in work and issues with the people that I work with, I become an emotional mess and a stressed-out disaster. I'm there almost seven days a week. It can be very stressful and I don't take care of myself. I stop meditating and get up out of the bed thinking about what has to happen, waking up at two in the morning thinking about "what ifs."

I sat down in a meditation after that and said, "I ask God and the universe, help me help myself find my way. I don't want to lose any more sleep. I don't want to live with what ifs because there is nothing I can do about it. I need to find my space. I need to find some peace." I just asked for help to do that. I feel like when I asked, I got.

I started sleeping. I started to get up and do my meditation every day. I stopped worrying about what fires I was going to have to put out today when I got to work. I just started letting go of stuff I couldn't do anything about, you know, who likes who, or what's going on with individuals at my business. I used to take all of that on personally. I don't anymore. I just can't. Who am I to even try and do that? I asked to please let me hear the answers and find my way. I am finding my way.

Before I got into the relationship, I used to think that I was putting so much time into the business, that I was almost unavailable to meet a man. After I got into the relationship, I said, "It's time for me to have a life." I really began to take time for myself. I still take time for myself, not as much. I don't come home as early as I used to. It's hard to say because I don't know any different. My days are like ten hour days. I guess for most people it's eight or so. I don't go to clubs, but I do go out. I go to the theater, to dinner, stuff like that. I go to museums, art galleries. I don't know if being out there is where you meet somebody. I always felt like the best place, the best way to meet someone is through someone. They come with credentials or recommendations. That hasn't happened. I don't think it has put me out of the loop. I definitely don't date clients. Maybe, but I don't think so.

I have to admit, I'm still shy. Having a business was the best thing for me. It forced me to communicate with people. It forced me to approach them. I like doing that. At home, I'm great. You take me to a party, it's like, "Oh God, help me," before I even get there. If I have to go to a networking thing, my partner likes that. She can do it. To be out there it takes everything that I have. I have to do some serious self- talk to go to a networking function or to go to a party. I'll go, but it takes a lot for me to do it.

When I was assertive in meeting the man in my last relationship, my spirit just would not let me be quiet with that person. I had to have that experience. I know that if I feel that again I will do it without reservation. There are times when I can do that. It has to be worth doing. It has to be a person worth doing that with.

I think it is a natural flow to be in a relationship, a partnership. I think most people feel that way. Many of the women who have given up felt that some of the men they encountered were users. Women know that. In knowing that they may close the door to men who are not.

The problem is that traditionally we've been taught that men are supposed to take care of us. They're supposed to do better than we do, financially. I think if we hold on to that old whatever, then we kind of miss out on even being open to meet the person that's for us. Some women are doing well. They may not be open to someone who is not doing as well. That could be a problem.

I remember being approached by a couple of guys, but deep down I knew they were not honest. They came out the gate playing a game. At this point in life, why? We are who we are. Why would you pretend or why would you want to play a game? We don't have to. I don't have any tolerance for that. I have no tolerance for lies. I've got to trust. If I feel like I can't trust, I don't want to waste his time or mine. I'll say that.

When I think about what motivated me to start a business, I think it was just destined to be. I was a secretary and I used to sell certain products for women. The products would just sell themselves. People would say, "Oh, if this is as good as my friends say then I want some." I didn't know the process of the effect of the product, so I took some classes and got my license. I never had any intentions of doing that. As I took the classes, I fell in love with the process and said, "This is my niche."

For several years, I worked out of my home. Finally, I said, "Why don't I start a business?" This was the 80s and everything I read said people were interested in what I had to offer. So, why not do something that I really love doing?

When I started, I never thought that it wouldn't fly. Maybe I was naïve, but I just thought this was something that was needed. I never thought of failure. Even when it was only 25 dollars in one day, it was never, "close the doors." I always thought it would grow and that we would be around, and we have been.

The large majority of my clients are women. The men that come in they love being catered to by women. Most men would prefer being treated by a woman. Men clients are wonderful.

I can talk with the women very easily about male/female relationships, but men are not that open. I have a male friend who comes to our business, but we usually keep it pretty professional.

When I discuss loneliness with other women, a couple of them got very involved in religion. It's God this or God that, or Jesus this or Jesus that. I think they are very lonely. Again, these same women seem to be kind of angry, a little bitter. One is about mid-fifties; everything is "God, God, God." Very bitter woman in the sense that if you don't practice her religion, you are practicing wrong. Lots of them get involved in religion and lose themselves in their churches. I guess it works for them. It appears that some women substitute church for a relationship.

I have friends who are very spiritual women who just work hard and take a lot of classes. They talk about the loneliness and they just move on. They acknowledge that it's there and know that it's there, but that somebody's out there for them.

I don't think about loneliness that much. I did after the surgery and I was suddenly by myself, but I don't deal a lot with feeling lonely. I do have really good friends and I do believe there is someone out there for me.

In the best of all worlds, and that special person comes into my life, and we establish a relationship, I see that relationship being very easy, just a natural flow. When we get together, there are no major hassles. I could be dreaming, but I don't think so. I just think at this point in life, things should be easy. Shouldn't be a lot of drama, not a lot of anger. It's like we've basically done what we wanted to do in life. We're together not because we need to be. We don't need anyone to take care of us. It's because we want to be, because we want to share and we want to have the experience. I think it should be easy.

If that person should come soon, I have never entertained the thought of having children, not in this lifetime. There are other women I know in my age range who feel differently. I have a friend who is 48. She still wants to have a child. She's single and if she meets someone, she thinks that she'll have a child. I think that's great for those who want them. They should have them, but not for me.

On the other hand, there are women who do not want to get married but want to have a child. I have two clients who have talked about that. One has a friend and she likes him. There's no relationship. She's considering asking him to father a child. Another one is thinking about artificial insemination.

I think that personally, it is a very selfish thing to do. There are a lot of children that need homes. I think that with both of them it's like wanting a part of themselves. That's okay. I think if you bring a child into this world, it deserves to have a mother and a father, a so-called "normal" household. You need everybody to raise the child. Just to bring a child in because you're hitting a certain age and you're thinking about menopause is not right. "Let me do this quick." I think it is a very selfish thing to do. It's not thinking about the child, it's just thinking about themselves. It's like if you really want to raise a child, then why not adopt a child?

You know, there are far too many young girls out there who are having babies. Single parents raised most of those girls. Most of them, I think, are just looking for love in the wrong places so they end up having children. As a mature woman, every opportunity that I get to deal with a young woman in that situation, I have a responsibility to help build their self-esteem. Their self-esteem is just under the rug somewhere with young girls. I don't think they really know what it is. I don't think they really love themselves. They're just looking for some recognition. They're looking for some comfort outside themselves. First, you really have to have it within, really be secure within. Then you can attract what you want.

If I were talking with a young girl now, I would talk about responsibility. What you put out there is what you get. I always say, "Do what you want to do. Don't do what somebody else wants you to do. You have to be true to yourself, that way you stay happy. If you start living your life to please other people, to manipulate other people, then that's trouble. If you are always honest with yourself then you're doing what you want to do, no matter what it is. Well, it does matter because you don't want to do something that is going to hurt someone else. If you're doing what you want to do, and you take responsibility for what you do, then that's fine. Do whatever, but do it with that thought."

When you lay down with this man, it's like, "Do I want to have this child? Is this somebody that I could possibly spend the rest of my life with?" If you say, "No," then I think you should be very careful about what you do. You have to think about the consequences. There are consequences for everything. If we understand that, and it doesn't necessarily mean that they are negative, then you can live your life and basically be happy. You live like that. You understand that. You take responsibility for that then life is fine. It's okay.

When I think about the children of these young girls, it scares me. It really does. We have to teach children responsibility. I keep going back to that. There's something inside us that tells us when something's right and something's wrong. Even if you haven't been taught, it's really my prayer that people will start listening to that whatever's inside them, start living accordingly.

When I send out the energy to the universe in my prayers, it's really that people heal themselves and start going within instead of outside for what they want. It's my feeling, as we mature, that we really go within. We start listening and we hear. It just seems like we're in the age that people are connecting more with their spirits. I feel like that by the time of the new millennium, they're going to connect more. There will be those who won't, but I would like to think that there will be more that will. We'll find that peace. I refuse to put out there that it's going to be treacherous. I refuse to.

I was raised a Methodist and, like most of us, you had to go to church. I was raised in the church, Sunday school, everything. All of that's fine, but I never understood. I was so resistant and went, but I never heard anything. I'm sure I heard some things that stuck with me. I know that there is a God; there is a power. I would have to say that in my 30s I can remember, and I had the business, somebody would come in and say to me, "You are doing so well." I would say, "But I'm not. I don't have any money. I don't have anything." They would say, "Look what you've done." I couldn't see it. I had to say that maybe I wasn't grateful. Then I would get in my car and drive home at night. Somebody could pull over in front of me a block ahead and I would "m-f" this and that. I mean "Get the hell out of here! I'm driving and I'm pissed."

Some days I could leave work and I would be in tears. One day I left work, I was in tears and I'm driving and something said to me, "Why are you crying?" I didn't know. I got home and dropped all my stuff. I sat down on the couch and I said, "Okay. I know I don't pray a lot. I don't do anything." I am pissed at the world." I looked at everything I didn't have. I sat down and I said, "I am so tired of being mad. I'm tired of being angry and I'm tired of the tears. I know there is God or a power. I need you to help me help myself. Show me what I need to do to get out of this rut."

At that point, I would never invite people to my home. I've always had a nice house. It was mine and you couldn't come in. Clients would say, "Why don't we have dinner?" "Okay." I knew that I would never have dinner with them. It was like you could come this close, but you had to stop right there. Never understanding why I was like that, I just didn't trust anybody. Didn't really care about myself.

One day I sat down and said to somebody, "This is nothing,"

talking about the business. They said, "How could you say that? You've really been blessed. You've got this, this, and this. You're healthy." I said that to my father and he said the same thing. Then it was like, "Oh, wow. Let me think about this." I just asked. I asked for direction. I asked not to do it for me but help me help myself, love myself, get out of this rut, see the blessings and see the goodness in me as well as in other people. "I'm tired of being shut down. I'm tired being closed and I really need you to help me."

As soon as I said that, I have to say in about a week or so, different people started coming as clients. Then I'd run into people and doors just started opening. Somebody says, "Listen, you have got to come and take this woman's class. It was a metaphysics class. She said, "You've got to take it. If you don't have the money, I'll pay for it. Come and take this woman's class. It's been miraculous for me." It was in the Valley. I said, "Hell, no. I'm not driving to the Valley for a class twice a week? No way." Then she said, "You can ride with me."

Then I realized, "You've asked for help. Help is here. You're saying, 'Get away from me.'" It's like not letting me out. "You don't have the money, 'I'll pay for it.' You don't want to drive, 'I'll take you.'" I realized my prayers were being answered. A way was being made, "I'll go."

That was like a beginning, then other things started opening up. People started coming and information was coming. Here I am today. I just studied; I've asked for truth. I asked for the strength to deal with the truth. I asked to be the best that I could be. I asked that for other people because we're all connected. It's not just about me. I want peace and harmony for everybody. I want abundance for everybody who wants abundance, although there are some people who don't want it. That's okay too. Whatever I want for me, I want for everybody. Once I start doing that, loneliness, it's not there on a daily basis. It's hardly ever there. It was there when I was sick, not having what I needed. It's like I don't have a lot of money. Today, I could probably say that I hardly have any, but it's okay because my needs are being met.

If I was at a podium with an all female audience talking about women without men, I would say that I do not think that we were meant to be in this world alone, as long as we're surrounded by good friends and family. I think that we need to see that and be grateful for that, not moan about what we don't have. We need to look at what we do have. Most of all, we really need to love ourselves, be at peace with who we are.

The physical part is not that important, as long as we're healthy. You know before a vacation we will say, "I got to lose fifteen pounds." Forget that. I used to be like that. I'll put on a bathing suit in a minute if I go to Jamaica. This is who I am. This is what I look like. Yeah, okay, maybe in somebody else's eyes, if I drop fifty pounds they would say, "You'd be attractive." I feel good now. So, I think we need to deal with who we are now, this moment, right now, love who we are right now. If we want to make some improvements, fine. Not necessarily improvements, but changes, that's okay. Appreciate who we have in our lives today: family, friends, co-workers. Deal with that.

Prepare ourselves for other relationships. Like I said, "He's coming, if we want it. If you don't want it, then let's just be happy with where we are. We're not alone. We're never ever alone, so I don't think we even need to think about that."

Ms. Johnson is a 39-year-old divorced mother with a daughter. She is in management in the communications industry. To survive the kind of childhood that she had is a miracle in itself. She is a testament of how one's childhood can influence one's adult life. In her case, it resulted in tragic consequences. She also reflects how when a woman has to protect the life of her child, she can display an enormous amount of strength. Her ventures into therapy also showed how this seriously aided in the healing process. In addition, combined with her spiritual path, she gained the tools that allowed her to be resurrected from near emotional death to the success that she is today. I don't know if there are many individuals who would have made it back from where she came. Now, she is able to send her daughter to a good school, buy a new house and car, and enjoy one of the most cherished possessions one can have, peace of mind.

I was born in Kingston, Jamaica, and spent most of my teenage years there. My childhood was chaotic in many, many ways. There was a lot of confusion. There were a lot of things about my childhood that I don't really consciously remember. There are some things I remember, but they don't make sense. They don't follow the logical order of things that one would expect to see in this world. A lot of what I will mention I have learned from talking with other people who I believe told me the truth, adults who were around when I was growing up.

My parents' marriage was extremely unstable. My father had a serious drinking problem. Growing up in Jamaica, the consumption of alcohol was something that people just sort of took for granted. They never thought that anything was wrong with getting drunk on a daily or weekly basis, or several times a week. When my father would drink, he would become violent. He became abusive, verbally and physically, to my mother. It terrified me. It was a very scary situation to be in.

Even after my parents divorced, which was a very unusual

and radical thing for my mother to do, my father continued to come around to the house and abuse her. Most Jamaican women would not have left their husbands, would not have gotten a divorce. As a child, I witnessed several incidents of abuse that probably scared the living daylights out of me.

There were times when I was sent to live with other relatives. My mother had a number of nervous breakdowns. She was hospitalized on several occasions. She was not a physically strong person. There were times when I was sent to the country to stay with my grandparents. There were times when I was sent to live with an aunt who lived in another part of the city. Moving from one relative to the next contributed to the chaos as well.

At various times, my parents would put the children in between them. They would use us as pawns in their struggle with their relationship. That was very difficult to deal with. I didn't get to see my father very often. Whenever he came, it would always be a special treat to see him. He was always an inaccessible figure. I never really felt that I had a right to demand his involvement, attention, or anything. It was kind of like, you take what you get when you can.

I am sure that the way my parents related to each other had a later affect on me. I actually ended up marrying a man who was violently abusive. It was like a classic repetition of that cycle. I didn't know he was that way before we married; it was a gradual process. Our total relationship probably lasted about seven years.

Initially, when I first met him, I was very young. I was in graduate school. He was ten years older than I. He was very, very attractive. He was tall and had black curly hair. He was a Creole. He had that New Orleans look. He appeared to be open and honest about things. He had a lot of stuff in his life. What scares me is that alarms should have been going off in my head when he told me several things about himself, but they didn't. Before I married him, I didn't know that he had been married and divorced. The grounds for his first divorce were "indignities," which is the legal term for spousal abuse. He swore that that was in the past, that he had healed himself and this was not a problem.

What I gradually found over the years was that verbal abuse would begin then physical abuse. Ultimately, I basically had to get away from him. I was very fortunate, because I lived in a town at the time that had a very forward-thinking, very progressive domestic violence program. They provided shelter to women. You could call them any time of night or day. If all the shelters were full, they would put you up in a hotel for the night, the weekend, or whatever it was that you needed to get out of the situation. They did require women to go into counselling after whatever the incident was. I was able to enter a counselor program to help me understand the situation that I had gotten myself into. I did not understand the situation that I was in. I didn't understand the cycle of violence that was going on in my home. I really, really believed that this person loved me. I wanted to be with him, even though I was so afraid and so unhappy. I was more afraid to leave than I was to be with him.

Part of how he manipulated me was to isolate me from my family, to make me feel like I had to make a decision between him and my family. It was like I was caught in the middle of this power struggle between him and my mom, which replicated the power struggle between my father and my mom.

He made me feel like I shouldn't listen to my mom because she didn't like him. She was against him. They had never met! All she knew of him is what I had told her. I basically was ashamed to admit to my family that this man was abusing me, and that I was so unhappy. He made me feel that to admit what was going on would be to admit defeat. He created the scenario of he and I against the world.

He not only isolated me from my family, but from all of my friends that I had, friendships that I had developed over years in this town. He would behave very badly around my friends. He was very jealous. He was very possessive. I couldn't see the difference between jealousy, possessiveness, and love. I thought they were the same things. "Wow, he must really love me, because he wants me to be with him all of the time (laughs)." He would act very badly when any of my girlfriends were around. Basically, he embarrassed me. I didn't want people to see the way he would behave, so gradually, one by one, all of my friends just dropped out. It became impossible to have any platonic male friends also.

I felt so secluded. That was one of the things I had to confront in therapy. My counselor said, "You need to begin to reach out to people who would be able to help you." She made me begin to think about my life without him. I could only see my life with him. I got to a point where I realized I wasn't happy. Gradually, the idea of living without him became more attractive. Without the counseling, I wouldn't have been able to really see that because he just began to control me, mentally. I am not sure or conscious just how that process occurred.

I started going to counseling when I had to escape from him one night. I called the emergency number and went into a hotel room for the weekend. It was in the dead of winter. I got away from him one Friday night. I was in town; we were living out of town at the time. I had literally nothing with me. I had no cosmetics, no food, I had no money. The shelter put me up from Friday night to Monday morning. They gave me money for a bus. I took a bus to go to the counseling center.

That was my rock bottom moment. I was about five months pregnant. After I became pregnant, the abuse got worse. I think I began to realize that the situation I was in was beginning to endanger my child. I realized there was nobody I could call. My complete isolation and vulnerability became very obvious to me. It was like I had to wake up and smell the coffee, that there was another life involved now. That was the critical factor. That was how I got into counseling. It was because I had to. I had nowhere else to go.

I wasn't sure why the abuse increased while I was pregnant, but apparently that is a very common thing. It's not uncommon in spousal abuse situations. My husband was extremely jealous and possessive, and just wanted me to cater to him. The fact that this was his child was irrelevant. That there would be someone else competing for my attention, that's what concerned him. I can't explain why, but I do know that it is not uncommon for abuse to get worse during a pregnancy.

I feel I have some responsibility for the total relationship, and its deterioration. In terms of the deterioration of the marriage, no. I really tried to be a good wife. I tried to do everything I could to make it work. The way I tried to do that was to yield to everything, to give and give and give and give. What resulted, I ended up completely depleted emotionally, financially, energy-wise, and just life. It was like I had taken on this leech that was going to just suck the life out of me. I tried to do everything that I could to make it work. He was not able to be a partner. He could only take, because he was so needy. He was a very needy, insecure person. I was too young to see that at the time.

When the counseling started, I don't remember us talking too much about my childhood. We dealt with very practical issues. I remember her saying things like, "You're in a very bad situation." She impressed upon me how dangerous it was. The fact that I was pregnant made me more conscious of how dangerous it was. When it was just me, I guess I didn't really care that much, but since there was another person involved, it was like my instincts made me feel as if I was waking up out of a nightmare, waking up out of a dream. That feeling that you get which is sort of unreal. I felt like I had just nodded off, just nodded out of life. I was in a complete state of...I don't know what it was.

I know part of the reason was that my father died. He died just before I met my husband. At the time that I met him, I was in a tremendous amount of pain. I had just gotten out of another relationship where that person had manipulated me, and abused me in another sense, abused me financially.

The key factor in therapy that helped turn me around, other than knowing that I was in a dangerous situation, was that I needed to put a plan in place to get out of danger. She began to talk about things like calling my friends and telling them, "I am terribly sorry for what happened. I'm sorry that I've been ignoring you, but this is what happened." She said that I needed to reach out and make connections with people outside of my marriage. "Not only was the situation you were in unrealistic, but you're going to need some help. You need to find some people who can help you."

At that point, I got in touch with my family. I got in touch with some women friends of mine. Even though we had been through whatever we had been through with my husband, we still had a connection. We still had a bond, as sisters.

I had always worked. I continued to work. I also began to put a little money aside. My husband had extremely high medical expenses. He was not a well person. He had migraine headaches. He had to get medication. He had to have very, very intense painkillers. He also had quite a serious drug habit. I didn't want to admit it at the time, but he would self-medicate. I don't think I was really dealing with a real person. I was dealing with a person who got high every day. All of my money was going into his expenses, as well as trying to feed myself and maintain a healthy pregnancy.

I just began to become selfish. I was very unhappy at this point. I recognized that. I had gotten myself into a very bad situation. I began to wake up and see the reality of where my life was. It was very depressing to have to confront that. I also realized that I didn't want to raise my child in that environment.

What concluded that series of counseling is when I left that state and moved to California. I called the counselor the day before I left. I let her know that I was moving on. I had to do a significant amount of, I don't want to say lying, but it was necessary not to let him know what my true plans were in order to get out. I had to tell him I was coming to California to visit my family, so that they could meet the baby. That was the story I had to give him.

I left my husband about six weeks after my daughter was born. I had to get his permission to take the child out of state. I was out of the house at that time. I had packed up my things and put them in storage. I was staying with some friends in another town. I told him, "I needed some time to get away, to relax with my family, and have them meet the baby. When I get back, we will go to marriage counseling." I had to have him believe that I was coming back, or he would have never let me go.

When I got to California, I basically crashed, emotionally. I just took care of my daughter. My husband would call and engage me in long conversations. He knew where I was. I had to give him that to get away. He continued to verbally abuse me over the phone, long distance. He tried to upset me. He threatened to come to California to kill me and to take "his daughter." Mentally, I was in complete depression. I felt that my daughter was the only thing that kept me going. I had no career. I had not worked in my field. I had no experience, other than my degrees and the work I did while I was in school. I felt like I had to start my life all over from scratch. I knew it was a great opportunity, but it seemed so hard. Leaving him and getting away was the hardest thing I have ever done.

To this day, I don't really consciously understand where I found the strength. I think about it now and, "Oh my God. I'm really glad that I did." It meant starting from scratch, and getting my daughter to an age where I could get her a babysitter and start my career. I had no money. I lived with my family for six months. That was the only thing that saved me. I had family here.

Someone suggested the idea of going on welfare, but no, I never thought about it. I started working part-time at a major university and I rented my own apartment. My mom had come from Jamaica. She took care of my daughter while I worked. I did some freelance work in the film business and television production. Almost a year later, I found my first full-time job that started me on a career path. Up to then, it was basically hustling and scraping. Whenever my uncle could afford it, he would give me money. I asked for money from my family. My family sent me money from wherever they were, whatever they could afford. It was my family that kept me alive, and I give thanks.

Once I was in my career and on my own, it was very difficult for me to relate to men. I think I went through a complete emotional shut down. I didn't date. I was primarily focused on survival. I still believe to this day that friendship is the most important part of a relationship. I was very fortunate, because I had a number of male friends who really, really helped me. They helped restore my faith in mankind. They would like listen when I needed to talk. They didn't put a lot of pressure on me. They treated me with kindness and respect. They didn't make a lot of sexual demands on me. They were encouraging.

It took a while for my mental strength to recover. Initially, when I came to California, I went through a six to eight week crisis counseling service at a mental health clinic. That really helped a lot. That was the first step towards me even beginning to function. I was just a basket case when I got here. I still remember the counselor that I had. She was a specialist in domestic violence. She really helped me a lot.

I wish I could remember specifically what she did, but I was under such stress at the time. The only thing I could recall is that I would sit there and cry and cry and cry. She gave me confidence that this was not the end of the world. That my life would get better. She was just there, and that was important for me then. I could call her at times other than when we were having our sessions.

A male counselor would not have been able to do anything for me, not at that point in my life. I was just in too much pain. It was hard for me to even make eye contact with men, on the street, in a shop, wherever.

After I did the initial crisis counseling, it took about three years before I was able to date and relate to men. At that point, I had begun to go into long-term therapy. What I found was, I could not, even though I would go out with men, and I enjoyed their company, I could not really let anybody get close to me, man-wise. Even if a nice man expressed that he likes me, I just wasn't able to let anybody get close to me. It manifested itself in a lot of anger. This is like my second wave of reaction now, still coming from the same situation. Going through long-term therapy, which lasted five years, helped me to recognize my role in what had transpired in my life.

When I got to the point of me taking responsibility for my life, I had to realize, "This is where you are, and you have to move on from here." That really helped. We talked a lot about my relationship with my mother, which at that point had seriously deteriorated. She was living with me, and she was resentful having to be here to take care of my daughter, even though she willingly came out at the time. We had to wait a number of years before she could become a legal resident. It was a very difficult and frustrating time for both of us.

I was very depressed, and I didn't want to do medication. I just basically talked it out in therapy. I don't think my mother and I have turned the corner in our relationship yet. We're still dealing with that issue. There's a lot of other stuff there too. My mother always felt that I was my father's favorite. I don't feel that way. She, therefore, always favored my brother. There was just myself and my brother, so there's this schism in the family of me and my dad versus her and my brother.

I was forced to do some things by the family that eventually ended up being very bad decisions. After my father died, my mother wanted me to take charge of his estate. My brother sold the house my father primarily left to me. He has not paid me a penny. I feel that is a great loss in my life. My brother is an irresponsible alcoholic, yet my mother will defend his actions. To this day, I suffer the consequences. I don't know if our relationship will ever be healed. We're at the point now where she's on her own. I'm on my own. We're kind of at a truce. That may be as good as it can get.

I had to stop speaking to my mother for a number of years because she has never really respected me. Again, verbal abuse. I was raised in an environment where children were seen and not heard. A parent could do anything to a child that they chose to do, whatever they wanted to do. There was very little protection of children.

My mother was very much unavailable, emotionally, for me when I was growing up. She had her own problems. She had this tremendously abusive marriage, even though she had divorced the man, he was still in her life. She had financial issues that she had to deal with. Raising two children in the third world was not a task to be taken lightly. When my dad didn't pay child support, she had to deal with the consequences of that. I had no role model on how to deal with relationships or any emotional support. They tried their best.

Before my dad passed, we had begun to communicate better. I had forgiven him for all of the crap he put us through. I reached that point as I grew older. He opened up more. I went to live with him and we were able to develop a relationship. He had remarried and I lived with him and his wife. My brother was with us then also. My father got cancer. We knew he would eventually die. We just didn't know exactly when. We didn't think it would be as soon as it actually was. I was away at school at the time.

Without those parental models, I didn't know how to relate to a man without confrontation. I knew what I saw in my friends' homes, but that's not enough.

At some point in the long-term therapy, I realized that I had to do more than just talk about my problems, which I would have to get out there and live my life, even if it meant pushing some buttons, trying to jumpstart things. I was still very afraid to let anybody get close to me. I had basically cocooned myself in this shell. I took care of my daughter. I did my work. I was in a demanding field that was very high stress. I worked long hours, weird hours. Working weekends, I wasn't available to date on a Saturday night. It was like work began to consume my life. These companies, they will mess with you if they can. I just had to begin to recognize the importance of relationships. I was in denial about that. I didn't have time for men. I didn't even want to talk to men. I noticed all this anger that started to emerge.

Just before I got into my marriage, I had found a spiritual master, Paramahansa Yogananda, a teacher who was very, very powerful and I knew would be able to help me. When I did get into my marriage, into that relationship, that was one of the things that also fell by the wayside in addition to all of my friends and my family. My husband was resentful of my spiritual path, absolutely.

I couldn't practice. There was no time to meditate. He needed to be catered to 24 hours a day. There was no time for me to have just for myself. Because I was new to the path, I didn't really insist on it. I didn't insist on anything in my marriage.

When I came to California, I found that path again. I wasn't conscious of this when I was coming out here, but this is where the headquarters is for that path. There were temples here. I was able to get back in touch with the path. I was able to begin attending church. When my daughter was three, I put her into Sunday school. Every Sunday, I would go to the service and she would go to Sunday school. She learned how to meditate. I've basically raised her on that path.

That helped me reach my center. I went through a spiritual rejuvenation. That's really the thing that caused me to begin to get in touch with my real feelings – my real Self, my soul, my higher Self. Specifically, it helped me accept the fact that I am a child of God. This particular path gives you some very powerful techniques that you can use to elevate your consciousness into the higher realms.

I began to regularly practice Hatha Yoga, which are very powerful body movements that not only strengthen the body, but also help to unite body, mind, and soul. I began to meditate more regularly. In meditation, you are not thinking. You are basically communing with the Soul. They have specific techniques to interiorize the mind so that you can get beyond thoughts and get into the higher realms of spiritual consciousness.

When you follow this path, any kind of emotional hang-ups or problems, you have to deal with them or they will get in your way. You'll be thinking about your problems instead of going beyond them. There are a number of aspects to this spiritual path that helped me. Number one, it helped me recognize where I was. Number two, to deal with what I had to deal with.

There are a lot of books about the teachings, a lot of lessons in the teachings about compassion, forgiveness, knowing yourself as a soul, being conscious of God, that we are one with God, and always have been. Yes, there is work that we need to do. The soul is right there. It always has been, and always will be. Through many incarnations, we evolve in trying to get back to God. On this path, I have those techniques to do that. I can't really discuss what those techniques are, specifically. One would have to take the lessons for themselves and study them. I don't want to say that it is secret, but it is confidential. There are many techniques that one can learn. It's not hard. Basically, meditation is what I am talking about.

ℰ

My daughter has been going through my turmoil since conception, really. She has dealt with it very, very well. I was blessed to have a child that was able to really hang. She could really hang out and deal with any situation I was in. She's very flexible. I've always told her the truth. I've always been honest with her. She's like my best friend. We communicate well. Whatever the situation is, I'll tell her the truth about it. That has really helped her to remain open.

The reason why I left my husband was that I didn't want to raise my daughter in that situation. What I do is fine with her, except when I start dating someone. Her immediate reaction to that person is negative. She doesn't want me to date. She just wants me to be her mummy. I think she's afraid of losing me. I don't know what that means. I've always told her that no matter where I am, what I'm doing, she's always going to be in my life. I don't think there is any real reason for that, but I have noticed that over the years. She's fourteen now. I tell her, "In another three years, you're going off to a university. What am I supposed to do? In another two years, you'll be dating yourself."

From day one, I have talked to her about boys. I told her the facts of life when she was eight or nine, in a context that she could understand. She's always known that she can come and ask me any questions about boys, sex, and birth control or sexually transmitted diseases. In fact, sometimes her friends come over and they have questions and we talk. They can't ask their parents. I just try to tell them the truth, and get it on a wholesome level.

The spiritual path that I acquired, I have raised her in. It is like second nature to her. I remember her Sunday school teachers would always tell me that she's a very spiritual child. I knew that. She has the techniques and she can use them whenever she chooses to. Right now, she's going through a phase where she's very busy. She just started high school. She likes to stay up late at night and talk on the phone.

I've been teaching Sunday school, and sometimes she doesn't like to go because I'm actually teaching her class. Apart from that, when I'm not teaching, she generally goes.

I spent my first 18 years living in Jamaica, most of my formative years. I would say that there are definitely some cultural differences between here and there related to male/female relationships. Jamaican women, generally speaking, are very passive. My mom was a very unusual woman to have left her marriage and get a divorce in the 1960s, in Jamaica. That was virtually unheard of at that time. I had an example in her in what she did that was not the norm of society. Most Jamaican women would have never left their husband, certainly, not if they had children. They tend not to be educated. See, both of my parents were educated people. I had an intellectual environment that was very stimulating on top of all of the craziness that was going on. I was surrounded by books, so I was exposed to other cultures and the realm of ideas through books.

I would say typically, Jamaican men tend to drink heavily. It's considered part of being a man. Boys are taught to "hold their liquor." "You gotta' be a man, so you've got to learn how to drink." Stuff like that. We look at it now and go, "Oh my God. That's intolerable. Why would you do that?" Kids down there can drink at 14 and 15 years old. They can go into clubs at 16 and order drinks. If you have money, it's not a problem. Different, different, different approach.

I know today, a lot of the friends that I am in touch with in Jamaica expresses a much more liberated philosophy. They are not willing to tolerate the same old B.S. that their mothers did.

As far as my own progress, I have been dating someone for the last five months or so. It's relatively new. I don't know where this is going. In the last seven years, I've had one relationship that lasted about three years. I've had another one with someone off and on a number of times. We never seem to really get it together. It was a good experience, and we're still friends. I've had a number of what I would call short-term relationships, six months, three months, four months, like that.

I've sort of been experimenting. I've been willing to engage in getting to know someone, having interaction with men, letting them get close to me, you know, allowing myself to be real. I try to be real with people. There are some people who date, but they are not really real.

Right now, I would say that I know more of who I am. I'm really looking for someone who can accept me for who I am, who can recognize who I am. I'm looking for someone I can be compatible with.

Earlier in my life, it was always about the other person. Now it's about what's right for me. It used to be, "Am I right for this person? Is he going to really like me?" Now, it's what's right for me here. "Is this person right for me?" I don't mean that in an egotistical sense. I mean it in a sense of, "What are the soul qualities that this person manifests in their life?"

This side of me has developed through my experiences, along with age and wisdom. In another sense, it's also developed because of the spiritual path. I now know, because I know myself, the qualities I am looking for in a partner. For a long time, I used to attract men who were very good looking, very worldly, but there was just nothing behind it. They would lie to me. They would manipulate me. Now, it's like I'm not looking at the package so much as what's behind it. I want to see what's behind the curtain.

In this last phase of my dating, it is still very difficult to allow someone to get close to me. I think I am very fortunate because I have met someone who has had a lot of experiences in life. He has a varied worldview, a cosmic view of people. He had no expectations of me in terms of I had to be a certain way, or do certain things. It was like I could just be myself. That was all I had to do. That was very freeing, very liberating.

I think a lot of men have expectations of women that – sometimes it's really a struggle for us to rise and to meet that. For me, it was just a matter of finding the right person, finding someone that I was compatible with at that time, as opposed to trying to fit myself into their program. I had to find the courage to speak the truth and tell the person exactly where I was at, what I had been through. "I am not really able to meet any of these expectations. You have to just accept me for where I am right now." That was really hard. A lot of women feel like we have to fit in with the guy's program. I got to the point where I was able to say, "No. It's our program. We're going to create this, and this is what's it's going to be."

I would have to find someone who was willing to accept these kinds of terms. That's really what it is. You're negotiating the terms of the relationship. Those were skills that I had never learned. I didn't know what it meant to stand up for myself. I didn't know what I wanted. Maybe part of me didn't feel that I was worthy of getting what I wanted. I had to come to the realization, "I am a child of God. I am worthy. And I am holding out for a real love."

A lot of my earlier interactions, during this second phase of dating, were always one-sided. It was like, either the person really liked me, but I didn't like them that much. I just kind of went out with them because it was something to do. Maybe they were kind of interesting, but I just knew that there wasn't anything really that deep.

On the other hand, I would really, really like this person and he would just, kind of, not be willing to look at the real me. They may have had an image of who they thought I was. They thought I was this exotic Caribbean princess, or whatever roles they thought. They had games and stuff. Finding that balance where it is a mutual thing, you have to search until you find the right person. That's just a reality.

With the right man or the wrong man, I don't think I will ever fall back into old habits of giving, giving, giving. I don't worry about that. I can see where people are coming from a lot quicker now. That has come with experience, with dating different kinds of men. I've dated an extremely eclectic mix of men. That is not something I necessarily or consciously was seeking. That is just the way it has happened. In a way, it is good because I do have a very universal approach to the world, kind of holistic, you know. Meeting different men from different cultures, at different stages of their lives has helped to broaden my perceptions.

Men who are into manipulation and control, and whatever, they don't even know that this address exists. I attract a different vibration of man right now. That's a good thing. Even if a multimillionaire playboy walked in the door and said, "I want you in my harem, x, y, and z." That does not interest me in the least. I know what I want now.

When the latest person I am dating comes to pick me up, in the last couple of weeks, my daughter has become extremely tolerant (laughs). I would have to say she's usually in her room. That's kind of where she lives now. She just comes down to eat and watch satellite TV. She has cable in her room, so she doesn't have to even come down if she doesn't want to.

We had a long talk. She understands that I am dating. She'll come down and say, "Good evening," and be polite. He wants to invite her to do some things with us. She has said that she would be willing to do that. Again, we're negotiating the terms. I don't feel like I want to pressure her or force her to interact with him. She will interact with him and get to know him in her own way. She actually said to me the other day, "Oh you know, he's a nice man." That's a good sign.

As much as possible, I am trying to provide a good model for her in male/female relationships. I've gone for long periods of time where I haven't been in a relationship. If I'm dating a guy, I don't call him every day. If I'm home on a Saturday night, it's not a big deal. If I choose to go out alone, to a party or whatever, I do that. I think I am a good model for my daughter. What concerns me with her are the music videos, all the heavy, heavy sexism, the women dancing in bikinis, or less, in these videos. Young girls need something to counter that. That's all coming from the male perspective. Even the women's videos, some of them, can be very negative. I really wonder what message they're sending to our kids, and what influence that is going to have.

I am the one who has to counter that with my daughter. We talk about these things all the time. We watch videos together. I give her a womanist interpretation. We argue back and forth about them. She swears, "Well, Mom, I'm not being influenced by this." I go, "Yeah, you are. It's subconscious. Just remember, your mother said it (laughs)." It has to come from me. She's my child. Nobody's going to raise her for me.

If I was sitting in my living room with a bunch of my

daughter's girlfriends, which has happened, and we were having an open conversation, and one of the girls raises the question, "What should I do if a boy I like wants to have sex with me?" What I have said to my daughter, and her friends is, "It takes time to get to know a person. You shouldn't be having sex with someone you don't know very well. The most important part of any relationship is friendship. If you can't be friends with someone, you have no business having sex with them."

I've always told my daughter that in her life, the order of things is, you get your education, then you have a career, then you get married, and then you have children.

When kids are going to have sex, they are going to have sex. That is not something that anybody can put a time or a date on. What is important to me, that she be emotionally mature, understand what she is getting herself into and take responsibility for it. I don't anticipate that she will become sexually active at an early age. She knows that it is important to take responsibility, use birth control, protect you against sexually transmitted diseases.

I don't think telling kids the truth is going to make them go out there and buy condoms, get on the pill, and go have sex. Knowledge gives them the power to choose. I would like my daughter to remain a virgin as long as possible. She knows that. We've talked about these things extensively.

In terms of me being a role model, I don't bring men into my home to spend the night. If I'm going away for a weekend, she knows where I am. She knows how to reach me. I don't want her to see me kissing or whatever. Yeah, a peck on the cheek, or a "chups," as we say in Jamaica. That's fine. I want her to see me relating to men more as friends.

If she's going to have sex, I cannot prevent it. All I can do is create an environment in which she has the support to do the right thing. That means basically being there as a parent.

I really despair at the young girls having babies today, that generation. What kind of children are they going to raise? Life is becoming increasingly complex. We're more and more dependent on technology which you need to have an education in order to deal with.

I don't know what is going to happen. It is very scary to me. I can try to be an example and raise my child with values about those things that I value, like: an education, being self-sufficient, to use your mind to its most positive potential, and to always remember, no matter what you do, you will always be a child of God. That's what I have to do.

Nadia

(Never Average Decent Individual Always)

Ms. Nadia is a 27-year-old single mother who is working and going to school. Her life has been very unusual. Her military experience caused some concepts to develop that affect her life today. She is extremely intelligent and wise for her age. She has a non-traditional sexual orientation that may be difficult for some to understand, but taken in the context in which she explains, it becomes clearer. She is an aspiring writer who I predict will one day produce some of the most dynamic books available, based on her own experiences and what her imaginative mind creates. She does have a tendency to be self-destructive, stimulated by depression. This could be her demise if she does not maintain control of her emotions. The contributions she can make to humanity far outweigh the personal disasters that she sometimes has to endure. I see a bright future for her.

I was born in Chicago, Illinois. I came to California with my family because I had no choice. We lost our house and my father was already out here. My childhood was interesting – basic two-parent home with brothers and sisters. I am the eldest of seven. There were hard times and there was dysfunction. Nobody's perfect. I guess, because of that, it makes me who I am today.

As far as my parents being good role models for me, they could be negative, and I would still find something positive out of it, at least what not to do. So, I would have to say, in an indirect manner, that they did provide a model. In the beginning, they were not that positive towards one another. I think it had to do with the fact that they were young and did not have a chance to find out who they were, then they started having children. Because of that, it made me not want to have children. I didn't want to get married. My parents used to fight a lot, physical fighting. There was a lot of tension and hostility. I think it had a lot to do with them both coming from broken homes, more or less. I saw it and I didn't want to put myself through that. So, in that case, I just wouldn't get married. That would be one less hassle I would have to go through. I would say that their relationship had something to do with how I would live my life in the future.

I moved out of my house at 17 years old. I had just graduated from high school and got accepted at the University of Chicago. I was a psychology major, minoring in English. That was the first time I left home. Being on my own in college was different. I think I am the most disciplined of all my parents' kids. I was always trying to do the right thing so I wouldn't have to backtrack. I wound up coming back because I was staying with my mother's folks and it didn't work out. They're crazy, simple as that. They didn't really like my mother and I heard them talking about her one day. I couldn't deal with it. I was only 18 then. Had it been now, I would have told them about themselves and kept on going. I felt it was better that I got out of there because it was a hostile environment. Eventually, something was going to burst. I tried to avoid confrontations.

I came back home. Eleven months later I left again to go to the Air Force. My dad was in the Air Force. My uncle, he was in the Navy. Everyone has their own favorite branch, being biased. My uncle told me, "If you go into the Air Force or the Navy, they are the best two of the four." My dad and I discussed it. I figured I could get money for school, do a little traveling, and grow up. I could get some experience, regardless of the fact that the majority of the people I knew felt, "The military is no place for a Black person." I wanted to see for myself. Experience is always the best teacher and will always be. Considering that I am an aspiring writer, the more experience I go through, the better my writings will be.

The Air Force provided some real intense experiences. For instance, I went into this clothing store – I was stationed in Montana, of all places. That's a very racist state. They only tolerate Black people there because they are in the military, and the military is bringing money to their cities. I went into this store to buy a leather coat. I stood there for about 20 minutes. There were five, all Caucasian, saleswomen. Not one of them came over to see if I needed help. The store was not crowded. There were one or two other customers. If there were five saleswomen there, someone should have come over and asked if I needed anything.

That's when I realized how alive racism is in America. You can read about it, see it on TV, but until you've personally gone through it, you really don't have a clue. Everything else is really second-hand information. It was like a slap to my face. My money was the same. It was not counterfeit. We're all living in the same country and I'm in the military. That supposedly gave me a little bit of clout, but it didn't matter.

I had a personal reaction to it. It made me not like White people for a long time. It opened my eyes. I began to see with eyes that had a little bit of wisdom. I was less naïve. I started observing a lot more. Like I said, when you don't go through it, someone being prejudiced against you, you don't really get the full understanding of it. After that happened to me, it was like a wall went up. I kept a lot of people, even Black people, at arm's length distance. I always felt that no matter what, people would treat me right because I would treat them right. It's not like that, so I had to do a bit of reconstruction.

It made a lot of my friendships a little different. I had White friends. I hate to say that because it sounds like, "Oh well, I don't hate all White people because I have White friends." It's just that things became a lot clearer, that no matter what, there's always going to be a difference. I choose to acknowledge it or be angry and do something destructive. Not so much as tolerate it, but do what I have to do to get mine. No one is going to give it to me. And most of all, become positive with it.

Another experience I had in the Air Force stands out in my

mind. I had a roommate who was French and Italian. Her folks didn't like Black people at all. She attempted suicide. I saved her life. She took sleeping pills. She woke up in the middle of the night. I thought she was sleepwalking. She told me that she sometimes sleepwalks. She woke me up, and I told her, "You need to get back in your bed." I was going back to sleep, but something told me to get up and check on her. I'm glad I did. She was really pale. She was just lying there and her pulse was very, very weak. I had to call 911 and the whole nine yards. We were friends, and it hurt me because I felt like I was partially to blame for it. She had a crush on me and I couldn't respond. That's not tolerated in the military. That took a lot out of me.

Considering that I am a very open-minded person, I believe in trying anything and everything once or twice, depending on how good it feels. Her crush on me was okay. It helped my ego. I'm not going to lie. I need my ego stroked. I couldn't show her the affection that she needed. Like I said, we were in the military. We couldn't walk around the base holding hands. That would have caused problems. Then there were rumors circulating, so I had to try to throw salt into everybody's thought process by dating the opposite sex. That caused problems with her. We got into a fight. It was stressful.

That was not the beginning of my being involved with women. I was about 16 years old. When that happened, I had a really good friend. I was always curious, but I never knew how to venture into approaching another woman and say, "I like you, this, that, and the other." She approached me and it was a budding romance. Everything went in stages. I can say that I loved her. That was probably the first woman I was ever in love with.

It wasn't something within me. She was the person that moved me. It's just who moves me the most: emotionally, spiritually, and passionately. At the time, I was in a relationship with a man who was abusive, not in a physical sense, but mentally abusive. Her friendship alone was soothing to my whole being.

Women share intimate relationships that could be classified as lesbian love. It's just that the physical is left out of it. At that time, she nurtured the part of me that he kept tormenting. It was very confusing for me because I was raised that homosexuality was very wrong, very bad. "My child is not going to grow up like that." But I felt within myself that if it was genuine love, how could it be wrong? That's what led me to further experiment.

The man that I was with was always down-talking me. He was older than me. Automatically, there was a control thing. If something was going wrong at home and I called him, he would say, "What do you want me to do about it? You make it seem like I'm always fixing your problems." With him, basically it was just a sex thing. He was this older man who had this younger woman. He was never comforting when I needed him to be. If I had a problem, I couldn't go and talk to him. If I needed money, I could never ask him for it. It was not so much of him taking care of me, in a sense that I couldn't take care of myself. We're already built as human beings to need that nurturing factor. Just because we're adults doesn't mean we don't need a hug, someone to pamper us. He was not giving of that at all.

In order for me to have been in that abusive relationship, I had to not know any better. Remember, I spoke about my parents and how they went at each other and how I didn't want to get married, but yet still, I was conditioned to that type of relationship. Even though he didn't hit me, he was mentally abusive. I felt that I deserved that.

That had nothing to do with me wanting to be with a woman. I was always curious, simply because I had read about it, because it was so taboo. Anything that's considered taboo is of course going to be more interesting. It's just like when you're 16, you're not supposed to drink. If you're at your house when your folks are having a party, nobody's around, you are going to try to take a sip of that wine simply because. That's how I felt about being with a woman. It was the curiosity that led me to want to experiment, not because of what he had done or not done. It started out as a curiosity.

See, I was a tomboy growing up. I'm the oldest and my father wanted a son first. I felt that I was inadequate because of that. I'm a daddy's girl. Dad is the end-all to end all to me. I played football, basketball, and wrestled until I got too old to wrestle. You know, I started developing. "Can't do that no more. Can't catch the football in the chest."

I always felt that maybe if I were a boy, my dad would appreciate me more. So, I went through that phase. It had nothing to do with being attracted to women. That was simply because I wanted my father's love. Of course, I understand that now. I've always been open-minded to new things. I felt that was the only way that I was going to grow. Once you've felt that you've learned everything, or there's nothing else that you can try, you might as well dig your own grave. Life is forever changing. Even when it changes, and it stays the same, it still changes. You can read a book, put it down and not pick it up for two years. Maybe even a month later, that same book, I guarantee, you will read something and say, "Oh, I didn't see that before." That's because you've changed mentally, or something that you are going through you can better relate, or for whatever reason. It's still going to be different. That's how I see things.

I've had male relationships after that initial encounter. I have a daughter! I don't believe in labels because it constricts you to having that type of behavior. If I were to label myself, I would be considered bi-sexual. Now, it takes a lot more than just a good-looking man to move me. He has to have something to offer. With women, I'm a lot more cautious in my picking. I know how women are. It makes it a little more difficult to be involved for me. With men, I appreciate them a lot better, having been in relationships with women.

Thinking about some of my past involvements, I had quite a few male relationships. I prefer to start with the one, and end with the one who changed my life forever. That would be my child's father. He was married, and I knew that. I was getting ready to get out of the service. I just wanted someone who would keep my bed warm. It was strictly for physical purposes. Of course, there was no plan for pregnancy and I did become pregnant. Because he was married, that made him less of a man to handle what he should have handled correctly. That was like the nail in the coffin that made me very, very harsh towards men. No matter what, I continue to love him, indirectly, because of our child.

Before I became pregnant, that was the best relationship I had with a man. It seems kind of odd to say that, maybe because he was married. He was taking from his wife to give to me. We shared. He was very comforting, extremely sensitive. When I was upset, he would make me talk. I have a tendency to shut down when I don't want to talk. I was used to not having anyone to talk to. He would make me talk. He appreciated me for me.

I didn't have to get all glamorous and dressed up like the mentally abusive man wanted. I didn't have to do things a certain way. He just appreciated me as I was. If I didn't want to dress up or comb my hair, so what? He came to see me as a person, not me as the outside package. I appreciated that. I got into that. That was great.

After the fact, he had to either tell his wife, which he decided not to do, or I had to leave and things just kind of went awry.

I had four months left to go in the Air Force. I left because I didn't want to lose the child. I especially decided to keep it. I had a doctor's appointment. I'll never forget this. I said, "I can't be a single parent. I can't do this. I cannot do this. This man is already tripping a little bit. I can't put myself through this." Then I heard the heartbeat. The connection was made. The bond was forming. There was no way I could terminate that life, or the beginning of a life. I decided I had to get out of the Air Force because everyone was trying to figure out, "Who's the father?"

I didn't feel it was my place to tell anybody that was going to tell everybody that he was the father. I wanted the news to come from him to his wife. I wasn't there to make any trouble. I had never met the woman. I got what I wanted. I was being selfish and petty. I can admit that now, but at the time, it was all about just having a good time.

I think when a woman becomes pregnant she plans on being a good mother. She ages maybe five or ten years. I heard the heartbeat. I aged five years. I was 22, so I was 27, maybe even 30, who's to say? I was concerned that there would be no stress or less stress so that I wouldn't lose my child.

I came home. He wanted me to put somebody else on the birth certificate, which I did not. As I told him, "It was not somebody else's dick, so why should I put somebody else's name?" He doesn't take care of her. I have a beautiful little girl and I'm not saying that because I'm biased. If I saw her on the street I would say, "Oh my gosh, she's gorgeous." But she is, and I love her with all there is in me.

There are times when I get frustrated because he has taken the cowardly way out. I feel a lot of men do that. My father took the cowardly way out. It seems to me that every man that has been in my life has been a coward. If I can be strong, how come they can't?

I would have preferred that he became honest with his wife, that he would have been a part of her life. He didn't have to stay with me. I'm an adult. I'll be all right. I made the choice. I know what I did. It was wrong. I shouldn't have, but okay, I can't go back and there's no time for regrets. He can be more active in her life. It's not all about just the money. I don't want her growing up feeling that she wasn't good enough for him to stay around, which is why I never say anything bad about him around her. I won't let anybody else say anything bad about him. We only know him as how he's done me. We don't know how he can be to her. She needs to have that hope.

My daughter knows who her father is. I've taken her down to meet him. There are pictures. She knows his name. She never hears me say anything negative about him because that's her father. She knows. The wife knows. When she gets older, I will explain to her – I don't believe in sugar coating anything to kids. They pick up on a lot more than what we give them credit for. When she's older, she's only four now, I'll tell her that I had an affair with a married man, the whole thing.

ℰ

It's possible that my bi-sexuality will have an effect on my daughter. Kids do more of what their parents do than what their parents say. If she should happen to come home from school one day and say, "Mom, I have a crush on a girl," I can sit down and I can handle that with her. I can sit down and talk to her about it. As I look at it, my experiences are a better way for me to relate to my child. There's a lot more same-sex relationships going on than people realize. They start at an early age. There are a lot of teenagers who commit suicide because of that. They don't have anybody to talk to, "I can't tell my parents. They're religious and they goin' kick me out." Uh uh, if that's who my child tends to be happy with, then who am I to say, "No?" That's how I look at it.

It's not something I would try to influence my child into. No, no. If I were a singer, I wouldn't push my child into that if that's not what she wants to do. Even now, I let her make her own choices. As parents, I think we have to learn how to let go a little with each stage, letting the child become independent. Because if you don't, and you try to live vicariously through your child, it causes conflict.

Right now, I let her decide. This morning she says, "I don't want to wear those shoes. I want to wear the other ones." That was her choice. She wanted to wear the other shoes, "Okay." It still went with the outfit, so it was no problem. If she decides that this is what she wants to do, I'm behind her 100%. I'm not going to tell her it's the best thing that has ever happened to me. No. Her relationship with men might not be like mine.

I think I'm a better mother to her than my mother was to me in the beginning, because I wasn't as young. My mother was 17 when she had me in 1970. I was 23. I had already done four years in the service. It wasn't like I didn't have a way. I'm a vet, who's going to tell me, "No?" Even if I have to work at McDonald's, at two different McDonald's jobs, I can still get a job. So, it's a little bit better for me. I'm more open. I'm more affectionate. My mother was not affectionate. Her mother was not affectionate. My father is. I learned to be affectionate through him. I love affection. I have no problem showing that to my child or anyone I'm involved with.

My dad will cry if he's hurt. He's just not very talkative, but I think that's most men. He enjoys hugs, kisses, and stuff. He's very affectionate. My mom is now coming around. She's more affectionate with my daughter than she is with me. That doesn't upset me. It used to, because I would say, "Why didn't she ever give that to me?" It took her a while to come around. I understand that as best I can because of the way her mother was. So, okay, no problem.

Because my father was so affectionate, one could probably say that had something to do with me being bi-sexual. To me, I think it is biological first and foremost, then the behavior, as you get older. I was a tomboy. I acted like one of the guys. I had no problem with that. I felt that would make me versatile. I believe in versatility, like a chameleon, change to your environment. It's a possibility. I won't say, "Yes," I won't say, "No."

There were other relationships I had with men, but they are irrelevant to me. You know how you sometimes take a lot of detours before you find the main highway? I look at them as detours. They're irrelevant. No biggy.

℘

All of the relationships I have had with women stand out. The first one was like I said, we were friends first. She would write me letters. She always thought I was so sexy which I thought was really fascinating. I don't think I am attractive. We used to spend time together and play basketball together. I love basketball. We would go out places. I always thought I was boring 'cause I'm pretty much a loner. She wanted to spend time with me. I said, "Wow. Where is the guy I used to date that was mentally abusive?" We very rarely spent time together. She genuinely loved me. She gave me the nurturing that I had lacked when my mother couldn't be as affectionate. In my late teens, early adult years, she filled the void that the boyfriend I was seeing was steadily making bigger and bigger. The only reason we stopped seeing each other is because I went into the military.

I've only had three real relationships with women. The last relationship I had with a woman was extremely negative. She used me. I got got. I was spending money on her. Basically, it was a financial thing for her. Not that I have much money. If I am into a person, I do whatever I can to help them out and what-not. But that's okay. You live and learn.

My mother met the first woman I was with. We were still just friends, so it was okay. But this one, I had told my mother about. I talked to my mom and told her that I find women attractive and that it's not going to go away. It's not just a phase. She met her. She said, "She seems like she's a lot of fun." She would prefer to see me with a man, of course. She just wants me to be happy. My daughter met her and adored her tremendously. We had never been physical, but she would come over. She would spend the night; she'd sleep on the couch. She was there all the time, but she was just using me.

You know how men use women sometimes, just for sex? Well, she used me for money. She didn't respect the fact that I was already struggling. The little bit of money that I had, she was always asking for it for this or for that. Her car would break down. She would need it for that. We went to a concert, and she said, "I want to get a new outfit, and I want to have this," you know. I was constantly trying to make her happy. Basically, the same things that I thought would work on her that I tried to do with the mentally abusive man, except I didn't give him money.

The end came when I got tired. I got fed up. I felt that was all she wanted from me. As long as I was doing what she wanted, everything was okay. I had to let her know. I wrote her a letter and told her that she was manipulative, very self-serving, and I couldn't deal with that. I'm not trying to change her, but because I can't deal with who she is, I have to go. I didn't want her back at the house. I didn't want her coming by. I didn't want her calling me, none of that. As far as I was concerned, she was dead.

My daughter has never seen me affectionate with another woman. She's never seen me affectionate with a man. I don't do that in front of her.

After that last relationship, I've been single ever since and enjoying it. Just taking care of myself. It's what I needed to do. I had to put myself first instead of others. I had to learn who I am and be comfortable with that, be complacent even. That's where I am now.

As far as the future goes, I don't even think about whether I will end up with a man or a woman. Like I said, it's whoever moves me. If I spend enough time with an individual, and that light goes on, "Hey, I can do this," be it a male or a female. I'm not in any hurry right now. When I look back it's like, "Wow. I was in a hurry to try to be in a relationship. I thought it was the thing to do." You can't love somebody if you don't even know who you are, let alone love yourself. I don't even worry about that anymore.

You know there are some stereotypical views about same-sex relationships; that one woman plays the man, the other a woman. You got to think about it now. It's not so much of playing the role of a man or a woman; it's that you always have one dominant person, whether it is same-sex or heterosexual. There is such a thing as henpecked men. That means the woman is dominant. Okay, it's the same thing. The last female relationship I was in, she would have been considered the man. She was the most dominant. She lives her life as if she were a man. She wears men's clothes and wears them well I might add, but she still looks feminine. That's just how she feels most comfortable. You have some women who just like to wear dresses all the time. Some women like to wear pants all the time. Does that make them the man because they're wearing pants?

It's the stereotypes that we need to get away from and really look at what is going on. It took me a while to get used to wearing dresses. I wasn't appreciative of my body. I don't mind wearing them now. I just wear pants to work. It's like a two guy's relationship. You are going to have one more dominant than the other. That's just the way it is.

I don't see myself getting married to a man in the future. I don't believe in marriage. I don't believe in it at all. I don't feel you should have to stand in front of a man of the Word and have witnesses to profess your love. If you two are committed to each other, that's it. That's basically what it is. To me, marriage is a business. If the man promises to do everything for you, you continuously give him ass. That's how I look at it. When I get tired of you, then what? We got to go through this procedure, so that we don't have to be together and let somebody else tell us, "Okay, you guys can go your separate ways?" Uh uh. Nobody told us to come together in the first place. Why should somebody tell us to leave? If it's working without the marriage, then why try to fix it?

As far as long-term family development, I don't want any more kids. I never wanted kids. I wanted a child. I have that. I'm through. I think you should know your limitations. I am 27 years old. By the time my child leaves, graduates from high school and goes off to start her own life, I'll be in my 40s. That's the time for me to start my life again. No thank you.

Some people are really good with kids. I'm not saying that I'm not. I'm good with my child because I know that she is my child, but as a whole, I don't like kids. I don't have the patience to deal with little people. I'm only learning patience because I'm a mother. I've never wanted a big family. I've never thought about getting married. I have thought about being in a longtime relationship. Yes. When it happens, I'll be ready for it. In order for that to happen, I have to be happy with me. There can be no compromising with someone else for me to change who I am. I'm not trying to change anybody. Why should I change for them? I have to believe that there is someone out there who's going to love me and appreciate me for me. But first and foremost, I have to appreciate myself. That's not going to happen overnight. Each day it gets a little better.

Right now, I am a lot better than I have been. I'm very sincere in everything that I say. I'm pretty much satisfied. I'm complacent. I'm not at peace of mind yet, but each day it gets there. I go to sleep every night, considering that I've been burglarized. I don't sleep like I used to. I don't get as depressed as I used to. When things happen, I don't feel like, "Oh, it's my fault. I'm a bad person." I don't feel like that anymore.

If I'm attracted to a man, that means I appreciate his physical appearance. When it comes to emotionally bonding, if I'm attracted to a person, and I'm in a relationship, there's no room for anybody else. I'm a monogamous person. If I'm in a relationship with a man and he's into to me, I'm into him and we're emotionally supporting each other, spiritually supporting each other, there's no room for anybody else. He's going to still see women that he is attracted to, "Hey, she's looking good." I may even see women I'm attracted to, "Aw, she's lookin' all right." Or a man, "Brother, oh yeah." But that's as far as it will go.

I think a lot of people have the misinterpretation of my sexuality. "Well, she wants them both at the same time." That's "ménage a trois." You didn't hear me say that. It just said that I acknowledge the fact that I find women as equally attractive as I find men. And that's all it means, nothing more, nothing less.

Women by nature are nurturers. You can see two women walk down the street arm in arm and nine out of ten times you won't think too much about it. "Aw, they're really close." You see two men doing that, "What the hell?" That's just the way this society is. Men have been programmed. When I say programmed, that means their behavior has been conditioned to not be open with their affection. When you see two guys give each other a pound, they may give a little hug, but they'll keep distance between them.

Most of the time, women will envelop each other. That's what we're used to. When we hold a baby, "Don't hold the baby like that." We don't hold a baby with distance. It's skin on skin. That contact is very important from the first time that you are entered into this world. It determines how you are going to be in this society, basically with men, as far as physical intimacy.

I've been with guys who were in a rush, so they didn't take time to make sure that I was going to enjoy the sex. They took away from the contact, the skin on skin thing.

My child's father was very patient when it came to that. With a woman, she knows exactly what a woman needs for her to have an orgasm. Whether it's oral or whether she has an add-on, a dildo, a strap, whatever you wish to call it. It's just different. The oral sex is better because a woman knows how to please a woman. The afterwards, with the holding. Most men, they'll hold, then they'll probably fall asleep. Sometimes you may just want to talk. You may not want to. You may just want to listen to the heartbeat. All the time, it's not about the actual penetration. It's about the fact that you need to feel loved. Sex gets so twisted with the love thing. A lot of the times we confuse the two. We think they're one and they're not.

You can make love to a person without actually having any kind of physical contact, by you calling them on the phone and saying, "Hey, I just wanted to say I miss you or that I'm thinking about you. I'm glad you're in my life." That's making love right there. Taking them out to dinner. Pampering them. Attending to their needs even before they have to ask. That's making love. I'm not saying that there are no men out there that can do that, but you can count them on both hands, and maybe have a finger or two left over. They're not raised to be that way.

Not all women can give you sensitive affection. The last woman I was with, she was just out for herself. But as a whole, yes. Well, she was sensitive too. She would call. It's nice to come home and have a message from somebody that you're into like, "I was thinking about you..."

A lot of men are just after the one thing, "just to get the panties." So you think, "Oh, he's just doing that because I haven't given him any yet." You wonder if he'll still do that afterwards. That makes a difference.

It is a rare thing for a man to be as patient and as sensitive as a woman. It depends on the age. If he's an older man, he's been around, he knows. Hopefully, he has a better understanding of women. If he is a younger man, I don't expect him to be patient at all. So, it depends on the age.

There is discrimination if you are not so-called "normal." I am not blatant with my sexuality. I think it is only important to those who I care about. They are those who would meet my significant other. As a whole, I don't go around broadcasting it. It's not that I am ashamed or anything. Why? What does it matter?

If I had to look down the road to determine whether I would lean towards a man or a woman, I couldn't do that. I've had bad experiences on both sides. They're both equals. That's how it is for me. Whoever would move me most. It's not about pitting one side against the other. Of course, you are going to make comparisons. You can't just say, "Well, I prefer this," without having something to compare it to for you to know.

I could meet a man today, and he could be the end-all, just everything that I need. That would be great. Then I can say, "I've chosen a man." Or I could meet a woman, and say, "I've chosen a woman." I don't even go out looking anymore. If it's meant for it to happen, it will come to me, whichever one.

If you're not true to yourself, how can you even say that you love God? How can you even say that you love somebody else? You are living a lie within yourself. Everything else is irrelevant. I couldn't say anything else because my daughter is going to do what she wants anyway. I would have to let her know that it would not be easy being with a woman. People still frown upon that. They feel that you're less than a person, that there is something wrong with you.

It's the same as being Black, although you get the argument, "You were born Black. You weren't born to love the same sex." You don't know that. I think it's a biological thing. I'm going to stand by it. Why would somebody choose something that they know people are going to hate them for? That doesn't make sense. Why would you choose a lifestyle that you know people are going to be blatantly angry and hostile towards you for? She would have my 150% support. I would let her bring her girlfriend home and everything, simple as that.

One of the areas of condemnation on my lifestyle has come from the Church. Some traditionalists say, "You're living in sin. You can die and go to hell." My theory on that is, let me worry about that. It's between me and God. That's all I say to that. I don't try to defend it. Why should I try to defend that? I am who I am. Just like I shouldn't have to defend being Black. I shouldn't have to defend being a woman. I shouldn't have to defend who I take to bed. Teen pregnancy, anybody trying to defend that? It happens. So long as you're not hurting anyone, what's the point?

Historically, I have heard people say that prior to the fall of the Roman Empire, homosexuality was the preference of choice and that it contributed to its fall. I would say that anytime you have greed, be it for money, be it for lust, or anything of those natures, you're bound to have instability. I think it was just the greed. They got so much into it that they couldn't help themselves. They lost their focus. That's how I feel.

That's just like with a woman. Cleopatra, she supposedly slept with so many men. Come on, that's greedy. You don't sleep with that many men. It's just greed. That's my interpretation of it. It's not that I am defending it. If they had been sleeping with a whole bunch of women, would it have mattered? I think so. Greed. If you start thinking with the wrong head or the wrong part of the body, you're bound to have negativities, some repercussions.

Whether bi-sexuality or homosexuality should be considered normal in society, I don't think there is such a thing as normal. No matter what, something else is going to come along and society will say, "That's not normal." What is normal? Of course, there are things you know that you cannot do, that you should not do. I don't believe in such a thing as normal. I use the word only because I have not found one that's better.

Some people say that if most men get together and most women get together, there won't be any families, meaning the death of society, the death of civilization. I disagree with that totally. You still have rapists running around. Unless a woman has totally given up on men, I don't think she could not have sex with a man. And vice versa, unless he's never been with a woman before, and he tries it one time, and "Oops," she becomes pregnant. I don't agree with that. In China, they only allow you to have one or two children. Maybe we don't need any more people. We can't take care of the ones we have anyway. There are so many kids in foster homes or being abused. As long as there are drugs, somebody's going to have sex with the opposite sex. Hello.

Fate has a way of presenting you with what you need whether you ask for it or not. Right now, I don't need to be involved. I have friends. I have men who are willing to help me in time of need, if necessary. I mean being horny. It's been a while. It's been about a month-and-a-half maybe. I was with a man. He was a very sweet guy, but there's no chemistry there. My head is not there for really all of that. Part of it is because of all I've been through. I'm taking a break. The rest of it is, I have other priorities. I need to get some things situated. Thirty is around the corner and I don't plan to make the same dumb mistakes I made in my 20s.

Originally, as far as career goals, I wanted to be a psychologist. Everybody and their mother wants to be one, so it's an overcrowded field. Plus, I'm the type of person who gives until it hurts. I think it would be detrimental if I became a psychologist. I wouldn't know when to cut it off. I'm a Spanish major because that's part of my heritage. My father's half Cuban. I was going into pre-medicine, so I might still go into optometry or maybe become a pharmacist. I haven't decided that. My all-time goal is to become a writer. I would write fiction stories based on my experiences. There would be some same-sex relationships because I've had those experiences. Plus, they exist, so why are we trying to close our eyes to it?

It burns me up when Afrikan Americans want to get on the bandwagon and talk about homosexuality. Not too long ago, and even today, we're still being ridiculed. People want to close their eyes to the racism and discrimination against us. One wrong is no better than the other.

There's still discrimination of same sex, but it sometimes supersedes the racism that is out there. I see it as a way for Blacks to be accepted by Whites, so they're going to agree with what Whites have to say. Homosexuality has been around since the beginning of time. It's not going to go away. You have a lot of individuals, even in the Black community, who are standing up saying, "Oh, that's wrong." But when the night falls, some of them are getting their groove on with the same sex too. You never know. Those are just things you need to sit down and think about instead of just looking at what the media has to say. The media has so much power in this country it is unbelievable. It's the same propaganda they were hyping up in World War II, which made Hitler rise. But that's another story. The more it changes, the more it stays the same.

I like to read. Anything that is going to help me understand myself as well as what's going on, I think I need to read on it. When I'm confronted or asked a question, I don't have to sound like an idiot. It's just that the subject of same-sex interests me first and foremost. I always ask, "Why?" There's never one answer to the why. There's usually quite a few. I'm very analytical. I tend to dig deeper. I am not going to be satisfied until it makes a whole picture in my mind.

I've doubted a lot of things. Maybe at the time I doubted same-sex relationships I was going through a depression. If I was speaking before a high school audience on the subject, the first thing I would say is, "Be true to yourself." I think that is the only thing I would have to use. If you're not true to you, you're in limbo.

I can picture a student raising his/her hand asking, "Well, if you do that, how can you have children?" There are many ways. It's obvious with women who were told they couldn't bear children. They've had it, artificial insemination. There are many same sex-couples who want to adopt. There are a lot of kids that need to be adopted. Teenage pregnancy is not going to cease. There are ways around that, just like I view a heterosexual and homosexual relationship the same. You're going to have your ups and downs. You can be in a relationship with a man and he is kicking your ass. You can be in a relationship with a woman, and she is kicking your ass. That happens. You can have one in the relationship that wants to be a dog, whether it is the man or the woman in a same-sex relationship. I view them as the same. A relationship consists of two people who want to be together and try to make it work. They're setting the same goals and nothing in life is perfect. Somebody's going to mess up some time. Somebody's going to be giving more than the other. The only difference is, there may or may not be children involved. In a heterosexual relationship, one may want to kiss and the other may not, that's a conflict.

If we think that the opposite sex needs to be together for the sole purpose of reproducing life, then we've lost the total meaning of relationship, or the reason why we're together.

Opposite-sex couples have the same problems same-sex couples do, for the most part. There can be emotional problems, financial problems, and what have you. You're going to have one who is going to be more dominant anyway. One is probably going to get emotional and cry, "Why you do this to me?" The other will say, "You know what, I tired of this. I don't have to deal with it." That sounds like a man and woman relationship. You can have that in a woman relationship. You can have that in a man relationship. I still say it's the same.

There's a stereotypical view that homosexuals go to clubs for one-night stands and that this is a common practice. What is the difference between a heterosexual going to a club for a one-night stand? People fail to realize that the sexual revolution, or evolution, is here. You can be revolting or you can be evolving. I did a term paper called *The Breakdown of the Black Family*.

I was getting some information and they were talking about the Sexual Revolution in the 70s. That's when one-night stands really became popular. Going to the clubs, group sex, swingers, and these are heterosexual people. What's the difference?

I don't know anybody who goes to a club looking for a relationship. You're foolish if you're thinking that. Nine of out of ten times you're already high, you're intoxicated off of some kind of drug, be it a stimulant or a depressant. You're looking to get your groove on. That is it. That is all.

I think the U.S.A. has the most problems with same-sex relationships. Europe, they don't have a problem with this. It's no big deal. Because our land was built by Puritans, these are the most freakish people walking around talking about, "Thus says the Lord," and they're walking around fuckin' everything in sight. That's another story. We need to get out of that mindset that homosexuals are sex-starved people. What about the man that has many mistresses? He's not sex-starved? Is he not sex-crazed? What about the woman, that as soon as her husband goes out the front door, Jim is coming through the back? That's not sex-crazed? What's the difference?

With interracial same-sex relationships, they're just asking for double trouble. They have the same problems, with more problems. I really thought about that because there's so much focus on being in a same-sex relationship as opposed to opposite sex. You may think it's just two girlfriends hanging out, or two guy friends hanging out. You really don't think too much of it. If it was a Black man and a White woman walking down the street together, "Oh my gosh!"

Any time that you do anything against the "norm," you're going to be ridiculed for it. My relationship with the girl that attempted suicide was interracial. See, but I'm open-minded. I don't discriminate against nobody (laughs). Knowing what I know, I'm open to that even now, but I have to admit I do prefer my beautiful sisters. When we talk about preference, it has to be the brothers and the sisters foremost. I enjoy basketball, but I prefer if the Lakers win. It's that simple to me.

I still play sports and I am very pleased to see that we have professional women's basketball. Took them long enough. I still prefer to watch men. Some women say that professional women's basketball gives same-sex women a sports outlet, but there's tennis, Billie Jean King, Martina Navratilova. Golf has several same-sex women. It's a bigger picture than just sports. What about the music industry? There are powerful women out there, corporate business types. You think she's not trying to get her groove on and using that? You have to look at it with an open mind. You have to think deeper than the surface in what you're seeing.

Attracting a woman that I'm interested in is not the easiest thing to do. I usually let them come to me. I'm cool like that (laughs). Usually, I go to the club and I'll meet them there. If it is someone on campus, we'll get to talking and what-not. I'll throw little things out and if they catch it, then I know that they're hip to it. You never really know. There would have to be a little time put into it. Eventually, sex is going to come up. Everybody talks about sex. I would probably use Ellen as an example, since she's already out. Depending on the response, then I would know whether I can go ahead and say, "Hey, maybe we should get together and do this and that," you know. I'm a little more cautious because rejection is rejection. Being rejected by one of your own is a little more severe than a man to me.

I've been rejected. It hurt, but I got over it. It usually takes me about two months, if it was a person I was really interested in. I have to sit back. I love to retrospect only because it helps me keep in touch with myself.

You know, I don't think that I am attractive. My mom never told me that I was. I used to get kidded a lot when I was growing up. I developed earlier than most of the girls. I would always wear baggy clothes to keep folks from bothering me, to keep the guys from messing with me, but then women started coming to me and that presented a whole new thing. I always thought that if I worked on the inside, the outside wouldn't matter. When I look in the mirror, I see a face and sometimes I see my cheekbones. I like my cheekbones because they're pretty high. I can see beauty in other people, not just the physical.

Not seeing myself as a beautiful or attractive person had an influence on my self-esteem in the beginning. I had very, very low self-esteem which is why I was probably depressed a lot. I know that I am not butt ugly. I try not to think about it. When I get complimented, I go like, "Wow."

At my job I get a lot of guys that come in and they're always complimenting me. I'm thinking that maybe they're seeing something else. Some I think are sincere, because they keep coming back and saying the same thing. It's good. I'm not going to lie. My ego does need to be stroked every now and then.

When I get depressed, I contemplate suicide. When I get really depressed, I call it my "blue funk." Sometimes I write. It's usually when I do my best writing, which is why I believe I'm a true artist. Depression tends to work for me. It's hard for me to write when I'm upbeat. I don't want to sit down. I don't want to keep still. I tend to sleep a lot. Don't eat like I should. I think about suicide.

I've come very, very close to ending it all. This past May, my best friend, she had to come over and keep me from...(sighs), she saved my life. I wasn't in a relationship. I was feeling really stupid about the last one I was in, which was with a woman. She used me. I was sick of school. I was feeling like a caged bird and I didn't know how to get out. When I came home, my apartment was empty because my daughter was spending the night over at her grandmother's. I just didn't want to go on. It was a lot of things. Sometimes I don't pay attention to things like I should. I was ready to end it.

Yes, I believe it was selfish leaving my daughter like that, but sometimes you have to be selfish. Nobody's going to take care of my daughter like I do. I know that. After my best friend came over, she said, "You can't leave your daughter. You can't leave her." She calmed me down, I sat back and I was thinking, "I can't get like this again. Something has to change." It had nothing to do with the fact that it was a same-sex relationship. I had baggage, issues is what we call them now, prior to my meeting her. I was constantly looking for someone to help me feel good about me. That's when I had to realize nobody can do it but me. No matter who it is, male or female. If I'm not feeling good about myself, it's not going to happen.

Low self-esteem had a lot to do with it. I know that I'm smart, I guess. I don't like to use smart or intelligent because we tend to measure it, and how can you measure intelligence? Really you can't. I know I'm not dumb, put it like that. I know that I can handle myself in a conversation. If I don't know something, I'll tell you, "I don't know." I have no quirks about being right all the time, or anything of that nature. I like to be right, but if I'm wrong, "Okay, I was wrong."

I feel that I'm not where I need to be. Then again, I don't know where that is. I guess I should be all right (reserved laugh). I've always wanted to just write. I haven't given myself the opportunity to do that, which is why I withdrew from school. I missed a lot of days. I wasn't happy. There was nothing outside of my daughter, and I don't want her to be the reason why I am living. That's not a good thing. When she gets her own life, then what in the hell I'm I going to do? I had to find a different way.

There's nothing now that can make me happy. Just be able to know that I can do what I can. I would say money, but money is not happiness. You can have all of the money in the world. Janet Jackson was on *Oprah* recently and she was talking about she's depressed. That girl's got more money than a little bit. That's when I told myself, "Wait a minute. Hold up. Money is not the answer." It would be nice to live comfortably. Peace of mind, calmness, being able to know that no matter what, I can still get through. That comes with having a oneness with God. I'm learning that slowly, but surely.

When I was seriously ready to end it all, I was going to slash my wrists. I have a really big knife in my kitchen. Every now and then when I am depressed, I hear it calling me. Sometimes I hear voices, but that's another story. Yes, I have been diagnosed as manic-depressive, and I was on anti-depressants.

There are behavioral scientists who say that people who are bi-sexual or homosexual usually have low self-esteem. That is probably true, which is why they said it. I think it is a generalization. It's the same thing they say about artists. Usually artists are depressed and they're crazy. I consider myself an artist. Aspiring, never-the-less an artist. Scientists have said that Black folks are lazy. If we're so lazy, how did this country get built? How did your wars get fought? Lazy people can't fight a war.

I think there is some truth about bi- and homosexuals having low self-esteem. When you're different, you go through a lot more than people who are not considered different. Who do you talk to? Who do you get to understand or relate to where you're coming from? Different people are not all in the same spot, mind you, which is why you tend to feel alone. So, of course you're going to have depression. It becomes overwhelming. You feel that you can't share your load.

When I look into my future, I see me having quite a few best selling books (loud, joyful laugh). I don't consider myself the next Terry McMillan. I'm a lot more explicit than she is, not in a nasty way. I'm very tactful with my explicitness. It's almost poetic. I would say that it is poetic. Yes, it is. I would be reaching out to a lot of individuals, mainly teenagers or young people – young adults who will walk in my shoes as far as experiences go.

You can write about love and I guarantee you people won't get tired of reading it. You can write about same-sex, and there's not that many people who write about that actually. I think that's my niche. I tend to understand it a little bit. I'm giving a different point of view. E. Lynn Harris is a prime example. He's a homosexual Black writer. I've read two of his books: *Just As I Am* and *Invisible Life*. He is very poetic in his writing. He's just not quite as explicit. That's okay. I can take care of that in my books. He gives you a side to same-sex male relationships that people don't tend to think about, that men can love one another. There's nothing romantic about two men being together to me, but men can love each other. Men are dogs even to other men. He presents that.

In essence of everything that I have stated, I hope no one was offended, for these words are based upon *my* opinions, which are based upon *my* experiences. As Shakespeare put it, "To thine own self be true."

Cynthia Stanford

Ms. Stanford is a 34-year-old divorced mother with two sons and a daughter. She works in a civil service occupation. Her primary struggle is to save her children from negative influences. Her time is so devoted to her children that it could be an obstacle to her having a social life in order to meet a potential mate. She is very dedicated to young people. When she is not doing something with her own, she is out working with other young people, primarily girls. Her background and the neighborhood she grew up in would instantly say that she is not supposed to succeed. The gang culture, and all that goes along with it, was not just in the community in which she lived, but had also touched her family. Through the hard determination that she has, and her strong religious convictions, she and her children seemed destined to have a successful life. This seems even more realistic in that she has just re-entered college. Her chance of breaking the cycle of self-destruction that permeates her family seems as assured as the sun rising tomorrow.

I was born in Los Angeles, California. My childhood was not too good. My mother and my father fought all of the time. I had a father who was very abusive, both verbally and physically. Often times, by me being the oldest, I saw it all. A lot of the times I had to help my mother heal. My mother asks me sometimes, "How can you remember those things, being so young at fifteen months?" But I remember watching my dad really abuse her bad, especially when she was pregnant with my brothers. He almost caused her to die. It was really ugly. Sometimes he would come in from work, walk in the kitchen, and just sock my mother for no reason. We would often run to my grandmother's house. He would come around to get us and threaten everybody. "You guys leave my kids alone or I'm gonna get you too," so we would always run back home.

In my childhood, I lived in a total of 17 homes before I was 18 years old, because my mom was always running. He would jump her. She would pack everything before he came back home and we would live in all kinds of project areas all over Los Angeles. There's not a place in Los Angeles I have not lived in. It was very sad times.

After that marriage ended, she went into another marriage that was just as abusive. This guy was more or less trying to sexually bother me in ways. We found out later that he was a Satan worshipper. He said that the only reason he wouldn't kill us is because my mother believed in Jesus. She ended up divorcing out of that marriage. When I turned 15, we moved away. That's when things started getting better.

I believe the reason my father, my mother's first husband, was so abusive, he didn't have any education. There were eleven children in his family. By him being the oldest, he had to drop out of school in the 10th grade and raise ten children because my grandfather had died. My grandfather was a very abusive man to my grandmother. I really think it is generational. My grandfather would do the same thing. He would come home and beat my grandmother, knock her up with a child, and go on about his business. My father did the same thing.

I have ten other brothers and sisters besides the three of us. That's just the type of man that he was. He was an alcoholic. He used drugs. A lot of that contributed to the violence. A lot of times it was guilt. When I was seven, he used to pick us up from the babysitter, and this one particular time, I saw him messing around with the babysitter. Me being seven years old, I went and told my mom. He whipped me for it.

A lot of times it was his own guilt. Whenever he would sleep around on my mom, he would come home and punish her for what he did wrong.

Now that I am older, I have discussed these things with my dad. A movie came out called *The Burning Bed*. It was a story where there were three children, just like we were, an abusive father towards the mother, running from place to place just like we did. We all sat down to watch it. He just came over to visit. We were all watching the movie. During the whole time we were watching it, he would say, "I wasn't that bad." I'm looking at him saying, "Yes, you were." My baby brother doesn't really remember anything. My other brother kind of. But I was there from the beginning and, "Yeah, you were that bad." At the end of the movie, she ends up killing the husband, setting the bed on fire.

My mom was sitting there crying because she was still remembering. I told him he was that bad. "The only difference was my mom didn't kill you. But you did exactly to my mom what that man did to his wife."

I never discussed the abuse with my mom's second husband. This guy had my mom so psyched out. He would do things like put different poisons in things. If we could have been seen at that time, we were all spaced out. We were in this far-out religion. Somehow, he talked my mother into selling everything that she owned and moved us to Oklahoma. He had so many things that he was doing to her and they weren't even married at the time. We were cleaning or something and she happened to open up this box. It had all this demonic stuff in there. We ended up escaping from him and moving back to Los Angeles. They still were not married.

He comes back to L.A., and starts seeing her again. After all the wrong and things that this man did, she still married this man. If you look at her in the wedding pictures, she really looks like she wasn't there. It looked like she wasn't herself.

I never had the opportunity to discuss anything with him because I hated this man. I really had to work through that. He was killed before we really had a chance to deal with it.

To try to explain why my mother dealt with this man, because she was a Christian, had to do with the type of church she was raised up in. It was Methodist. It was one of those type of churches that didn't really deal with the spirituality of what is really in the Bible. They dealt with more of social functions and things of that nature, so she really didn't know. But by her being so young, it was more or less her trying to find herself and find out about all these different religions. I think we belonged to at least four Jehovah's Witnesses, Hare Krishnas, Self-Realization, all these different things. It was like she was really trying to find herself. When she got involved with him, he opened her up to his world, although it was a dark world on his side. The part she was seeing was like the meditation side of it, the spiritualist side, from his point of view. She didn't really start getting into it until she found out that he was putting spells on her.

Then she met this old woman who started talking to her about how to get out of it, what kinds of things she needed to lay around. It was real weird for me as a kid, you know. Once she started laying things down, I can really say that God started opening up her eyes because then, that's when she really got saved, while she was in the marriage with him.

She really started reading her Word and she really started trusting in God. That's when he really started feeling uncomfortable around us. That's when he threatened her with, "If you were not a child of God, I would kill you."

ℓ

As I got older and was able to look back on all of this, for a long time I didn't like men. I didn't trust men. I didn't want to be touched by men because of my stepfather. When I was twelve, I was asleep one night and he came in the room and began to massage me. I kept my eyes closed because if I woke up, he would be able to use that against me and say, "I will kill your mother." I started making these loud noises and he fled the room.

From that, I didn't want any men touching me. I didn't trust them at all. I really threw myself into sports just so I could stay away from home. I didn't want to deal with it.

I didn't get out of that until my first marriage. I wanted it to work so bad because it never worked for my mother. I used to always say to myself, "I will never let a man hit me. I would never let a man do these things to me." But yet, I wanted to identify with a man. I didn't really have my father.

When my first husband came along, I threw everything I had into the relationship. He was about 5'9", light brown eyes, bald-headed, and a nice build. He was showing me a different side of a man. You could really feel good about yourself. I didn't know how good a man could make you feel until I met him.

Incidentally, we met at a friend of ours 21st birthday party. It was really like love at first sight. We met in August. In September, I had my engagement ring. We were married the following July (laughs). It was like a head-over-heels thing. One bad mistake that I regret was dropping out of college for it. I ended up being pregnant and kind of gave up my dreams.

I had always been told by my father's side of the family by the women that, "When you're married, you have to give everything to your husband. Your husband is your world. Your husband is your life." He was a minister, so I'm like, "I have a Godly man," so my life no longer mattered to me. Everything was him. At the time, I didn't really know. All I know is that my marriage was great for the first two years. It was excellent, no arguments. Everything was good, but I didn't have anything to identify myself with. I virtually lost my own identity. It was good as long as he was happy. I didn't work. I was the complete housewife.

About three years into the marriage, he lost his job. I didn't know that he lost his job from stealing. As things progressed, I found out that he was on drugs, using cocaine, and that's how he lost the job. All of a sudden the money wasn't there. The marriage really started going down.

I woke up one morning and asked myself, "If this guy trips out and leaves me, how are you going to support your children?" At this point, I only had two, my sons. That's when my aunt called me about a job. It's funny; the Lord will take care of you when you most need it. I took the job. My husband couldn't handle it. I was making more money. When he couldn't pay the bills, I would pay them. I didn't even think about it. I didn't ask him for it, I just did it.

Sometimes I think if I could identify the wrong things that I did in my marriage, it was that I never gave him a chance to be a man. I immediately started taking responsibility. I refused to be like my mother, stuck. It's like, if you can't get it done, if you can't find a way to do it, I'll find a way to do it. It probably really made him feel less than a man. I'm sure it did because I really took charge.

Because of my childhood, I was a very strong-headed female. It really started falling. The more I was taking care of the business, the more he was just lying around at home, gettin' high, and not doing anything.

I tried to tell him to get off of drugs. I tried to work with him through it. Another mistake, he wanted me to go to a drug rehab with him. I went a couple of times but then I stopped. I was all into it and he wasn't. I said, "This is your sickness." And I admit, when I was younger, I would get high with him. I think that caused a lot of the problems. I never did cocaine. I did marijuana. But I quit. I quit cold turkey. I don't think he could handle it. That was the difference in the relationship. Before it was okay; we were both doing the same thing.

When I got pregnant with my daughter, while I was lying on the table having her, he starts laughing and says, "You know, I had you on cocaine." I said, "You had me on what?" He said, "Yeah, I was putting it in the marijuana." I'm like, "What!?"

Right then, right there, I knew, "You're not for my life. You're against me. If you can try to addict me to something because you're addicted, then that's telling me that I cannot trust you." That's when I started looking at ways to get out of the marriage. It was about eight years into the marriage and I still (with emphasis) wanted to try to make it work. Everybody was saying, "You ought to get out. You ought to get out." I was saying, "No, God is able. God is able."

What really made me get out was, one night he called and said, "Could you come and pick me up?" I had to put my kids in the car and we drove to the corner of Western and Wilshire. He was passed out on the sidewalk. Just out of it. My kids were, "Mommie, what's wrong with Daddy?" It was like, "No."

My family on my father's side, no man, and it is 113 of us, not a man is saved. Every man had a drug problem. Every man had some kind of alcoholic problem or gangster or something like that. I said to myself, "I am going to break this mode with my sons." When my sons looked and saw their father lying there, I said, "No. I have to get out for the sake of my sons. I can't make it work." My sons were totally stressed out, crying every day. All of the grades fell in school and I was not going to accept this.

When we got home, he flipped out. I didn't know if it was PCP or what, but he started to try to get violent. The minute he tried to hit me, I flashed back, naturally, to my mom. I beat him up so bad. Then he started hitting on my sons. I had to defend my children. I got him out. I ended up having to call the police. While I was at work, he went in and stole everything. That hurt me. It hurt me bad, but I filed for my divorce that day. I didn't wait.

He did things like on Christmas Eve, I go to wrap my children's gifts, he steals all the gifts and sells them for cocaine. It was over. I had no more feelings. I had no more love. I had no more of anything. It was just over.

I got to the point where I would talk with older women because I really wanted to understand this thing, and they would tell me, "Well, you just stay there. You have to do everything you can to try to make it work." Well, that was old school. That was okay for them. But that was not okay for me. I was raising boys and then my daughter comes along. I didn't want them to have to see an abusive mother in an abusive relationship like I did because my childhood was horrible.

Even now, my brothers, they're in penitentiaries, they're in and out of trouble because they don't understand why they are going through the things they are going through. It was just ugly. I had to. I had to get out of it.

Then in my family, every last one of the men are in some kind of trouble. The only thing I can say is it must be generational. If you read in Genesis where Abraham was talking about how the problems of your father will last for generations to generations. And literally every generation on my father's side of the family, from my grandfather, from his father, all the way down, every male child has some kind of problem. I refuse to let it go through my sons. That's why I do so much. Everybody complains, "You are always so busy. Don't put your whole life into your sons." I tell them, "No, I have to," in order to break that mode. No male in the family has ever been to college. I have to break that mode. I can't let my sons go down without at least me trying.

As far as the women, on my father's side, they have problems as well. They were in abusive marriages. That's also generational. My grandmother, even though she went through all of that, she was abused. Her daughters were abused. All of the women in the family were abused. There were drug problems. That's why I had to snatch myself out. I started looking at my family, "I don't want to be like that." They're better now. They've given their lives to the Lord. They've gotten away from those abusive men. But it took all of what they went through in order to see. I'm like, "I don't have to go through being beat on just to see that I am a good woman."

A couple of women have broken away. We're the strong ones in the family. We're the ones that keep everybody together. 113 from one woman, that's a lot of people. Only one girl graduated from college out of the whole family.

I know that many people think that when women come out of bad relationships they turn to the Church. It's a hospital. That's where you go for your healing. In my particular case, I lost it for about a year. I felt as though with my husband being a minister, a man of God, I was okay. He knew the Word of God, so everything was in him. I went to Texas and there was this lady. She was having a home church. We were sitting there. She was going around prophesying different people. She said to me, "How are you and the Lord?" I said, "My husband's a minister." Anytime anyone asked me anything about God, I would say, "My husband's a minister." I never said that I was actually a Christian. She prayed for me and she let me know, "You are a woman in Christ."

When I divorced, I think I became stronger in the Lord. It's a hospital. It's a healing place. The Bible will clearly tell you when you are by yourself, "I am there as your Father. You are never alone because I am there with you." That's been my stronghold.

There are some women who use it as a crutch and do not go back to another man. Some do. My mom tried it. I even think that she does that now. Even with what I am dealing with, I can't get into a relationship because that is fornication. I am learning that there are Godly men out there. You just don't have to have sex when you are in a relationship. That was always a thing with me. I always thought sex made the relationship. In the past year, I'm learning that it is not even about sex. You can have a relationship even without that.

A lot of women do that though. They say, "I'll just stay in the Church and that way I'm covered." But you're not because you're still in bondage. You have to get out there. You have to get out there and try, even though I've had a couple of bad relationships since my marriage, not abusive, it was just something I chose not to deal with.

After the marriage, I involved myself in other relationships immediately. I don't know why, but my whole life, I've never been without a man. I've had boyfriends since I was 15. I didn't know how to be by myself. I didn't want to be by myself.

This particular young man, whom I started seeing after the marriage, was a childhood sweetheart whom I should have probably married, I sometimes think. He was about 6'4", an athlete, light brown eyes, and he was bald-headed. I guess I like bald-headed men. We started a relationship and it lasted for four years. He was smoking weed and all that, and I'm like, "I just got out of that. I'm more than that now. Whatever man I date or whatever man comes into my life, he has to also be an example for my sons and my daughter. You're not trying to make yourself better. You've been in the same position that you've been in for the last four years. I need to see growth."

My children would talk about him. They would say, "Momma, he smokes." And I say to myself, "Naw, I'm on a mission. I have things I'm trying to do with my children. No, he's not the one."

Then another relationship, a guy I was with in the beginning would say, "Let's take the children and go play golf, and let's do this and that with the children." About three months into the relationship, the children were no longer involved, although he had children too. And I'm like, "No. I am a package deal. If you date me, you also date my children. There will be some times when we can spend some time alone, but I have three children. I am a single parent. My children need my time. If you can't come in and be with my children and me, then we can't have a relationship." So that was the end of that.

After that, I've been into myself lately. I'm single now. I'm learning to love myself all over again. I've learned that I don't need a man in my life, I can support me and I can be happy. I always thought that I would be unhappy without a man, because all of my friends have men and they all look so happy.

Valentine's Day was really hard for me. It was the first time that I was by myself. It was a little difficult. A little teary eyed, but I made it through. I thank God. I think, more or less, I have been throwing myself into my children a lot lately, seven days a week.

My middle son, he was having a problem in school. I started working with him one-on-one, so now he has brought his grades up two grade levels. That's my joy. That's my healing.

I'm sure that the time will come when I will need that personal companionship. I still have those feelings. I think I'm just trying to wait for the right one to come along. I'm learning to not just jump into it because I need a man. I love men (laughs). I love men. I really do, but this time, I'm going to take my time. I don't want to choose. I know the Bible says, "He who finds a wife finds a good thing." That's great, and I want to wait for that. I don't want to go out and try to find him. Whenever I try to go out and find somebody, it's always the wrong one. I feel that God will bring the right one. He'll bring the right one to me. He'll come.

℘

The problem with a lot of young girls in relationships today is they are trying to find that comforter. I have a lot of teenagers that I deal with. A lot of them come from broken homes or the father is not paying that much attention. A lot of times they are trying to find a father figure.

My goddaughters, they think the thing now is to have a man. Everybody needs to have a man. It's okay to have companionship, but you don't have to sleep with that man. Some of the girls that I deal with have more than two or three partners. Things are too serious now to just be out there doing things. That's basically what I talk to them about. They just feel, "Oh, this man, he's got a car. He's high rollin'. He's this. He's that."

What they need to understand is they can take care of themselves just as good as that man can. That way, you don't owe anyone anything. You've taken care of yourself. A lot of them try to keep up with the Joneses. "My friend has a man. I feel bad if I'm by myself." In time they will learn. Some have to learn the hard way. Some listen to what I say. Some won't. I have had a couple come back and tell me, "You were really, really right," and they are doing very well.

Getting back to father figures, there are many girls looking for their fathers in a man. I didn't because of the way my father was (laughs). I would never want a man like that. My goddaughter now, she's in a relationship situation where her father's around, but her mom just died. The father never advises her, "No, you shouldn't do this. You shouldn't do that." Now she's in a relationship with this guy and she figures, "Oh, he has this, he has that." He's promised to give her a car and he's promised to give her this. She's really kind of cut her relationship with me. She's backed up a little bit. I don't force it. She has to learn it on her own. This guy is talking down to her, making her feel real bad about herself, telling her she's nothing. He cusses her out, the whole nine yards, just trying to be a daddy.

I feel so bad I just want to hold her and let her know, "You don't need this in your life." She has a very good job. She's a strong female when she wants to be. I think she sees so many of her friends in relationships she just feels that she needs to be a part of that. Her friends see him and say, "Oh girl, he fine." That keeps her there. He's supposed to have all this money. His parents are rich or whatever. I guess she's looking for a savior so she won't have to work, and she will have someone help take care of her daughter.

At one time, she even thought she was pregnant by this young man. She gained like fifty pounds when she really wasn't pregnant at all. It's really psychological, trying to hold on to this young man. He's really nothing to hold on to. I feel so bad I want to tell her, but I can't step in right now. She has to learn like I had to learn.

In my day, everybody would tell me the same things that she's going through, and its like, "I don't want to hear anything you tellin' me." Eventually, I had to go back to those same people and tell them, "You know what, you were right. I was wrong." She'll come to me. She usually does.

Presently, we have an epidemic of teenage pregnancy. The reason for that, parents are not talking to their children. I had a group a couple of years ago. The ages were from 8 to 17. I would often show movies, have books, have care packages, talk about condoms, but I had to get a release from the parents. My pastor was the one who said, "You shouldn't talk to them about that," at the time. He has five children. He's like, "I don't want my daughters watching R-rated movies." So a lot of times they didn't come to those particular classes.

Later on, his 15-year-old daughter was hanging out lights one Christmas. She starts complaining that her stomach was hurting. They rush her to the clinic and the doctor comes out and says, "Did you know that your daughter was nine months pregnant and getting ready to deliver?" They had not a clue that she was pregnant. That naturally shocked them.

Then the 14-year-old girl ends up having sex on a bench at school, and she comes up pregnant while the other one was having her baby. She had her baby two months later. They didn't want to talk to their daughters about reality and things that were going on. That's bad.

These days you have to start talking to your kids very, very early. Last year, one of my sons told me, "Mom, guess what? I said, "What?" "It was two girls and a boy in the bathroom having sex." At first, I didn't know how to take it. At the time, my son was 11 years old. After thinking about it, I knew a woman who would give a sex education class. I called and told her, "Well, I know how to deal, but for me to try to tell a male child how to do all of these things, I don't know." So, I set up a class with her. I talked to my sons about it very openly and let them know, "If you feel like there's something, or if you feel like you're ready, let me know, we can talk about it." Then my 10-year-old says, "Mom, what if I'm ready now?" I said, "No, darling, you are not ready yet" (laughs). That lets me know that at 10 years old, those kinds of questions are coming up. They're dealing with it in elementary schools. They took the class I set up and now they are very aware of what's going on. Girls are starting to be interested in my son, but he's not really interested. He keeps it on a friendship level. That's because we talked. We let them know that it is a very serious thing; it's not just sex.

The problem with teenage pregnancy is no one talks to them.

They don't know. They get all of their information from their friends who nine times out of ten have it all backwards.

An organization I am working with, I have 200 girls. I had three girls to come up pregnant before the program was over, but we never knew. I had one young lady who, she had her baby at 2:00 a.m. She was at our banquet at 1:00 p.m. the next day. Her mother wanted to beat her, but another lady reminded her, "Well, you did the same thing when you were 15." Generational and not talking to them can lead to serious consequences.

I have classes and I let the parents know that this is what we are dealing with. Teenage pregnancy is on a rampage. Somewhere we have to let these young women know that there are other ways in their life without them having to have a child and become a mother at such a young age.

Another element we have to look at, there are some girls who have babies because they did not get the love and nurturing at home. Having a baby means that they have someone to love them exclusively. That is so true with my mom. That's why she had me. My grandmother abused her. My mom was in the juvenile system since she was 13. She ran away from home several times because my grandmother would beat her. She made her the man of the house. She had four daughters. She had a real bad childhood, so she would run away. If she didn't come home at a certain time, my grandmother would call juvenile services and they would lock her up.

She got pregnant and my grandmother found out about it. She had her go to this doctor. She told my mom that she was going through a routine pap smear. At the time, my mother was 16. The doctor ended up performing an abortion. My mother didn't know it. Neither did my dad. So the next time around, when she was 17, she got pregnant with me. She didn't tell my grandmother until she was four months pregnant. That way, she couldn't get rid of it. My grandmother had her locked up in juvenile hall until she had me. So, my mom went to foster care. I was all hers. I loved her unconditionally. When she turned 18, she married my dad immediately.

She still tells me that I was her love child because at the time, she thought that no one loved her. I have a girlfriend who is the same age that I am. She has eight children, all by different fathers, except for two. She was sexually abused as a child and the same thing with her. She has children because they love her and those are hers. At five years old, her mother left her at the Greyhound bus station. She called for her grandmother to pick her up. Her grandmother was very abusive. She didn't have anyone at the time to love her.

Everybody tries to figure out, "Why does she keep having all these children?" That's because she needs people around her, those children are hers. No one will ever be able to take them away from her. They are very close. She continues to have children, and I really think that's why.

I know I have talked about sexual abuse a lot, but these are sick people. But once again, people need to be aware. You can't trust everybody. The people who are closest to you are often the ones who abuse. I was sexually abused as a little girl. My mother still doesn't know. I tried to blot it out. It was my cousins. This is really emotional because I've never really talked about it since I was a kid (gets emotional).

You think that the people who are closest to you are okay because they are family. It's not like that at all. You have to be very careful. You have to be very involved in your children's lives in every aspect. People who you think are not abusing your children are abusing your children. You have to look at that child and be able to know the difference and know whether that child becomes withdrawn or not. Look at the different attitudes within that child.

I psychologically dealt with the sexual abuse by jumping into sports. I did every sport involved. I stayed away from home. My mother never knew. I kept to myself a lot. I blotted it out. I stayed away from those who abused me. If I saw them, I would go another way. A lot of them that I see now, they act as if they don't remember (speaks quietly).

I don't say anything. I don't want to bring it up. It was a very ugly thing. My mother was sexually abused. She saw this one guy and she totally freaked. Some people deal with it in different ways.

Sad enough, this is a common thing among girls and women. Why? I don't know. I know a lot of men for some reason like younger girls. My goddaughters almost fell into it. They were involved with this 26-year-old guy and at the time they were 14. We had to threaten him and let him know, "You will go to jail or you will lose your life. Stay away."

For some reason they like younger girls. I don't know if it is a sick mind. I don't know what causes it. It's bad. It's not only in girls; it's in boys too nowadays. You just have to be aware. You just have to be involved in your children's lives 100%.

Everything my sons do, I am there. My son went away on a trip and it was the first time he was away from me. If a coach says, "You want me to take him?" "No, I'll take him." It's really hard for me to trust.

The music videos of today have a definite effect on our children. Oh yeah. Even with my own, although I don't allow them to listen to it at all, I did an exercise with them one day. I had some old school rap tapes when we were in school. I compared it to one of theirs. The raps back then were dealing with higher education, trying to make yourself better, or something like that. These videos now are sexually motivated, half-naked women, drugs, gangsters, robbin', all negative. They were able to look at it and say, "I don't want to be like that." So now, even if they come on the radio they turn. I don't have to turn. It's brainwashing our children. It makes them think, "Well, I hear it on the radio. I see it on the video, so it must be okay. It must be okay to be this way," and it's not.

With my brothers, the younger one was a star. There is no way that he should not have gone pro, but he didn't want to get his education. He had letters from every university in the country it seemed. Instead, he wanted to get high. He wanted to do all of these negative things. One thing I appreciate, even though they didn't make it, they talked to my sons and let them know the reality of it.

My brother decided to become a gangster at the age of 29. He's in a real serious situation right now. He gave his life to the Lord a couple of weeks ago, but he was involved with this stripper. They ended up fighting and now he's in jail. He was getting ready to do this thing with the Crips and the Bloods, some kind of truce thing. My thing to him was, "God took you off the streets because that was getting ready to be a very ugly situation."

He was into all that negative rap stuff and I told him, "Keep it away from my sons." Right now, they don't need to be brainwashed. One of my sons is 13 and he can go one way or the other. This is the age. I don't want anything negative around them. Nothing but positive. "If you have to do these things, you need to go to your house and do those things."

My older brother, he had to go back for something he did. He'll be out next month. He's been a very positive influence in my sons' life, because he's gone through all of those things with the gangs, the music, the selling of drugs, and all those things. He is trying to turn his life around because now he has sons and children of his own. He lets them know, "You guys, it's nothing out here. It looks good. The money looks good, but it's not."

The reason a lot of our young boys are involved in gangs, some are trying to find families. They are so close-knit. They have so much love for each other that they couldn't get at home. When a boy is in a gang, for the most part, they always have each other's back. This is what my brother tells me.

He tattooed himself recently. He put on there, "Trust No One," because he and my mom were having problems. The only thing I could see was, he held on to the gang real close because my brother and my mother, they didn't get along. I wasn't about to deal with the negative stuff around my children. My mom was living out of town at the time and she wasn't going to deal with it. These guys loved him. Whatever he needed, money, whatever, they had it for him. All that he couldn't get from my family he got from them.

They refuse to turn their backs on the gangs because they're the ones who have been there for them all along. As you know, once you're in, you're in. They say that's your family for life. They are looking for home. Looking for family. Looking for love.

Not having a father in the home for my children during the early part, it was hard for them, especially for my youngest son because he was closer to his daddy. My oldest son was there from the beginning and he saw everything. That was his dad and they were very tight for 10 years until he started tripping out on that stuff. My daughter never knew any of the negative things about him, so it was always, "My daddy, my daddy, my daddy."

Now that he's not around, one thing I noticed was he's never come to a game or anything. Yet, I am there for everything they ever do. I won't talk negative about him because that's their father, so I call and tell him, "Your boys are playing in this game. Can you come?" He came to this particular game and they got excited, "My daddy's here! My daddy's here!" I think they might have played one of their best games ever. But the thing that I know hurt him most, being their father, is that after the game was over they didn't run to him. They ran to their coaches. All of the men in the gym hugged them and he had to sit back and watch.

My thing is, "You're doing this to yourself. The door's open for you to have a relationship with them. You don't have to stay. I don't want child support." Everybody says, "You're crazy. You should try for it." No, because that's not what it's about. "I want a relationship between you and your children." I said, "If you guys ever want to talk about your dad, we can talk about it or try to call him on the phone." Now my oldest son is to the point of, "Whatever.

I don't care because I am going to make something out of myself."

They used to cry at night. I told my son a couple of months ago, "The way to get back at your father is not to turn to the negative side of things. But the way to get to him is to make something out of yourself and become a strong young man. Then you will be able to say to yourself, 'I did it. My dad wasn't there for me, but I became a man.'"

I looked at them and they really took that advice. Right now they have so much, I don't want to say pride, but I guess I can say pride in the things that they do. Everything has changed for them. I keep positive men around them where they don't miss out too much. I know that's their father and all, but now, they are looking at their dad because he still has a drug problem. He tries to cover it because he remarried, but they know.

When they come from him for a week or whatever, they are so happy to get home. It's okay to be with him for a couple of days but, "I want to come home to my momma." I think my older son is starting to see him for what he really is. Like I tell them, "Don't take it out on him, because his father did it to him too." He didn't know his father for 18 years.

The thing I tell him, "How can you do this to your children?" In the beginning of our marriage, when we had our first child, he was always saying, "I will never treat my son like my father did me." He would say that over and over and over again. But yet, this is what he's doing. He doesn't call for months at a time. They see him maybe every five months during spring break or something. I just tell my son, "Don't get mad. Make something out of yourself, someone that I can be proud of."

Right now, I play the role of the mother and father. On Father's Day, our pastor had all the fathers stand up in church. I stood up boldly (laughs). I can't teach my son to be a man, that's why I keep them involved with positive male role models. I'll get in there and play football with them in a minute. I'll tackle him. I was a little tomboy myself. A lot of things like that physically I can do, but the sexual type things, I often have to say, "Go talk to your uncle because I don't understand your body and what you are going through." When it comes to things like that, I'll either call his coach or I'll call his uncles to deal with the real men issues. I dare not try to teach them to be a man. I am not a man. I can't teach them to be men.

Having them involved in sports allows them to be involved with other men. I've known single mothers raising their children and a lot of the boys are kind of soft. They only have that nurturing side but they don't have that strong physical side that a young boy child needs to have.

In our family we have no men like that. All the men are strong, even though they trip and they have their problems, but they are all strong men. That's what my mom did with my brothers. She raised us by herself. I stayed home. I was in sports. I still had to cook meals and all that kind of stuff. They were doing their sports and manly things because she kept them around men.

When we were children it was very hard for my mom. The one thing that she would tell me was, "My children will be something in this life." Although she had to work and was a single mother, she made sure that we stayed busy. She kept us involved in sports and different programs throughout the community. She worked hard so that we would not end up stuck in life.

She was able to go back to school and she maintained a 4.0 grade point average. She made sure that my dream was fulfilled and that was to go to UCLA. I thank my mom because she made me the strong woman that I have become. She has always told me, "You can make it. Just trust in God."

I look at her life, I look at my life, and I am dealing with a lot of the same things that she dealt with. My mom made it, and so will I. I admire her for what she did with her children because I also do the same with mine. She gave my brothers every opportunity. They had the same opportunities as my kids. The only difference is they chose to go left rather than go right.

There have been times when I have almost given up on men, that it was just a hopeless case. Every male I see has some type of problem. Why do I have to have the problem because they have the problem? But that is very temporary. I learned that all men are not the same. There are some good men out there. It's just a matter of locating them or finding where they are. They are out there.

You know; thinking about all this, the most important thing I could say to young people would be, first of all, learn to love God. Second, most important, learn to love yourself. That way you never have to depend on anyone but yourself to make it in this life. What happens is you don't owe anyone anything. The only thing you owe are praises to God. That's it.

Margaret Richardson

Ms. Richardson is a 52-year-old divorced mother raising a son. She holds a top administrative position in education and has traveled around the world. If ever there were a person who can say that she was raised in the "old school" way, she would be it. It is as if she grew up in a time that is unknown today, but whose values are currently needed now more than ever. She is one of those rare individuals who is financially astute, and was able to use that knowledge during and after her marriage to successfully prosper and get back on her feet following financial disaster. The ordeal that she went through provides many lessons for us all to heed. The significance of the foundation that her father laid for her should illustrate how important and influential parenting can be, particularly during difficult times. Many parents tell their daughters to be prepared and independent. She is the classic example why.

I was born in New York City. I had what I consider a very happy childhood. I didn't have any substantial problems. I came from a unified family, a mother and father that stayed together until he died. There were grandmothers and grandfathers in the home. I think I had the storybook normal things that young people grapple with as they're growing up. I didn't have real issues in terms of not having enough money in the home or not enough emotional support. I had all of those things.

I didn't feel deprived economically at all. In terms of emotions, I probably felt somewhat deprived. I had an extremely strong father who was an attorney. It was very important to him that I met certain goals that he had in his mind related to education, how I lived my life, my values, and my morals. Those were things that he was up front with. They were out on the table, and he expected me to live up to each and every one of those things, and I knew it.

For instance, if I would get a B on a report card, he would say, "Well, a B is okay, but I expect you to get A's." If I came home without books from high school, he would say, "Until you are getting straight A's, I expect you to bring home books every night. And I expect you to study." He was very strong. In retrospect, I see all of those things as extremely positive. But in terms of the self-concept at that time, he was not the type of person who hugged you and loved you and kissed you and anything that you did was fine. I probably didn't have, what I perceived to be then, as emotionally secure a home as I would have liked, where everything I did was right and wonderful. It wasn't that kind of home. Looking back, I appreciate what he did, but he was demanding.

My mother played the normal post World War II wife. He was the boss. My mother and I, being the two females, were and always have been very, very close. I guess that's by virtue of me being an only child. We do a lot of things together often, frequently. I saw her as the normal female of that time living in a home where he brought home the money. He made the decisions, like what kind of car to buy. He may have consulted her about the color, but the big decisions were his.

My parents provided the best model for male/female relationships that they could. I think times have changed right in there. In my age, by virtue of being a child of the 60s, when all of the different things were beginning to happen, women were beginning to find their feet in the world. Perhaps it wasn't modeled the way I would like to see it modeled now, the way that I would like to see women modeled in their own homes now. I don't blame my parents for that. I don't see how they could see any different. They were married in the 40s, just after he got out of the war. That was that whole post-war, World War II thing. You come home, buy a house in the suburbs, the big developments, that type of thing.

For the time, it was a very normal life. It didn't give me the skills for a relationship or maybe I didn't use them correctly. Maybe they gave me the skills to live in a relationship in a particular way, but by virtue of being on the cusp of a new world, I chose to live my life a little differently. I do believe it had something to do with the 60s and 70s and the turmoil that was going on at that point in time.

Being an only child, I suppose it did make me self-centered. I've read all of the information about only children. I have never had that personal feeling about myself because I always felt that my father wouldn't allow it. They didn't allow me to be self-centered. They didn't allow me to think I was wonderful and grand. Everything in the world had to go his way. I don't think I am as self-centered as only children are, quote/unquote, supposed to be. I'm really tuned to other people and their needs, trying to make things right for them, trying to make things work for my family and friends.

Since I have had to get out and work, which was one of the consequences of my divorce, I've gained a lot more confidence in demanding things from other people, or not taking things off of people. I'm talking about my job. That then sort of carries over into your personal life. You realize how to manage people on a professional level. I'm a much stronger person now than I was, but in a different way.

The extended family, my grandmothers and others, had quite a lot to do with my development. The grandmothers always felt, the grandmothers were more dominant than the grandfathers, that they could monitor me, tell me what to do, what not to do. They always talked to me about values. Back then it was about what ladies did, what ladies did not do. That was a frequent conversation with them on both sides. Moreso with my father's mother than my mother's mother. My mother's mother lived in New York, so I would spend every summer with her. She was a very good mothering influence. They had a lot of influence on me as a child.

Looking at the social revolution of the 60s and 70s, as compared with today, I think I would have to compare it on a number of different levels. Emotionally, probably for young people, what they're dealing with and what's happening now, the emotional struggle is probably the same. All young people go through a period of wanting to get out from under their parents, to be grown, make their own decisions, and all that type of thing. That was the same thing that was happening in the 60s.

The social revolution in terms of civil rights and the social revolution in terms of the women's movement will probably never happen again. I don't know if we will ever see that kind of social revolution again. These young people out here now think they're probably going through and doing the same things that we did. I don't see it that way. I think we had a lot of different issues to deal with. Some of the issues are not the same. There was always peer pressure, but the peer pressure wasn't in terms of things that are now life-threatening.

You always told your girls, in that day and age, "Don't get pregnant." That was a big thing, "Don't get pregnant." If they got pregnant, many of the girls would go off to visit Aunt Susie or Aunt Jane and have the baby, then came back and everything was fine. Therein lies the difference in what I see happening now, in terms of girls getting pregnant. There's nothing wrong with it now. It's fine. It's accepted.

The things that can happen to young people out here now are so much more dangerous than they were when I was young. We didn't have drive-by shootings. You could go out with your boyfriend and not have to deal with that. We didn't have AIDS. I know there were some social diseases out there, but the stuff that is out here now will kill you, so there is a comparison. Narcotics were there, obviously, when I was young. I'm not talking about the kids of the 70s. I'm talking about the kids of the 60s, now. That's basically when I was in high school. You knew drugs were out there someplace, and I suppose there were people who tried them. I wouldn't say that didn't happen. The proliferation of crack and the way marijuana is promoted in popular culture, particularly in the rap songs, was unheard of in my day.

I have friends with young people now; their kids are stoned on this stuff day in and day out. I didn't see that happening, at least in the circle that I grew up in the 60s. It is a much more dangerous world now for young people, and that is emotionally, socially, and economically. It's just dangerous.

The women's revolution of my time, theoretically, meant the ability of the female to be on equal status with males. I guess primarily, that would be in the work force, as I see it. I don't think women have really reached equal status, emotionally, with men. They haven't reached it in economics either. I think there is still a glass ceiling for women. They have much more opportunity in the world now than they had before. That comes from the post-World War II generation, where the men went off to war. That's the beginning of it. The women had to maintain the family. They went out and got jobs in factories and sometimes worked in the home.

When women work along with a man who they're married to or in a relationship with, and bring home the same amount of money or more, things begin to happen in the relationship because of the egos involved. This last generation of men are what I call "on the cusp" of this whole women's movement. It happened when we were in late high school or college. Men then were raised differently. They were raised in the old way of thinking, and yet, for so many of them, the women that they are involved with do work because they want to, or they have to work in order to maintain a standard of living in the economy that we're in. That does crazy things to a relationship. My hope is that the next generation of men will be used to it and it won't be quite as hard. It has been very, very difficult for men who are 45 years and up, I would say.

I think the so-called free love movement had an effect on our relationships. Anything that affects the whole world or a whole generation, it may not affect segments of the generation or population as much. It affected the generation that I am in. Women certainly look at sex more openly now than I was raised to look at it. Young girls look at it differently. They tend to look at it more like men look at sex. That's the residual of that whole movement in the 60s and 70s. It's much freer. I don't know if that's bad. There are some dangers such as sexually transmitted diseases that we didn't have 20, 30 years ago. They weren't as life-threatening. That is one of the real dangers with it.

The other thing that is a danger, men of a certain age, I find, verbalize and want an open sexual relationship. Deep down, they don't really want it. Again, that's the dichotomy of those men who were raised on the cusp of all of that happening. Theoretically, it's interesting and intriguing and that's what they want, and yet, deep down they don't really want that type of thing. If they want it at all, they only want it for themselves. They don't want it for the woman. Again, a dichotomy of equal rights of women, and where they are in terms of men.

$$\wp$$

My first interest in boys started while I was in New York one summer. I must have been eight or nine and I said to my grandmother, "He's my boyfriend." I remember in the 8th grade liking a boy who was in my class. My next door neighbors were boys. The house next to that was one boy. I used to like them, but we all played together. Being an old school teacher, you begin to see it around the 3rd grade or so. That's basically when it began to happen for me.

When I began my somewhat first relationship, my father was relatively strict. There were lots of rules. I couldn't date until I was 16. My parents had to know the young man. He had to come over and meet them, grandparents and all. He had to go through all of that. Most of the guys that I dated, initially, were boys that were in a group that my parents had. They tended to know them and know their parents, knew the parents' value system. We all tended to live in the same neighborhood. We all went to the same schools. I went to a private school all the way through. We all went to these private schools in the area.

Parents were in clubs that had spin-offs for the young people. The parents' clubs would give a dance for the youngsters. It was sort of our own group. I realize now, and I don't know if they did it on purpose, I suspect they did, but it was a tremendous control factor on who you went out with. In retrospect, it was very good. It was excellent because it really controlled a lot of extenuating circumstances. Those boys knew the parents. They knew your father. They knew they were in trouble if you went home and said anything went wrong (laughs). All of those things were really good control factors.

I became involved in my first serious relationship in college. I am going to take serious to mean, because I don't know if young people really know, emotionally. I think they do, but I'm not sure. My first sexual relationship was in high school. My first sexual relationship that meant anything was in college. It lasted a number of years. I don't regret it. I see the guy now. Actually, we're friends. We even live near each other. We are close friends. When my father died, he was one of the first people over. If I go away, I can call him up and say, "Will you take in the papers for me?" He's more than willing to do it. That turned out to be a very nice relationship.

I believe we met at a fraternity/sorority function. I don't remember any problems in the relationship. I guess that's why we are still friends to this day. I can look back on it and say I was not in love with him. I don't think he was with me either. He actually was out of school and in the armed services. He was a little bit older. I might have been 19. He might have been 22. Maybe that was positive. He might have been more mature.

We broke up harmoniously, but I wouldn't consider that a love relationship. It was just a very nice relationship. In the end, we just stopped seeing each other. We began to see other people. See, I basically was young. We stopped seeing each other for a year or so, then he called up and said he was going to get married. He's still married to that girl. I just think it was moving on, maturing.

From there, I just dated other boys in college. I don't recall any of them being deep emotional relationships. They were all nice guys. I don't remember a lot of them. I was never one for fooling around with a lot of men. It was never anything that I was interested in doing. I wasn't even interested in dating a lot of men. I usually found one guy or so, maybe two, that was about it. I never dated a lot of guys.

When I was a junior or senior in college, I met the man I married. We were in a sociology class. I stayed married to him for 22 years. He was getting a master's degree. We just started talking. Of course, this school was White, so there weren't a lot of us. You sort of acknowledged someone who was the same color in the class. There was a bonding, maybe much more now, as I listen to my son and what goes on now. You sat together and met wherever the recreation point was for your group to meet between classes and after classes.

As far as I can recall, he just started asking me out. We just started dating, exclusively. We eventually started talking about marriage, what he wanted to do in the future, what I wanted to do in the future. He went into the hospital for a hernia operation or something, and I went to visit him every day. In his mind, that sort of solidified things, that I would take the time to do that, that this was a relationship that could work. I remember something about him asking me to marry him in the hospital. Of course, with my upbringing, he had to get down on his knees. He had to propose. He had to ask my father for my hand in marriage. I was raised in a very formal home. He did all of that.

For us to stay married for 22 years and end up in a divorce, a couple of things happened. For me, part of it was – he was a very dominant male – I assumed that I was in this relationship that I was raised in. The man was dominant. Some of these things we had discussed before getting married, that I would work until we had children. At that point, I would stay home. It was such a male-dominated relationship, that initially, when we first got engaged, he told me he didn't want me to work at all. I told him, "Well, you know, I've gone through school. I've got these degrees and they would be wasted if I just sit home and do nothing." He finally agreed that I could work. I said to him, "I will only work until we have children. At that time, I will stay home and take care of the children, and you." That's what we agreed upon.

I noticed in the relationship that there would be times when he would be dominant. Then there were times when he would expect me to make decisions and do things. I recall saying to him, "I'm confused. Half of the time you want me to be in a relationship of 20 years ago, and the other half of the time you want me to be in this new world relationship where I'm equal, and I can make any decision that you make."

He said that he realized that, but that was the way he was. I think I had a man who was mixed up in terms of the women's movement and the old way. Intellectually, he understood the women's movement. He was very intelligent, extremely bright. He has numerous degrees in several areas. I used to tease him and say that he was a professional student, 'cause he liked to go to school. He's got degrees in law, accounting, and several different areas.

He would vacillate back and forth between when he was dominant and when I was dominant. I couldn't always read the situation. I would say, "Okay, I'm going to let him make the decision." He'd say, "Why didn't you make the decision and do it?" "Because I thought you were going to make the decision." That was the beginning of the end, as I recall it.

He then decided that he didn't want to stay in the profession that he had trained for. He wanted to get out and go into some other things. He went to school and prepared himself for these other things. Once he left his initial profession, he never could seem to get a grip on what he wanted to do. He would go from scheme to scheme. He bought a picture frame company. That didn't go well. Then he did something else, and that didn't go well. Then he got a job, and that didn't go well. He could always get these jobs, and good jobs.

He went back to school and got an accounting degree, came out with the degree and was immediately hired by one of the top seven accounting firms in the United States – no experience in accounting at all. He just had a degree. He was a very personable person. He could talk you into just about anything, so he talked himself into all these different jobs.

Then there seemed to come a time when he was bound and determined that he had to be rich. It didn't make any difference how he did it, he just had to find some profession that was going to make him rich. That, I think, was the beginning of the downfall. Being rich wasn't anything that was extremely important to me.

One of our differences was he was raised very poor. I was raised, depending on sociologically where you want to put those breaks, very upper middle class. In the Black culture, probably upper class. In general, if you put the Rockefellers in the upper class, obviously we were not there. I never wanted for anything. I had a brand new car at 16. I went to private schools all the way through. We traveled.

He was raised with a father that worked in the factories. There were times when his father was laid off for long periods of time. They just didn't have any money. At some point, maybe he saw that he wasn't going to be a millionaire, and it began to bother him. He was just at a stage where he had to make money. He would get these good jobs and then he would quit them. He would come home and say, "I quit that job." By this time we had a child, we were married 10 years before we had our first child, I worked all that time. I invested the money. We had a couple million dollars in property. I invested in property.

My father had been in that, and his mother before him. I sort of understood the business. I had taken this money and invested in all of these things. I said, "You can't not work. If we want to build this thing to where we both can retire and not worry about it, and keep up our lifestyle," which was very good, "you have to work." We lived a nice lifestyle while we were both working, but it was like

I could never get through to him.

He'd quit one job and then he'd get another one. Then he'd quit that one. There would be this interim where we would have to live off of my salary, and the money that was coming in from these other business ventures that we had.

Finally, he went into one business venture that just ruined us. It ruined us financially. It took absolutely everything that we had. I would plead with him, and plead with him, "Don't do this. Get out of this. Get a job." I was dealing with an absolute brick wall. He just didn't understand it. Then he would get so deep into these things there was no getting out.

He lost all of the property. He lost our home. This home that I am in now is after him. We had a five bathroom, five bedroom home and a huge acre of land. He lost it all. We had to move out of the house. The buildings were all gone. The cars were gone. They came and got my car. I had a Mercedes. They came and got it out of the garage, just took everything. We were still married. He said to me, "You need to go back to work." I said, "All right. Let's start again. You go out and get a job. I'll put the baby in daycare. I'll go get a job, and we'll start all over again." We were young. He didn't want to do it. I said, "I'm going to take the child and go to my mother's. I'm going to get a job. If you get a job, and we're going to start all over again, you can come. If not, you don't bring anything to the table at this point. You're dragging me down to the point where I can't make it, and this child won't be able to make it."

He promised that he would get a job. We moved in with my mother. My father was dead by this time. I got a job. I went out and was hired immediately. I would get up every morning and go to work, bring my money home. He would turn over in the bed and say, "Good bye." He would stay home all day and look at television. That's all he would do. Of course, I was extremely depressed. I would come home from this job, get in bed, and pull the cover up over my head.

He had a degree in all of this. He had a degree in everything else: sociology, psychology, I mean PhDs. He had more than one PhD. I'm going under, not figuring it out, not really knowing why. I later went back to school, took some courses, and realized that I was in a deep depression. I could always manage, because I didn't have any alternative. There was no money coming in. I had to go out and find a job, bring the money in, and feed us, which I did. Fine.

But then, and again I go back to the dichotomy of the male/female thing, and this male of my generation. The roles were reversed. I am now the breadwinner, but he still wants to be dominant in terms of making the decisions how the money's spent, what's done, what isn't done. I said, "You can't do that. You can't put me in the breadwinning situation and then tell me I have no say because you're a dominant male and this is your family."

That was the final straw. That was the point where there was no return. He wouldn't accept the fact that I could make decisions on my own. I could deal with the family, but I was saying to him, "I'm not going to just support you, and have you sit here." He couldn't deal with it.

It took us six years to actually break up, but that's what really did it. I simply think that he, whatever was happening in his mind, whatever made him decide that he had to put everything into all of these businesses, was beyond me. He produced movies. To show you how bad his luck was he produced a movie with Richard Burton, who was one of the co-producers. Richard Burton died three minutes before the end of the film. The film could never be finished. All the money that was put into that film was gone.

It was like he was just out there. He'd say, "If I throw this money into this, this business will work and I'll be rich." There was another scheme of buying and selling diamonds, running them back and forth from Amsterdam. I'm going, "You're not paying the house note, and you're running diamonds back and forth." It was just something in him where he had to make this big money instead of working on a job and bringing home the little paycheck, and we just take the paycheck and live happily ever after.

It took about six years for me to realize because I think I really tried to keep it together. I tried to support him. He would go into other ventures and I'd take part of the money I'm earning, he's not working, and say, "You need this to make this venture go. Here's the money to do it." It got to the point where I said, "There's no reason for my child and I not to have things in order to give him this money that's basically being squandered. It just isn't making good sense."

My father would have said, "This is the wrong man. You need to get out of this." Finally, we did break up. It wasn't easy. He really blames me. He feels that I should have stayed and supported him in whatever it was that he was doing, whether he had a job or not. I certainly feel that for a certain amount of time it was my duty to support him. But ten years without a job is too much for me to stick in (laughs). He resents me to this day.

Six years may seem like a long time to leave a person, but I was always trying to support him. Underneath all that, I was afraid to be totally out there on my own, alone. I let it go on all those years, and I shouldn't have.

My mother, who was sort of monitoring this whole thing, sat me down one day and said, "You know, Black women call it love. White women get a divorce." I thought, "Umm, well okay. It's time for me to get out of this." He's been gone four years and he still doesn't have a job. That tells me that the decision I made was the right one. He wasn't going to change.

He got to the point, after he had lost all of these things, he would say, "I don't want anything because I don't want anybody to be able to take it away from me again." I would say, "No. You go out and make it. You have it. You run your business so that you don't allow them to take it away from you again. You don't bet the house on a scheme, so when the scheme falls through, the house doesn't." You learn those things, but I could never get across to him.

When I finally decided it was over, I couldn't stay in it any more, I told him he didn't have to leave immediately. I knew he didn't have any money. "Put some money together and go find yourself a place." At that point, when I knew it was over, I started seeing other men. I said to him, "Our relationship is over. This isn't going to work. I have to go on about my life." That bothered him very much.

When he realized I was seeing other men, he became very hostile. He talked about me terribly to our son. He wanted to blame everything on me. Interestingly enough, he got our son to believe him for a long time. The child was only twelve. He and the child had been very, very close, because he basically was the mother. He was home with this boy; I was working every day. He became the nurturing person for this child.

When he had moved out, he finally said to my son, "You move out with me. Leave her." My son must have initially said, "Okay." He came into my room and said, "Daddy wants me to go and live with him. I can't do it. I don't know why. I can't do it. He's outside. I'm going to tell him I can't do it." That was the beginning of the change in the relationship between my son and I. I don't mean that the child didn't love me, because he did, but he was under the influence of this man.

In the time since then, the horror stories that this child tells me that his father told him are horrendous. We would just go, "Well, those stories aren't true. That didn't happen. It didn't happen that way." But again, his ego was all tied up in it. I think he felt he had lost. I had said to him, "You have got to go." I think that hurt him, so he had to denigrate me. Of course, the only person that it would make any real difference to was my son.

Now that the child is older, we laugh about it. We tell stories about the stories that his father had cooked up (laughs). There were times when it was real trauma for the child. The child didn't know who to believe. He finally, on his own, went to some friends, people who knew us through the years and asked them. They basically verified what I was telling the child. "No. He didn't work. He was a moocher," all that type of thing.

In time, the child came to realize that, in fact, I was telling the truth. To show you more about this man and what I was seeing and feeling, and why I had to get out of it, he left me with atrocious tax bills. I got a tax bill for $1,839,000. A tax bill. Those are the types of things that I had to work through. I had to call the IRS. It turned out that he had never filed income tax for X number of years, our joint income tax.

Again, he wanted to be the man. If I had said, "Let me take these taxes to somebody and have them do it." "No. You can't do that. I'll do it." He would never do it. So, for years of not filing taxes and by us having had this property, when you don't file the tax, they take your last year and estimate it on that. So, these years where we were making lots of money, they just took that amount and upped it and six years of that amounted in this huge bill.

I had to work through all of these things. I had to come out and tell them, "Look, this is his bill. He didn't do certain things. I will file whatever taxes you want me to file, based on the information that I have." It took me years. I paid all of the bills. He left me with huge bills. When he didn't have money to finance his scheme, he would take a charge card and charge it up to the limit, or get the cash off it. My credit was all messed up. I had to work out the whole credit thing. I had to pay off the IRS. I had to just start from point A.

He took $3,000 and put it in my son's bank account, in my son's name. He didn't tell my son. So, my son goes to his account and finds out that he has $3,000. He comes home and he says, "I have $3,000 in my account. I don't know why, and I don't know how it got there, but here it is. What am I going to do with it? It's mine. It's in the account." I said, "Whoa, wait a minute. I'll bet you anything that's your father."

The child, at that point, wasn't completely convinced. "Oh no, he wouldn't not tell me." I said, "You know, if you take that money out, he is going to be angry." The child took it and did what he wanted to do with it. "All I can do is tell you what I think. Technically, it is your money. It's in your account. But you know you didn't put $3,000 in there." He drew the money out. He did a number of things with it that he wanted to do.

When his father found out, he called here, balled the child out, and told him he would never speak to him again. He told him that he was not his child. He has never spoken to that child again, over $3,000.

Sometimes I look back and say, "Could I have seen all of these things? Were there characteristics in him that I missed?" I was young, 20 years old when we got together. What was it? There were certainly characteristics in terms of wanting to dominate. That didn't bother me. I came from a family where the father was the dominant person. That didn't strike me as odd. I was willing to do that. What I don't believe I saw, I probably didn't see it because I was raised in such a cloistered atmosphere. Maybe if I had been out there, as the kids say, in the streets and gone with a whole lot of guys and all that kind of thing, I would have seen symptoms of other things that I honestly, honestly never saw.

When I met this guy, he was hard-working. He had to put himself through school. He lived on 10 dollars a week. He ate biscuits and Kool-Aid in order to go to school, to get these PhDs. He had scholarships but he didn't have a lot of money. He is what I considered to be a hard-working, dedicated man. He changed. What circumstances that did it, I don't know.

We stayed together so long because I kept saying, "We can make this work." Again, I came from a family that stayed together. My grandparents were all together. My parents were together. I didn't understand separating and divorce. You just got in there and helped the other person get over the hump, and then everything would be okay. It didn't work that way.

The change may have occurred because I think he thought he could depend on me. As I said, I went out immediately and got a job and supported him and the child. I think the change came when everything went out the window. I think that he was probably in some form of depression. I couldn't get him to go get any help. I said that to him, I said, "Why don't you go talk to a therapist? Go see somebody." Well again, that's a male thing, particularly a Black male thing where they don't want to do that. I could not get him to go. He told me *I* was the one that had the problem. I said, "Wait, I work every day. You sit home and watch television. I don't think I have a problem. You're the one with the problem."

Something snapped when he lost everything. He's never really been the same person after that. I think he lost his confidence. What I don't understand is, he continued to come up with these different money-making schemes. There was still something going on in the back of his head that he could do it. I understand from people who know him that he's in another scheme now. It's not working, but he's not getting it.

I've tried to wrestle with myself, "Should I have done something differently? Should I have really stayed in it and, 'You sit here, and I'll just be the supportive wife that goes out and works and takes care of you. That's what love is supposed to be.'" I don't think so. I think I made the right decisions. Life's not always easy. That was difficult for me because I'm on the cusp of the traditional family, and yet I became this new woman out here that's got to go and make it for herself. Those were not easy decisions for me to make at all.

To get back on my feet, I worked. One of the things my father taught me, by virtue I suppose of him being an attorney and having to think rather logically about things, he always said to me, "Whatever you do, if you come home and tell me that you have done something, I'm going to ask you your thought process. If I determine that you thought as logically as you could, whether you made the right decision or the wrong decision, it's going to be fine. If I determine that you didn't think a situation through clearly, that's when you're going to be in trouble."

I took that advice and I took each little bit. I took the taxes and year after year after year I just worked through it. I took the bills. I refinanced the house so that I could take that money and pay off all of the bills. Therefore, I could pay at a lower interest rate on these charge bills that he ran up. He left me with all of them. I was continually funneling money into his projects. It's been ten years. He filed for bankruptcy. That was on my credit. I got all of that off. I moved up in my career.

When I retired, when I got pregnant, because that was our agreement, I was Director of Administrative Services for a school district. I had a really good job. I left it because that was what we had talked about. By the time this child was in the third grade, I had to go back to work. I just went to the school board and said, "I am overqualified. I have all of the credentials. I am overqualified to teach, but I will take a job teaching in a classroom if you'll give it to me." They were kind enough to give me an assignment immediately. I didn't take that assignment. I went to another place and got a job. That really worked out well. I think I stayed in the classroom about a year and I moved on up. I have an administrative position now that is right under the head of the company, and I make really good money. I keep my own hours. I travel. It turned out to be a really good job.

That goes back to my father because I said to him, "Why do I have to get all of this education? I'm going to get married. I'm going to have children." He said, "Because you never know what's going to happen down the line. You may need to go out some day and work." Lo and behold, that's what happened. All that education he was giving me came to serve me. It's taken me about ten years to get straight, but I just did one thing at a time.

My ex-husband had put all of our furniture in storage. I had furniture from all over the world. He wouldn't pay the storage bill.

He wouldn't tell me where the storage companies were. He had them in a couple of different storage places. He lost all of that. All of that is gone. I had no bed. I literally had to start from the beginning. The child's bed was gone. His bedroom furniture was gone. I had to buy him. I had to buy me. I had to buy cars. I drove a little beat-up car 'til I could do the other things, and got to the point where I could buy a nice car.

I worry sometimes about how my son is taking all of this. I don't know how deep down in his head, psychologically, where he is and what it has done to him. I don't know how he'll relate to women and that bothers me. I did have him go into therapy for a while. These are some of the things that concern me about the next generation.

I said, "You really need to go into therapy and talk to someone." He said, "Men don't do that." I said, "Oh my God. I've worked so hard on this kid." It's a throwback to "men don't do that kind of thing." He went for a while. I promised him that if he went, I would not ask him any questions about it. "Tell her whatever you want to tell her. I don't want to know what you said. If you want to talk badly about me, fine." I don't know what happened. He did not go for a long time.

What I see in him are some qualities that I think are very good. I'm worried about those things that I'm not seeing. I worried because everybody takes these experiences in their lives differently. If I see it happening, I can talk to him about it. It's all of these things that I know go on in his head that I cannot see and I can't feel. He and I have a very, very close relationship now.

He said to me just recently, "It took me a long time, but I realize now what I have. I realize how hard you worked to give me all of the things that I have." When he called from Europe the other day, he's on his school break, I said, "Do you need some more money? I'll wire you some more money." He said, "No, I'll live on what I have. I realize that you have to sacrifice in order to give me this, and I'm not going to ask you for any more money. If I have to eat at McDonald's every single day, I will live on the money that you've given me." He stayed longer than planned, and I sent him the money anyway. Call it a mother thing. When he returned, he didn't spend it, but he did ask me if he could use part of it to invest in the stock market.

I see those as very positive things. He must have felt the weightlessness of living in that household, because he's very frugal with his money. He saves his money. He's 18, and he's invested heavily in the stock market. He got a 24% return on his money last year, and he's just a freshman. He says, "This is the money that I'm going to have later on. I'm not going to let certain things happen." Those are positive things. He's not into drugs. I always say to parents, "Your kids don't tell you what's really going on. They only tell you what they think you can deal with." So, if they're on drugs, you don't know it until you find it out. They don't just come and say, "Guess what, I'm doing heroin."

He called me from Amsterdam and said, "We went into a cafe and you can order marijuana just like you order food. We ordered a marijuana cigarette, and I took three puffs. That stuff's for the birds. Why would anybody want to do that?"

He talks to me about sex and his sexual experiences. I can say to him, "The stuff that's out there will kill you. Be very careful." It doesn't mean that I don't want him to have sexual experiences, but I want him to think about it. I want him to be careful about it. We do a lot of talking. He hasn't been in a real relationship with a woman, so I can't get a grasp on how he is going to treat her, and probably won't know that until I begin to see a relationship.

I know for a fact that his father not speaking to him hurts him tremendously. Interestingly enough, it doesn't hurt me. One of my friends said, "Oh, I'm so depressed." I asked, "Why?" "I've been divorced from my first husband for 25 years now." I said, "You know, I don't feel that way at all about not being with my husband. I feel liberated. I feel great. I feel wonderful." I think I've come out of it pretty good. (lowers her voice because she feels this) I'm sure there are going to be repercussions with the child. I don't know how. All I can do is be there for him, try to walk him through it, help him through when those things hit him in the face. I tried to do as much as I could along the way, but I know it's going to hit him.

Right now, in terms of male/female relationships, I've had one serious relationship since I've been divorced. That lasted for about four years. I tend not to be one that fools around with a lot of men. I've dated a number of men, but they didn't turn into any kind of serious relationship.

I'm in a quasi relationship now. It's the beginning of one, so I don't know what's going to happen or how it will go. The interesting thing about it is, his personality is very similar to my ex-husband. That scares me – very, very similar – extremely dominant personality. It makes me wonder in some kind of way if that is the kind of person that I'm attracted to. Actually, I think it is. It's too new a relationship to determine where it will go. I've known him for about two years. We've only been sort of serious for about four or five months, maybe.

I don't think the young relationships of today are going well at all. I just look at the kids that I know. Young men don't treat women with the kind of respect that I would like to see. I have to frame everything. I led a very sheltered life, so there were probably lots of things going on out there that I, 20 years ago, 40 years ago, wasn't aware of. They didn't enter my frame of reference. I think these men treat women very badly.

I have a co-worker that has a son and the boy's girlfriend just had a baby. He refuses to marry the girl. She is an absolutely lovely girl, darling little baby. He says, "I was just out there having fun. I'm not going to take any responsibility for it." That's very, very scary to me. It's not even for my son's generation, it's the generation after him. I don't know where they're going to be. They aren't going to have the kind of parenting they should have. Parenting is so important. I realize in my life, I have fallen back on my parents' parenting so often. Those were the things that kept me going when things got rough in a relationship. I don't think that these young people have the skills to give it to the next generation.

I think the generation of our children is in peril. I think they are going to have a very difficult time. That's why divorce rates are so high. People don't want to work situations out that may be difficult. I feel good about the fact that I tried for X number of years to work the situation out. I didn't just say, "Six months, I can't take this anymore. Good bye." I feel very good that I tried. I can say to him or anyone else, "Hey, I really tried to make that work." It wasn't until it was shattered completely that I said, "Okay, this isn't going to work. It's been 25 years of my life, but I just have to move on." I don't see that in a lot of young people today. I see them, "Oh, this didn't go right. You didn't do that the way I want. Good bye." I don't think that's good.

I think there are more negative influences in our society today than positives. There are just so many negative things going on in the lives of children. Without a strong family they are going to have a very rough time. That then affects the next generation. There must be something positive. There's always something positive, but I cannot think of a positive thing that is going on in terms of relationships.

The most important remark I could say to young people regarding relationships is to make sure they have communication with the significant other. If that takes a third party, both should be open enough to go to that third party and get some help, learn the skills that will allow them to communicate with each other so that they can really understand what's going on in the other person's head. So that they can work together, whatever it is. It doesn't have to be material things. Whatever it is you want out of life. You can't read someone else's mind. You really need to communicate and talk about things, what your problems are, and where you see yourself going. How your lives fit together.

One of the most important things I would say to young people is, make sure you're in a relationship with someone who understands communication, understands communicating, and knows how to do it. Those communication skills are probably skills that a lot of people don't have any longer.

Children don't play in the streets and communicate with each other anymore. They sit in front of the TV, the computer, or play video games. Those are all solitary things. There are so many communicating skills today that these young children don't even learn. That is really central. If you can understand the other person, then you can begin to make decisions in your own life that coincide with the other person. You've got a real understanding of what they're thinking. That can get you to the doorstep of having a successful relationship, but that's only the front door!

Yvette Mackeka

Ms. Maceka is a 41-year-old single mother who is a top executive in the film business. She is very confident, independent, and knows what she wants. She comes from a very secure background that allowed her to enjoy many things at an early age. Her non-Western spiritual belief is a main factor in keeping her balanced and centered from negative behavior. When trouble and physical ailment was surrounding her son, she knew how to gather the support of her family and friends and to put him in the presence of positive men when his father was not around. She is also a very strong advocate for women and points out the abuses of power some men have used to suppress many women. She is not a strong supporter of marriage, but the feeling seems to surface that if there was a man that she could really groove with, that song may change.

I was born in Dallas, Texas. My father passed away when I was 14. Prior to that, we moved moderately because he was an executive. His job offers came every three to five years. He was not around a whole lot because of his schedule. My mother was a housewife and kept very busy. Around 10 or 11 years old, I began to see that there was some unhappiness between the two of them. At that same time, my father became very ill with his heart disease. For about three years, he was on and off with heart problems.

My father was very strict. My mother was the buffer. She was the one who would try to balance out the strictness. For the most part, we were middle class, economically. We always lived in nice places and had nice things. We had wonderful friends and good influences. We went to good public schools. My father didn't believe in private schools. He had gone to private schools all of his life. He felt that kids should have a better social idea of what was happening. We were always involved in extra-curricular activities. We got exposed to a lot of different things.

I'm not sure if my parents supplied a good role model for me, but if it is about a father who was there, supportive, and cared for his children, yes, he was. My mother was caring and supportive of her children, yes. It was a time when people stayed together whether they were happy or unhappy. I don't know if that is good or not. I believe that created a kind of tension in the household. If in fact you are staying together because of the children, that can cause problems. However, they did provide good parenting.

As far as the two of them getting along with each other and providing an example for me, there was too much role-playing there. I saw my mother role-playing. I saw my father role-playing. I feel that in order to have real tenderness exchanged, people have to be happy with themselves and be sure that they are doing what they really want to do – at least striving to do that or endeavoring to discover what that is. I don't think that was acceptable behavior, per se, at that time. I think it was more of, "You're supposed to be the housewife, and that's supposed to work," regardless of the inconsistencies or something that should have been prescribed for them. I just thought they were role-playing.

I started getting interested in boys very early on. My sister and I were very popular. We were twins. My father was in a glamorous industry. He was well-known and popular. That carried a lot of weight. We were just popular. I remember getting attention from boys. I started to have an interest in them at the age of nine. We kept things very clean, very innocent. We didn't fool around or play around. We would do homework together or participate in certain after school activities together. I had three brothers, and guys would come by and play with my brothers. That was usually the excuse, "I'm going to come by and play with your brothers."

We'd all go swimming together, go-cart riding together, or ride bikes together. It was very social. There were never any touching or holding hands. As far as it would go would be, "So-and-so likes you." It wasn't anything like, "Would you go with me?

Would you be my girlfriend or boyfriend? Can I call you my girlfriend?" We never went that far.

When the issue of how to deal with boys came up, that was a taboo subject. We didn't get advised (laughs). It was more of witnessing things. Watching our friends' older sisters interact, watching movies. A lot of it was instinct. At times, you realized that certain things were going to happen: holding a boy's hand, kissing them on the cheek. There was never any advice. I felt my mother was anticipating it with terror, as opposed to a person you could go to get counsel. It was something to be avoided. She was not very helpful in giving you a forecast.

In retrospect, I definitely think that was a hindrance for me dealing with relationships. I wound up doing things out of peer pressure rather than having some type of frame of reference, even if it was just from a conversation. It would have been nice to have a feeling of, "I could say this, or do this, or be coy. I could be slick. I could be this or that." It was more out of peer pressure when you start doing things when you're hanging out. "Well, everybody else is doing it." It's not having your own self-identity about things or your own feelings about things.

Much later on my brothers might make a comment. I'm the oldest. They were always impressed that these guys wanted to hang out with them anyway. That being the case, they didn't make any value judgments. They would say, "He's okay. We're all going to play basketball. What's wrong with him?"

My first serious relationship started off trusting. It was very fantasy-like. You know, if you watch enough TV, you think things are supposed to be a certain way. If the bubble burst, it would be very disheartening, very discouraging. It started off with a mutual friend who was actually dating this person. We were just friends. We had gone to New York together. We were all hanging out. I hadn't seen this friend of mine for a long time and I remember my sister had started dating this person. This other guy came with the guy my sister was dating. That's how we began to talk and hang out. It was months afterwards when we got together. That relationship lasted three-and-a-half years. It was a blast. We had a lot of fun.

We always had like puppy loves in high school, but this was more serious. We were all in school running around. It was the kind of thing where we took weekend junkets together. We included friends. It kind of taught you how to be with other people. It had its rocky roads. We broke up a few times, but we always ended up getting back together. The breakups were never for long. We had a lot of fun. We...had...a...lot...of...fun.

After going through what we went through and spending wonderful times together, I realized I was outgrowing him. I remember one evening I was just looking at him in almost a frightening way. I was actually kind of shocked that I didn't feel the same. Something was missing. I tried to push it toward the back and eventually realized after two or three weeks' time, something had changed, that my life had just picked up and moved on. It wasn't the same feeling.

Coming to terms with that, I decided to be mature and honest. At least I would try. We went for a ride one day. I explained to him that I thought we should date other people. We both had been together since we were young. It was our first serious relationship. We needed to see if dating other people would bring us back together even stronger. We were in college at the time. After that, I just started dating other guys. The sad part, I enjoyed being in a relationship, primarily because of the ease of it. It was less to think about. It was nice being in one. It was also nice to say that you had a boyfriend. "I have a boyfriend. My boyfriend is so-and-so and blah, blah, blah."

Not too long after that, maybe a year, I don't really remember, I got involved in another relationship. I met this person through a friend. A friend of ours had gotten married and I met her husband's friend. I kept saying, "I want a boyfriend. I want a boyfriend." They said, "You should meet this guy. He's going to be living out here now, so why don't you meet him?" When I first saw him, I wasn't impressed at all. We went out. I thought he was a warm person. I thought he was personable. I thought he was sexy. He became more enticing as I got to talk with him and spend more time together. I really liked him. Physically, he wasn't doing much for me. At the time, physical was important. More important than it is now. We lasted about three or four years.

We definitely had breakups. He was living with somebody else, another woman. I didn't know about it. I remember being extremely naïve and just trusting. My friends were telling me that this guy had rented this house and he had a roommate. The roommate was going back somewhere and he was doing certain things with his life. It never dawned on me for a second to even think that anything was going on between those two. I can whale it now. It was not something that I would even question. I thought everyone had such good intentions to a degree. We started going out and hanging out. I figured it wasn't even a thought, an afterthought or second thought. It was just nothing.

We went out one night and hung out for a while. The next day he called. We were supposed to go someplace, but he told me he couldn't go. That's when I realized something must be up. It just hit me right then and there. A frightening thought occurred to me. I called a mutual friend and said, "This just occurred to me, but..." They said, "You know what? The person who is his roommate?" I said, "Does this happen to be an ex-girlfriend or something like that.?" "Yeah." I said, "Get real." That's when I was really upset. At that point it was over.

We didn't talk for months. Later on, he called and said something had happened. To make a long story short, this went on and on and on. By that time, I believe I had fallen in love with him. I had one of these hopeful feelings that somehow things would work out, so that he would be able to do what he had to do. The excuse I kept hearing was, "She can't go back now because the money thing is not right. She's moved into another part of the house, and so on." I realized that was not true, but I was too far gone then. I was too involved at the time. We broke up on and off a lot. Finally, she had moved out and we were starting to be more consistent, more serious. Then something just snapped. I said, "No, I don't need this."

I realized that you can't change anybody. I came to the realization that I couldn't change this person. If he had these tendencies, he may not stop because of me. Something just went flat. It wasn't as if I didn't have feelings for him; it just wasn't worth it. I came to another feeling about myself, and I wasn't going to subject myself to that. "Enough. I don't want to be part of it." It wasn't the end for him, of course, but I was through.

My responsibility for that relationship was being involved in it at all, realizing I was having hopes on things that were not going to work out. What I was going through at the time was thinking that it was more important than what it was, really putting a lot of emphasis on a relationship, which I still do. I was compromising myself, based on lack of self-esteem, lack of self-worth. At the time, it didn't even dawn on me what it was. When you start getting involved and ask, "Why am I in this?" you start examining yourself. "What am I doing?" That was my negativity. He didn't give me anything. I didn't need anything from him. It wasn't anything that I was plotting against him. I respected him.

I didn't realize it at the time, but as I got more and more involved, it just came out to be my lack of self-esteem. So, it was an opportunity for me to look at that. When I realized what I was doing, and kept working on it, it served its purpose. It didn't take me long to get him out of my system. It's funny with me. When I'm done, I'm done. When I'm with you, I'm with you. I'm honest about things like that. I was with him until there was no longer a reason in my heart to be there. I just dated a few guys after that, a few relationships. I was available for about a year or two, maybe less.

I had my son when I was 34 years old. I was not married. It was a serious relationship; we moved in together. We bought a home together. It was as serious as it could get without actually saying, "I do." We didn't get married because something told me that he wasn't really the one. I don't know how much I believe in the institution of marriage. I believe in two people being together, understanding that they want to be together. I don't think marriage keeps you together though, loving somebody does – having a mature person, someone who has a solid foundation in life. If those two people have the same thing going on, they can stay together. They don't have false expectations. They know how to problem-solve, work out problems, let individuals be individuals. I don't think marriage keeps people married. I think it's a great ceremony. I'm not saying that I wouldn't mind, eventually, possibly walking down an aisle one day just to say I did it.

Having my son was not enough of a reason to get married. We're all programmed to a certain degree. Coming from a situation where my parents were married and I thought all of my friends' parents were married. A couple of them weren't. It did come up in my mind, "I should get married." But then I thought, after we got together, I said, "Well, no." If it was not going to work out, it's going to be easier not to have to go through all that hassle.

When my son was born, we stayed together only eight or nine months after that. It would have been less. I think the fact that I was pregnant kept us together longer. We started falling apart early on. After I was about five months pregnant, it wasn't a good relationship. He was unstable. He was getting his businesses together and he was fairly insecure.

I was making more money. A lot of his insecurities were in full swing at the time. We clashed. A lot of things went to discussion and I told him, "If you need to leave, you need to leave. Please feel free to go." He said, "No, I'll be here." After our son was born, we definitely made a pact, made an effort. We bought a house, his business began to pick up, so we decided "We should be able to make it."

At that point, he started seeing other women. He was really going through a lot of changes and started womanizing. I said, "If that is what you want to do, you do that." I haven't ever said I was going to date somebody else because somebody is dating somebody else and I'm dating them. Practicing infidelity I would say.

When people started calling the house and hanging up, that's when I knew something was wrong. Just punk stuff. They wouldn't call and leave a name, just call and hang up. There were just tell-tale signs. A woman knows. There were times when he would stay out late. One of his tell-tale signs was, he would yawn after saying something, and he wasn't sleepy. "You lyin'. You're yawning again, so stop telling that story." He'd say, "Oh no." "Yes you are." He was a character.

One day I woke up and just said, "You know what, that's it." That's how upset I was about it. Some of his friends told me he said, "She's not mad anymore. I'm worried." I just was not going to go through that anymore. We had enough. I didn't think it was good for my son, so we were left alone.

I think it can be a problem with the male ego when the woman makes more money. Not with all men, just most men. With the role-playing thing, you grow up thinking and believing that it is something to be worried about, something to be aware of and not have happen to you. I don't see where it is a problem. If a woman has a problem with it, she also has to deal with the stereotype, to have someone not making more money than she is. If that's not a problem for the woman, then why should a man be worried? I think it is a belief system, a program we have been trained to follow. When the situation arises, that's what we go to think. That's all we have to think is that. It makes you draw emotions that aren't positive.

When my son's father and I split, my son really felt it. He

definitely felt it. His father was very close to him. After a while, he stopped coming around. That's when my son got asthma. It was strictly emotional. It really affected him. I had to seriously pray that it would be resolved, and it was. It was resolved through lots of love and behavioral adaptations, making the effort to have family support and family outings, pointing out other positive male role models who were Black in his environment that he loves. I was constantly endorsing his father even though we weren't together. He never hears me talk about him in a demeaning way. I don't believe in that.

Now, my son wants us to get back together. His father just left town the other day. He was here for his birthday, the entire week. My son's entire mission during that period was to try to get us back together. That's not going to happen at all. It's not there. I love him as a person. No matter what happens, we'll always have a bond. The last relationship was with a guy much younger than me. He was mature in some ways, and immature in others. There was mutual respect for each other's lifestyle, time, schedule and responsibilities. It worked out.

As far as dealing with his immaturity in the beginning, I reverted to playing the female/male female role thing. It tended to circumvent some of that. We didn't really go there because in a lot of ways, he was very mature. The maturity comes after a while when you realize that he was limited because of experience and time. The ways that he would deal with troubling or difficult situations would be immature. If he was in a spot, he wouldn't admit it. Early on I kind of determined I was not going to react to it too much, just didn't make a lot of sense to. I believe that it made him a little spoiled, a tendency to be a little too comfortable.

I never felt that I was playing the mother role. He had a very strong mother figure. She was very prevalent in his life, very strong influence. There was no necessity for that. I did see where I played being the wiser one, the one who had to set a tone for things. In my first relationship, I kind of outgrew the person. We were in an age transition, from childhood to adolescence. In this last one, because he was younger, I'm not sure.

I am in a glamorous kind of business and it used to keep me really busy. Now, because of my responsibilities with my son, I definitely make time for him. I'm quite involved in several different activities and that type of thing. It does make it difficult to be still or be in one place for a very long period of time. It's not always because of the job. I think it's because of who I am. I enjoy and need to be in this kind of situation. I like being involved, but if the other person is insecure it can have a detrimental effect on a relationship. I believe you fall in love with the person and what they do, not so much falling in love with a particular situation or predicament. If that is what you're looking for, I'm not the person for you anyway.

When you fall in love with a person, then you fall in love with what that person is and does for a number of reasons. You wouldn't want someone who's just in love with the idea of you, or just hiding behind certain things. I don't believe I do that. I want to take the time to hang out and be with friends and have warm intimate moments. I cherish those kinds of memories when I'm busy, busy, busy. I do what I do because I like being involved. I like being there. It's not to be used as a substitute for something else. Being involved with someone who falls in love with you is because they want to be involved with you. You and what you do. When they start trying to change you or make you do something to fit their own needs, that is not going to work out.

In the last relationship, I did not involve him with my son, even though he needs that male strength. It would have been too confusing for him. He's involved with his father. That's all he knows. If another person really becomes that other person, then he can be more involved. I don't want him confused. He's too young.

℘

I decided to become a Buddhist because I wanted things. I

didn't feel I had enough control over my life at the time, especially not over my emotions in what I have gone through in my life – things in general. My father died early. I realized how emotionally depleted and drained people can be. I didn't like that. I didn't like the explanations I was getting from other religious sources about things.

The convincing factor came from the person who told me about it. It was something about her. It was her. I had been told about the practice twice before and I wasn't interested. She was very cool, very warm, very hip all at the same time. She was classy and down-to-earth. She was just a quality person and a people person.

There are a lot of uppity, bourgeois things around me. My father was raised in that. My mother was down-to-earth, but she had that bourgeoisie about her too. They had a bourgeoisie kind of attitude. They were all highly educated. My father's family was all doctors and things like that. My mother's parents were more into college education. They had another kind of arrogance.

But to meet someone who was very hip, very classy, very nice, but down and easy to talk to was a revelation in itself, someone who you could relate to, who would relate to you even. That's what drew me in. It had an effect on my whole being. It is feasible to say and highly probable that I might not be able to talk about these things in the way that I have. I don't believe that I would have had the spiritual resources to deal with some of the things I have had to deal with.

Based on our philosophy, there are certain things you have to deal with. There are certain karmas, certain ways that you were brought into this world that you now have an opportunity to work out, to look at, and to change. Without some really strong spiritual energy and confidence in something, especially in the belief of the philosophy, it's hard to face up to that stuff, no matter what you are doing. I know that if it wasn't for the practice, I would not be the person who could find the resources to rebound after difficulties. Now, I can look at something, not always right away, with a little objectivity and say, "Somehow I will get over this. I'll get through this," or look at myself and say, "There's something about me that attracted this. What? Let me change that about me."

If I work on things that way, it's easier to get through something. It keeps you focused. It has helped me to take responsibility for my part in a relationship. I've experienced a lot of opportunities to change my karma in my love life, in this lifetime. For some reason, that's just what I've got to do. Some people have great fortune in relationships. They meet the right person right away. They meet two or three great guys and all of sudden marry the last one.

I believe, based on the changes I've been through in relationships, primarily because I've had the fortitude to continue and kind of foster better relationships with these guys, what it's done for me is keep me from doing something really crazy, like killing somebody (laughs). Doing something that in the long run, would just be really bad, something that would be life-altering.

When I had my son, I wanted a child. That was life-altering, but that was something I chose to do. If I didn't have this practice, this spirituality, I might do something that would not be the best thing to do. If I didn't have something to keep me harnessed, or to keep me on some type of positive route, it could turn out really ugly. Now, we could break up and still be friends. I'm still friends with everybody.

If I had a partner who could not relate to my spiritual belief, there would be a lot of static, a lot of irritation, a lot of friction. There's a tendency to want to belittle or put down or change someone in their belief systems. You can't do that. You've got to follow who you love and love them for who they are. If you fall short of something that you feel is above and beyond anything that you would ever do, if that's the case, then walk away.

No matter how much I love someone, how impressed I am with him or his spiritual belief, I would never leave mine. I don't think two people have to have the same religion. I think that if what you do is part of you, and is you, and doesn't interfere with that person's lifestyle or belief system, and you two relate to each other, that's all that counts. Be supportive of each other. All you have to share with each other is life experiences and your life condition, where you're at, your character. Once those things match or they complement each other, how you do it, how you get there is solely up to you. A lot of people who have the same religion don't make it. It doesn't really have to do with spirituality; it's how you practice what you do.

The type of business that I am in is conducive to getting along with a lot of different relationships. Whether it is conducive for finding a partner, I don't know. I used to say, "No." Then, in the later years, I've come to see people get together and do well. They get married and support each other. They have children. I think it depends on the people. I think you can find someone as long as they are mature.

I've heard discussions where some men have said that some women are trying to be like men, demanding and controlling. That is probably true. I believe it's true. What they don't like among those women they shouldn't like about themselves. You have to take stock of where you're at. Sometimes if that person is not for you, all those things become real heavy. They tend to be the most prominent things in a relationship, the things that bother you about a person. That's when you should walk away.

As far as women trying to be men, I think we're going through a metamorphosis right now. We're going through some type of change. Some of the things or actions that we're assimilating, or trying to make it in this patriarchal society, you will see women assuming certain role-playing too. They feel that's what's acceptable. That's what other men are looking for, so they can get ahead. So they can secure a financial or business position.

One thing I realize about life in general, everything changes. Sometimes some men want to keep things a certain kind of way. That's not going to happen. There's cross-gender stuff happening. I see a lot of men getting involved in very primary female activity-based things – cooking for instance, designing clothes, occupations that used to be more women-oriented, so to speak. Men have become the status quo in some of these job markets. For women who are climbing the corporate ladder, getting more involved business-wise, it's important. Many women today don't want to play that domestic role. They don't want to just stay at home and be a few things to a man. They have to have their own self-identity. I don't think it's all been worked out yet. I don't think we have a master plan yet. I think things are evolving. Eventually, it'll make more sense in time. Then we'll start evolving again, and things will be all weird once more. It will be something that you can't put your finger on. Looking at someone and judging that person for where they are at is a waste of time. There's nothing you can do about it.

Life in general is evolving the way it is supposed to. I believe that a lot of women would like to be less assertive because a lot of men are not around. They haven't assumed the position, in terms of, quote/unquote, the role-playing of being the male provider, the main provider for a family's economic stability, especially in Black families. Hopefully, things will even themselves out where people are comfortable with the sharing of responsibilities. We're not going to get around that. Either gender is making up for what the other one hasn't done. They are not fully or 100% doing them. It's funny, but until this society finds a way to give people that supplemental support spiritually, emotionally, it's going to be difficult to see one gender being totally one way, or the other gender being the other way. It's not going to work.

I don't see it weakening men. I think they have to get stronger. Women are strong because they've been suppressed. Any oppression just makes you stronger. We know that as Black people. Look at Nelson Mandela. Look at South Afrikans. You push a spring down long enough it's going to pop back pretty high. I don't get why people haven't seen that women have been suppressed. You suppress something, quite naturally it is going to garner some kind of strength. You have to start resisting. Stop resenting. Let things be. Listen and grow and change yourself. The more you repel change the worse it is going to get.

Men don't have to worry about it. They just have to adjust. Women have to do the same thing. Women are doing what they have to do. They are having to do this. If men were doing what they were supposed to do, then they wouldn't have these kinds of things. Men have abused their positions. They have abused their authority. Women are saying, "No, you don't know how to behave. You don't know how to make the position you want the women to be in worth her time." It's a thing of suppression. If it was one of appreciation, "I appreciate the role that you play. I won't take advantage of this. I won't say that I have control over you because I have money, because I go to work every day. I meet more people." Women have had to deal with all those different things. Men don't understand that. It's cruel. It's ridiculous.

I think I'm a product of stereotypes and all that, so when I see a Black man with a White woman, I don't like it. I base this on a lot of what I've seen and heard. Not because I don't think it's right. My brothers date White women. My uncle, my mother's twin brother, is married to a White woman. We have a very mixed family. There's Japanese, Indians, and Whites in our family. I still at times have a problem with it. I think it is because I've been programmed to have a problem with it. Some of my best friends are mixed. My son's best friend is mixed. What's interesting is when you can feel someone's just with somebody else because they feel it shows status, or it shows that they have entered a certain kind of zone. That's like, "Well, okay."

I feel the same thing about the industry I am in. Some Black men, who become stars or whatever, feel that Black women are no longer good enough for them. They want to show that they can pull that kind of woman or they're attracted to that kind of person. If you wear a sticker on your neck (laughs), you are going to get attacked. I don't think people understand that.

If you truly fall in love with someone, that's fine. If it is just something that says, "I can do this now. This is my trophy. This is the new nomenclature, a new broach I am going to wear, a new medal." They are the ones who are going to suffer.

If my son came home from school and he brings home his first love, and she is a White girl, I would have to pray a lot, but I would leave it alone. I've gone through that with my brothers. Bringing home White girls was like, "What's this about?" This happened early on. I've never dated a White guy. I have them as friends. I knew they had other intentions, but I never seriously thought about it, so it was never an inclination.

On the other hand, my brothers were into it. Primarily, because they felt a White woman would be more forgiving, less demanding. Their standards wouldn't be as high. They always felt that with a Black woman they had to have a certain kind of car, certain kind of money. I think we're taught to want those things.

It seems that relationships don't last today the way they used to. One of the elements I think people need is common goals, something to fight for together, something to do together, a common purpose. Nowadays, people don't do anything together. They don't fight together. They don't grapple together. There's really no history, no reason to be together. After you hit a hard time, it's like, "This is just extra baggage," as opposed to someone who means something to you and has struggled with you. You realize this person is important to you because of the way you have handled things together, what you do together, what you build together, what you are able to learn together in particular situations, based on the fact that you have common goals. Maybe we don't have common goals anymore because this person is fine. This person's got money. When it's all said and done, the materialism wears off and all the surface things are used, "I'm not interested anymore."

Sexual involvement, approached in the wrong way, can get in the way of having a meaningful relationship. The way sex is projected throughout society, it's a way to control people. We all know that sex is just sex. It's better after you haven't done it for a while instead of doing it all the time. Teenagers keep going through it over and over again. What adults do, I believe after a while, is that it is not the end-all or be-all. You've got to like the person. This is a person you can hang with for a minute. You can be there to love them if you don't make love at all. What if they can't make love? What if they're sick, out of town for a long time? What are you going to do?

People keep bombarding you. The message that society gives is unbalanced, the programs that we get. The subliminal message that we get is that sex is all that important. It's primarily to control you. It's not that important. It's important for obvious reasons. It's the way we conceive. It's a way we can enjoy loving someone, but it can't keep you together. If there's no love there it gets old.

There are tons of music videos today that project sexual innuendoes. I think the ones who are doing it were influenced that way. Cartoons have tremendous sexual innuendoes. They're just put a little more innocently, but the message is always there. Because of our society, in general, we lack so many standards.

There are probably two things that are motivating the number of teenage births today: the fact that it is a result of unprotected sex, just passion, let's get involved, don't think about the consequences of sex. The second thing is I think girls think it is a way to hold down a man. You get pregnant you'll be involved with them forever. There are a bunch of other reasons, but those are probably two of the major ones.

Some girls didn't get the love and nurturing they should have received as a child and having a baby sort of guarantees that. It's almost like a substitute for lost love. But once they do that, they may realize that they are not really ready for the responsibility. More often than not, I still think it is the first two reasons I gave.

If I was sitting down in a room with a group of girls talking about relationships, I would let them know that a man is not going to make you happy. That's something they have to build for themselves. They really should work on finding out who they are, what they think their purpose is. Based on that, try to strengthen their relationships that they do have with men through strengthening their own ideas, their own values and principles. When they do that, they can determine when something is right, when something is not right, when it's time to move on or do other things, if it's time to hang in there and make it the best relationship. It's important that they do that. If nothing else, they will be able to have a much more valued relationship rather than something that just winds up being a negative, where at the end they wonder why they even did this.

They should always demand and give respect and show that they really appreciate men. It's important not to take advantage of anybody. The more you know about who you are, what you're doing, what you can do for yourself and for others, you kind of avoid stereotypes and learn to appreciate a man for who he is, what their contributions are and how it complements what you two have. To begin a relationship with a whole cluster of expectations and cliques, you are just bound to find out, eventually, what's cool and what's not.

I mentioned earlier about my hesitancy regarding marriage What's important is companionship and resolving to work with someone toward a goal, toward wanting to maintain a great relationship or maintain a certain kind of companionship for the sake of your children. I don't think you necessarily have to get married to do that. People get divorced. I don't think getting married deepens the relationship, per se. It can be very symbolic, very heartening and very endearing. "You did this and it kind of means something."

Basically, what I have seen, it does not keep people together. I have friends who have great relationships that are not married. And there are people who have great relationships who are. There are some who have been married and divorced a thousand and one times. I have more friends in great relationships who are not married than the ones who are.

When children get involved, they know who their mother and

father are. They can say, "This is my daddy. This is my mommy." These people are together. They are building a wonderful home and they are happy. Children know. They benefit from that.

If my son ever approaches me about how to deal with a relationship, I would probably tell him, to follow his heart, go on his instincts. Be extremely respectful and communicative. Be appreciative and loving, supportive. Treat someone the way he would want to be treated. Don't ever take that for granted. If you treat someone other than the way you would treat yourself, it is not going to work. If he could do that, he would eventually find out if that person is there for him, or not, if he really felt that strongly about that person.

Loretta Fuqua

Ms. Fuqua is a 47-year-old professional woman who is divorced and is raising a young son. She is very romantic and can be emotionally needy. She may have a tendency to give too much of herself in a relationship. She seems to be a very sensitive person, which means it is going to take a sensitive man to understand her needs and not run over her – someone who can understand and fulfill her emotional needs, someone who can be that positive male role model for her son. She is the kind of woman who wants to give so much to the man she chooses to love. If her mate does not understand this, he may use it to take advantage of her, which would serve to lower her self-confidence and possibly turn her away from ever wanting to have a relationship again. There are some women who are so gentle that they almost seem out of place in this hard society. She is right on the edge.

I was born in Chicago, Illinois. The 67° below wind-chill factor is what drove me away. My childhood was basically okay. There wasn't anything particularly unique about it. I have an older brother. I guess you could call us a middle class family. We lived in an apartment complex in Chicago that was considered one of the first successfully integrated housing projects. I was exposed to a lot of different people at a young age.

My parents were normal kind of folks. I think my mother was a woman ahead of her time. She was one of those women who was very open, very honest. She didn't mind sharing things with me. My dad was more closed. He wasn't emotionally demonstrative like my mom. I knew he was there. I didn't think he didn't love me, but he didn't know how to show it, physically. He was always there when I needed him. He would be there in terms of my mom's backup. She was the primary disciplinarian, but we knew if Dad found out, that would be our butts. Nothing abnormal, my childhood was cool.

My mother provided a good model for me. My dad, in terms of how I should act with boys or men, it just didn't happen. We didn't even go there. What I learned was mostly from my mother. I'm sure he was good for my brother. My dad raised my brother as opposed to raising me. My mother raised me, although she raised both of us. He interacted more with my brother. I guess it was a guy thing. He felt more comfortable.

I remember times growing up when my father would make statements that just totally missed where I was, what was going on with me. I used to think sometimes that he didn't like me because of it, but I knew he did. When you're young and you're in that situation, you ask, "Why doesn't Daddy do this or why doesn't he do that?" My mother would say, "Oh, you know he loves you. That's just not his way." You kind of accept it after a while.

I could easily talk with my mother about boys. I couldn't do that with my father. My mom and I could talk about anything. We had one of these relationships where she'd come in at 3:00 am with some barbecue, she'd wake me up, we'd sit up, eat and talk.

I think my dad would avoid me. He would sometimes say, "Ask your mother. You go talk about that with your mom." He would always defer to her when it came to talking about boys. He would tell me what not to do. Like, "Don't get pregnant. Don't do this." In terms of discussing a man/woman relationship, no way.

My mother, we never really sat down and said, "Let's talk about boys." It would just come up. Say she was in the kitchen pressing my hair or something; something would come up on the radio. I distinctly remember a situation where she's doing my hair, this song comes on, "If he loves you so, it's in his kiss." I would ask, "Mom is that true? Can you tell if someone really likes you if they're a good kisser?" She would say, "No, baby. Somebody could be a good kisser and not care anything about you. It's more physical than emotional." So I'd ask, "How do you know if someone likes you?" "The way they treat you. They respect you. They don't try to take advantage of you, physically. How you play together. Do you talk about those things that you like?" Our conversations about boys were basically geared around something else that may have brought it up.

I had a lifelong love when I was little. I used to get on punishment because of him. There was like three blocks between my building and his. If I was late coming back from playing, I'd get grounded or something. I shouldn't have been over there playing in the first place. It was all because of him. My mother would say, "You should let him come over here and play with you. You shouldn't be getting in trouble playing with him." She was tolerant. She was patient. We laughed a lot about things regarding boys.

The concern was what good girls don't do. You don't have sex. You don't let a guy feel you up. You don't stay out late. When I became a bit more interested in those kinds of activities, she was tolerant. She knew that my boyfriend and I would stand in the doorway and kiss before he left. She just let things take their course.

I didn't start dating until I was about 16. I went on a quasi date. My dad took me and picked me up. I used to hate that, but he was always there. We never talked about anything related to boys. His concern was who the parents were, what did they do, that kind of stuff. He'd do like the background checks.

When I was a senior in high school, I was dating a guy who was going to college and he wanted to have sex. I came home crying. When I cry my eyes swell. I'd come home and my mother would say, "You were out with your boyfriend?" "Yeah." "He asked you to have sex?" "Yeah, but I said, 'No." "You're upset about it. Okay. You're be all right. He'll still be there. He'll still like you. Don't worry about it." I think that was kind of a threshold for me. I didn't really realize at that time how much my mother knew what was going on without me even saying it. It just made me feel a little more comfortable. Now, as adults, we talk about everything. As I was growing up, it was more of a guidance/direction thing.

My first serious relationship was with my oldest son's dad.

We met in school. He was a basketball player. I was a freshman. I just got there. We met. We liked each other. We started seeing each other. We started dating and stuff. I got pregnant. We stayed together until my son was about three years old. He was physically abusive, so I needed to end that relationship. We're friends today. Then, it was a bit problematic.

The naïve thing on my part, I was trying to get pregnant. It wasn't like it was a surprise, necessarily. I was in this mode of, "Yeah, we're going to be together. We're going to have this baby." I was a sophomore when my son was born. Everybody was up in arms. They'd say, "You're not going to finish school because you're pregnant." But I stayed and finished school. It was rough, but I did it and he was there. We had our ups and downs. I don't think we were both prepared for what we got ourselves into. We did things sort of by the seat of our pants as most parents do.

In terms of our relationship, if there had to be a commitment, we knew we were with each other, but we also knew that we didn't have to be. We could go our separate ways. As things got progressively worse, we did.

When he actualized his physical abusiveness, it was always precipitated by some type of argument. It was usually something I would bring up. It could be a situation where I was trying to correct him or I said something he didn't like. It could be something he did or didn't do. One example was we were in New York at one time. He's from New York, originally. We had gone into the mall and these two brothers – we were separated in the store – these guys came up to him and ran a pigeon peck, whatever the old folks used to call it. People show you a roll of money and say, "Hold this for me." Then that person feels compelled to give them something of value in return. Well, these two guys came up and it worked.

He comes rushing me out of the store saying, "Come on. Come on." I said, "What happened? What's going on?" "I'm holding this money for these two guys. They trusted me." I had bought him this wonderful Longines watch. Back then, that was like a big deal.

"I gave 'em my watch to hold for me, to show them that I was trustworthy. They gave me their money." He's rushing out of the store like he's got something. I started laughing. I said, "You fell for the oldest trick in the book. Who's going to walk up to you and give you their money?" I knew what it was called then, I don't remember what it was. There was a street name for it. "That's one of the oldest cons in the book. You fell for it."

We get out in the parking lot and he pulls it out. He's got a wad of paper cut in the size of paper money, covered front and back by a dollar bill. I'm cracking up. He's pissed. He is really pissed. We get in the car and he starts hitting me, telling me to shut up and stop laughing. These people took his watch, and whatever cash he had on him. He gets angry and hits me.

There was another time when we were arguing. It all centered on him getting angry about something he was saying. He literally threw me across the room and fractured my hip. Whenever he got angry, he would try to lash out, and if I was in the way, I would get the brunt of it.

I stayed in the relationship because I used to think it was my fault. I would think I made him mad and that's why he did it. We were living together and I was trying to finish school. I thought it was best for me to stay so I could do what I had to do and that was finish school. He never hurt our child. He was always nurturing and caring as far as the baby was concerned. I needed the help, basically.

When I graduated, we tried to make a go of it living in New York. I got a job. We were staying at a relative's house. It didn't work there either. He would still have these outbursts. He wasn't as physically abusive then. He knew there were other people in his family around and he didn't want to show that he was abusive. As we got older, the incidences occurred less, but we both knew that the writing was on the wall. I just got tired of it. My options grew. I finished school. I knew I didn't have to stay with him. We had already planned to come to California. That's how I got here. We didn't have any family out here. I always wanted to live there. I had visited San Francisco. It was a little too cold. I wanted to come where it was a little warmer, so I said, "Let's go to Los Angeles."

We moved to Los Angeles and he decided to go nuts again. That's when we finally separated. We had an apartment. He got angry because he found out that I was seeing somebody else. I wasn't sexually involved with this person; I just had a friendship at the time. I've had male friends all my life. This guy went to the same college we did. He was like another friend I knew here. He knew that I would go visit this guy. He knew that I knew him and that he would call the house. One day, I guess it just got on his nerves. He wasn't working, so there may have been some other things going on.

We even went to counseling. That was something people didn't really do way back then. I'm thinking, it's a new place, a new situation. Perhaps things would be okay. They weren't okay. Fortunately, he didn't hit me. He just took it out on my things. Fine, I can get new things. I came home from work one day. He had cut up all of my clothes, cut up all of my pictures, tore up my diploma in little pieces, just real vindictive stuff. Everything I owned, he tore up. He called me at work to tell me he had done some redecorating at the apartment. When I came home and found all my stuff destroyed, I called the police. They escorted him out and I moved. That's how I got away from him.

I went back to Chicago for a few months. I sent the baby to his grandmother in New York. It was during the wintertime. That's why I said that 67° below wind-chill factor blew me out of there. It was a bitter cold. I had gotten a job teaching part-time at Chicago City College. It was good money for like four hours a day. It was flexible enough where I could work out the babysitting situation. I was just trying to regroup. I needed to start over. I decided I didn't want to be in Chicago. I didn't want to deal with that cold weather, so I came back to California. One friend let me stay with her for a while. I got a job waiting tables and doing other sundry things. I was eventually able to get an apartment and I've been here ever since.

Meanwhile, I started dating my husband-to-be in 1985. We

got married in 1990. We were living together all that time, so we said, "Well, okay, we'll get married." We got married and all hell broke loose (laughs). We were together for about seven years.

Prior to getting married, our relationship was fun. We had a good time. I had my place, he had his. It was nice. He was smart. I enjoyed him. I enjoyed his company. I thought that we could make a go of it.

I initially didn't want to get married. There were a few things I was concerned with. He would travel a lot on his job. There were issues of trust and fidelity that came up a couple of times. He'd be out of town two-and-a-half weeks of the month. I was expected to stay home and run the house, make sure everything was taken care of. I didn't have a problem with that. My problem came up when strange women were calling the house. I got a sexually transmitted disease. There was physical proof of things happening.

When he came back, first there was denial. Then I said, "This is not about denial. Let's deal with what we have to deal with here and what we're going to do." I still loved him. I wanted us to be a family. I had my oldest son, we had the baby. We also had his nephew, so there were three young men in the house. There was so much else going on that we needed to work on this. We needed to focus. Business-wise, he was fine, but family just didn't seem to be his priority.

A situation developed that was really the straw that broke the camel's back. I got a call at work from a woman who said she was the mother of his daughter. He supposedly had another child. There was a time when we were separated. He had a relationship with this woman and she ended up having his child. This was before we were married. We had separated. We were still seeing each other during the separation. The premise was we were going to work on the relationship and see where we were going to go. In the interim, he had a relationship with this other woman and a child came of it.

When we got married, I didn't know about it. We supposedly

resolved all of our issues. We went to counseling, premarital counseling with the pastor. He asked us to write down what would cause us irreparable damage to our relationship. He said, "Most Christian marriages end in divorce. What makes you think yours won't?" We talked about what we had going for each other in terms of common interests. We have a family unit and all those other kinds of glorious things. When he asked us to write down those things that would cause irreparable damage, I gave him my list. My husband gave him his. To my husband, it seemed like a blueprint for "things to do today." He went down the list one by one in terms of his behavior.

It wasn't the issue of having this outside child, per se. It was the issue of him lying, and me finding out from somebody else. "If you're my partner, I'm supposed to be your number one who you trust. You let me know what is going on, not somebody out there in the street. If you have an issue or something that you know might blow up in your face, regardless of what it is, I'm your wife. I'm the one you're supposed to deal with it first." It hurt me that I had to hear it from somebody else. To add insult to injury, he's gonna lie. Then he really goes off.

One Saturday he came up to my job. He tried to break into the door with a crowbar. He had both the kids with him. He's crying. What happened, after I found out about the baby – it was a Labor Day weekend – I had talked with this woman. I met her in the park. It turned out that the woman who called was the other woman's sister who was upset because she had asked my husband for some child support, something for the baby. He said, "No, that's not my baby. You can't prove it, etc.," so she called me at my job.

I don't use his last name. I use my maiden name. She called and said, "Are you Ms. so-and-so, also known as Mrs. so-and-so." "Yeah." Then she goes into this thing about this baby that belongs to my husband. I said, "What is it that you want? Why are you calling me?" "I just thought you should know because I know you didn't know." She went on to tell me that she knew when I was getting married and her sister was coming to the wedding pregnant, and all this other kind of crazy stuff. I said, "Fine. You want to talk to me. Let's not talk here. This is my job. Let's meet someplace and talk."

I hadn't said anything to him. I go meet this woman. I told her, "I am going to have my son with me. I have to go pick him up. If there are kids, they can go play on the side and not hear our conversation."

We met. She produces this child that is supposedly my husband's daughter. She said, "I was really afraid to meet you. I didn't know if you were going to cuss me out or what." She turned out to be the aunt, not the mother of the child. I told her, "I don't have anything against this woman. It's an issue that my husband and I have to deal with, but don't call me at my job. If there are any more issues that you have, you address them with my husband. Don't call me."

She said, "I called you because he won't talk to her. I thought you should know about it." "Now, I know. Thank you very much. We'll handle it from here." We were married at this point. I found out about this baby after we were married.

I went and talked with the woman and I'm pissed. He has another son from his first marriage. Both the boys were there. I made sure there was food in the house; I went shopping. I said to him, "Look, there's food here. I packed my bags because I was going to be gone for a couple of days. I just need to get away and think things over."

I hadn't said one thing to him about the phone call. He starts going off, "Oh, some bitch called you on the phone and you are going to believe her." I turned around and looked at him, "Oh, you know what I'm upset about?" "You're going to believe some bitch before you believe me." "I don't know what to believe. I want to go away for a couple of days to have a little peace and quiet and I'll come back. I'll be back. Just let me have these days."

I ended up just going over my girlfriend's house and crashing overnight. We sat up crying, talking about what's going on, what I should do, how I felt and all that. I was basically feeling just betrayed. It wasn't even the issue of him being with another woman. Even having an outside child. I just felt that the rug was snatched right out from underneath me because that was a time when we were really trying to recommit to making the relationship work. To do that, and not tell me this situation existed was like a slap in the face to me. I felt like "Boo Boo the Fool."

All this time, I'm sitting up here talking about, "Yeah, we're going to work on it. I'll recommit. We'll do these things and make everything okay," and then this situation comes up. "You still want to lie to me and I'm the last one to know." I felt betrayed, just a complete lack of trust there.

We even tried to resolve it going back to our pastor for counseling, to have him address this situation. He felt that the pastor was going to jump on me for not being the obedient wife. He thought he would say, "Listen to your husband and do what you're supposed to do. Be a good Christian wife." The pastor looked at him and said, "Why didn't you tell her about it? If you two are supposed to be trusting, why not tell her?" "Because I knew she would get upset, so I never would have told her." "At what point do you think you would have to let her know?" "If the girl was grown and came knocking on the door, I still would have denied it."

This was his attitude. Oh no. This is not okay. We are on completely different pages in terms of what we feel about trust. He didn't think it was not okay. When he goes out, part of his job is to entertain people. He was a professional athlete. They had to go out, and yes, there were women involved. It was just a mess. It was like a real big betrayal of trust. I felt kind of stupid.

I'm trying to go through all these changes to stay with this man and he's not reciprocating. He was not willing to do what I felt it takes. Then he told me that I was being unfair and judgmental, that the baby wasn't really his. I said, "You still don't get it. It's not the issue about the baby. If she couldn't take care of the child, fine. You have a problem. You need someone to take care of this baby? This is my husband's child, fine." We had all kinds of kids in and out the house. That didn't bother me. What bothered me was the distrust, the lies – one thing on top of the other and on top of the other.

It got to a point where I didn't know what to expect when I got home. I didn't need that. I already worked in a field where I'm making decisions. Stuff could happen at the drop of a hat. There's stress involved. I don't need to come home and try to wonder what my husband did today, or didn't do.

There was this one incident. I have a company car that I drive to work. He took the car that I'm supposed to drive for work only, to take one of his friends to the airport. He didn't tell me about it. I'm asleep when he does this. I get in the car the next morning. I opened the ashtray and there's a joint in the ashtray, in my work car. If I had gone to work and they had done a spot inspection or something, that would have been my job.

That wasn't the first time he had done something to undermine my job. These are things your employer looks at you for, "You can't get your personal life together, we can't have you dealing with our clients." Part of my thought was that it was just his way to control me. I thought he was thinking, "If she doesn't work, if I jeopardize this, then I have full control. She'll have to be totally dependent on me." I'm not a dependent person. At least I don't think I am, not in that way. I've always been able to take care of myself, financially. Emotionally, I might be dependent. I just felt that he was trying to undermine what little stuff I did have going.

Like I said, issues of trust and infidelity are two things that are very important to me. I figure, "If we're going to make this commitment, then let's make the commitment and do what it takes, however ugly it may be. It will pass in the scheme of things. There are negotiable issues."

When we made the list of irreparable things, we didn't go as far as to say if he did these things what would happen. Then when it happened, I was faced with, "Now what the hell do I do? Do I want to stay with this man? Do I want to commit to the relationship?"

I told my mother, "Mom, I don't want to stay with him. I'm really upset." She said, "Just stay for the sake of the children, so they'll have a dad, so that they will be a family unit. If you have to, just have an affair. Get what you want outside the relationship, but stay in your marriage." That was her advice to me. "It will be better for the children in the long run." I told her, "I'll try. I don't know." I'm just not from that old school "do or die" kind of thing. I did try to hang in there a little longer, but I just couldn't. It just didn't get any better. I chose to divorce him.

He was very upset. He said that he didn't understand why I would want to leave him. When I sat down and tried to explain it to him, he got real defensive, very emotional, saying that I wasn't being fair. That those things that happened, how did I know that it was even his. Little things like that.

"It doesn't matter anymore. I'm at a point right now I don't know what to believe whatever you tell me. You tell me one thing, you're someplace else. You're supposed to do one thing and something else happens. I don't know what I can count on anymore. As much as I would like to think that it is going to be okay, it's not going to be okay. That's how I feel."

Then it got to a point where I wasn't even in love with him anymore. I didn't want to hear him use the bathroom. If I saw the toilet seat up, I got pissed off. Every little thing he did started bugging me. I knew that wasn't good.

It was really an ugly scene the night I was preparing to move out of our house. He had gotten drunk. He drank like a bottle of Tequila Gold or something like that. He was throwing things up against the wall in the house. My son was watching all this. He's yelling and ranting and raving. I said, "Let me just pack and get my things ready. The movers will be here in the morning." "Why? You're going to have to sit me down and tell me." I knew he was drunk, so I didn't really want to get into it. I didn't know where this was going to go. I called one of his friends, "You'd better come get your boy." His friend said, "I'm not going to get in the middle of you all's stuff."

My husband said, "Tell me. I'm not going to let you move until you tell me exactly why you're leaving." "Let me put John to bed, then we can sit down and I'll tell you everything you want to know."

It was kind of funny to me, because we sat down on the couch and I said, "First, we're going to say a little prayer, because I have to ask for forgiveness, because I'm about to rip you a new asshole." That's what I told him. "You asked me, so I'm going to tell you, step by step. You don't know anything about friendship, trust, loyalty, fidelity, those things that were paramount in our relationship. You just chucked them to the side and I'm supposed to say, 'Okay?' Slap your wrist and say, 'Don't do that anymore honey, because I don't like that?' Not only did it happen once, we're talkin' two or three times. I get a sexually transmitted disease for something that you are going to deny? It's not worth it. It's just not worth it. You are not the man I thought you were going to be in this relationship. I can't be the woman I want to be with you, so we got to go. It's just that simple. We have got to not see each other anymore." I moved out and got an apartment. He sees John as we agreed in the child support arrangements.

When I left, he didn't do anything out of the ordinary. I think his position was that it was my loss. I'm the one who's crazy. His social position was, "She's the one who's crazy. She's the one with the problem, not me." I don't know if it occurred to him for us to get back together. Frankly, I made it clear that we wouldn't even if he wanted to. I wasn't hearing it.

Whatever else he may have gone through, I really don't know. I didn't try to keep track. I do know that he was concerned about time with our son. I told him, "I am not going to deny you access. I don't have a problem with that. That was never an issue with us." The boys were okay. "It's just me and you that had problems. I've made too many sacrifices and done too many things during the course of our relationship for you to treat me like this, for you to ignore those things that were important to me." That was it.

As time went on, he would purport to not know. "I really don't know why. I'm a good man and I'm a good this." "Yes you are, and you'll probably make a great partner for somebody else. I don't have a problem with that. It's just that you and I can't be together anymore." He was absolutely in denial.

When we were dating, everything was great and fun. When we got married, I think his point of view was, "I got you now." I found out later that he had made a comment to one of my friends at the wedding, "I got her now." That kind of flip, "Ha ha, she married me," that kind of thing. He saw it as some kind of capitulation on my part in me marrying him. I guess part of it was. I figured if we're going to be together, let's do it right and make a go of it.

℘

The problems we were having caused my oldest son to freak out. It caused a lot of turmoil. There were two different camps: his side and my side. My son and my oldest son were on my side. His nephew, who he had adopted, was on his side. Being a jock, a lot of the issues centered around who was good in sports and who wasn't, who got what attention because of that. My son was more the artistic type. He liked to draw and paint. He liked basketball, but that wasn't his life. The other was a jock, straight up. All he wanted to do was play professional basketball like his uncle, my husband. They had that bond. My oldest son didn't. If he didn't perform, they would tease him and dog him. I used to say, "That's inappropriate. You're an adult. You're not supposed to act like one of these kids. If there's something he's deficient in, you're supposed to give him guidance and counsel, not stand over there and say, 'Yeah man, you ain't got no game, or you don't have this.'" He would do that with other boys around.

Consequently, my other son felt he didn't have any support

because that's the guy I'm living with. He's there. He's unhappy, so he causes a wonderful scene and goes to live with his dad.

It started when something happened and he was upset. He was just upset about being there in that situation with my boyfriend and I. We had been living together but we were not married. He didn't like the other boy. They got along, but they didn't get along. He was just very unhappy. He would attack me. His thing was, "Mom, you're not doing this and you're not doing that. I'm not getting this." We get into this argument and he called me stupid. "You're stupid. I could just tell you anything. Your boyfriend lies to you and you believe everything he says. Anybody can lie to you 'cause you're stupid." Of course, I went off. Then his father kicks in, "Yeah, you're not taking care of my son and this other man isn't there." I said, "Fine, you want the job?" I packed his stuff up and set it outside and told him, "Your dad will be here in an hour to pick you up" (laughs).

Of course, I'm in tears and crying and all that stuff, but, "I got your stupid." So he went to live with his dad which was okay, but it wasn't okay. He stayed with his dad most of the time. There was a kind of a back-and-forth thing every now and then. Eventually, I told him, "This isn't the flop house. You're in one place or the other. You chose to be with your father. That's where you're going to stay. Maybe you two need each other." His dad really didn't do much for him while he was growing up. Fine. He wants to step in now, great. "You are getting big. You're 6'2". You're bigger than me. You're feeling your oats. You want to stretch out a little bit. Do it on your dad, not on me."

I didn't get any support from my boyfriend at the time. He was into other things. The family issue just wasn't his priority, necessarily. He prided himself in having a family, though. He would say publicly, "I'm such a good family man. I'm a provider and this is what I do." When it came to the daily nuts and bolts, it just wasn't happening. If it didn't seem to serve his purpose or a goal that he had on his mind at the time, then there really wasn't time.

Even at issue now, when my son goes to visit him, he tells me, "He works all day. He doesn't really spend time with us. We're just there all day doing nothing. When he comes home, it's late. We're just there with his new wife." This was always an issue. I told him, "It's your dad. He loves you." I'm giving him the "he loves you" speech. When he can spend time with him, he does. When he does it, it's always these grand elaborate gestures. They do Disney World. Or there's some social thing involved that he's planned around it, which is okay. The boys enjoy it. But those events cause the boys to ask, "What are we going to do today, Dad? Where are you taking us now?" Opposed to the everyday kind of, "Come play with us. Come spend time with us. Come hang out with us." It's not like one-on-one. It's always a time with a group. It's always a situation: "These are my sons. This is my family. What a man and father I am," kind of thing. The opposite happens in the home. He doesn't really interact at home. From what I understand, he still has the same problem. I am still hearing some of the same stuff from visits. Those are issues that are ongoing with him.

℘

I still have my stuff going on with me. I have issues in dealing with men. I seem to have a tendency to – I've been called accommodating, but it wasn't a compliment. It was more of allowing people to take advantage of me. I'm just not real clear in terms of relationships. At what point does being accommodating become a negative? Or at what point does being emotionally needy become a handicap in a partnership?

I just had a relationship with a guy. We were together for four years. We ended the relationship. Some of the issues were my being too emotionally needy, him not being able to count on me for things. One of the things was we were sharing a house together. I said, "I'll do the curtains and the decorating stuff." Didn't get around to it. I just put some stuff up on the windows. I didn't really buy furniture nor do anything like that. I did do some other things for the house.

Refinishing furniture is a hobby of mine. I just haven't got into those things in this particular setting. In terms of our relationship, it became an issue and he asked me to move.

Before that, I had asked him to marry me. It was February 29. I think they call it "Sadie Hawkins Day," where everything is reversed. I said, "Fine. I'll do a little reversal." I went out and got a little token kind of ring, fixed dinner. I asked him if he would marry us, meaning my son and I. He gave me some flip answer like, "Boy, somebody could get messed up if they say the wrong thing." Just a totally inappropriate answer for what we were talking about. I took that as a, "No." Two weeks later, he asked me to move out. When he did, I wasn't surprised. At the same time, I was asking what were some of his issues. He said I was too emotionally needy. I didn't do the curtains. I didn't decorate. He said, "I didn't commit to the house." I have books and stuff in the garage; "You didn't bring your books in from the garage after you bought the bookcases." I'm like, "These are not issues. This is bullshit. Curtains are negotiable. Books only have to be brought in. What are some of your real things here?"

As it turned out he really wanted children. I wanted to have kids. We tried to get pregnant but we didn't. What it came to, "If I stay with you, I'll be giving up my chance to have kids." I told him, "You knew this when we met four years ago. Why is it suddenly a bigger issue now?" At our failed attempts to get pregnant, it was always my failure, then our failure. He said, "Let's not try anymore. It's like an emotional rollercoaster when things don't happen." Later he said, "When I said we won't try and get pregnant anymore, I expected you to really just focus your energy on getting the house together. When you didn't, those things just colored the relationship. You're so needy. I just don't have the emotional energy to give to you and your son."

I'm sitting there thinking, "I'm gone eight to ten hours a day. So is John. Where does all the emotional needy stuff come in?" I'm not one of these cling-on kinds of people who has to go everywhere together, do everything together. He took his vacations. I'd take mine. We'd have time. He had his things to go to. I'd have mine. Those were all things that I thought were okay. We still enjoyed things that we liked to do together. I really didn't see what his point was. But it turned out that I was draining him emotionally. I didn't follow through on decorating the house. The fact that he wanted to have kids.

I don't want to make it sound so trivial, the house and decorating and stuff. Then he says, "It's not that I don't love you. I do love you. I care a great deal about you and I love John. But there are other things that I want to do. It just isn't working out." "Okay." I didn't even argue on this one. That was in March. I moved out in June.

During the course of the relationship, when I stopped wanting to make love to him, he tells me, "It's really turning me off now. That was the one thing I could count on." "Sorry to disappoint you. I'm only good for sex?"

Leaving that relationship really threw me for a loop. By that, I mean emotionally. It put me in a place, "You're too old for this shit now. You need to be real clear on what you want from a relationship, and where you want to go."

Hindsight is 20/20. People show us who they are. We know who they are and we stay in spite of it. Maybe we have expectations that our being together might change something. Even as much as we want to think that, it doesn't. I generally think I am pretty accepting and pretty open. When I see somebody I'm interested in, I can say, "This is something I can deal with, or this is something I can't deal with." If I can't deal with it, and I still want to be with this person, I'll try to put it in a place where it's manageable.

"When you have this little quirk thing, just keep your little stuff over there and I'll put mine over here. And that will be okay.

We'll know that those are your areas and these are my areas." When he would go into his little funks, not working for a while and needed his creative space, I could give it to him. That just meant he could be sitting in that chair and I am over here. He's not interacting, but at least I know he's in the same room. I still have access if I need it.

I don't have to be in your face. I don't have to know what you're doing all the time. "You okay over there? I'm okay over here." That's all right with me. This is where I was questioning, "Where does emotional neediness become a deterrent or a handicap in the relationship?"

It's my feeling that if you're going to love somebody and you're going to be with somebody, it's because you want companionship. You want someone to lean on, to be able to tell your troubles to, sharing your friendships with him and that other kind of stuff. You want that person to be your friend. You want that person to be your confidant. You want that person to be the shoulder at night when you're tired and you're stressed out. If that's not part of being with somebody, why bother?

Financially, I can take care of myself. I don't need that from a relationship. What I need is the emotional stuff that people want, the love, the affection, the attention. It just kind of threw me for a loop. It's like, "Where do I put it without it being put upon? Is it becoming a burden to the other person? What do you do with that emotional energy, that emotional need, so it doesn't become something painful for that person and for you, so you can both get what you want out of the relationship?"

The other part, I guess there is some kind of lesson that I'm not getting. Even when I try to go back over my other relationships, what did I give up? What did I sacrifice? I had to come to terms with the fact that this is the first time I've ever thought about being needy after leaving this relationship. And I am. I am a needy person. I like to be loved. I like attention. I want to be fussed over every now and then. That's what I want. I didn't think it was a bad thing, but when I first left the relationship, I kept thinking, "You know, there's something wrong with you, girl. You haven't got this stuff right yet. If you don't learn your lesson, you are going end up going through the same changes in each relationship." Then I started asking, "Is it that I choose bad men? No. They're nice men. They're friendly. They're outgoing, but something happens during the course of the relationship. It flips or it turns over or whatever."

I'm no angel, but in all of my relationships, there's been fidelity. I never messed around. I'm what they call a "serial monogamist." One at a time is plenty for me. There are some things that you don't have to worry about. You can find me. You don't have to worry about me sneaking behind your back to do something with some other man.

I take that back. That was one of the other issues. He was out of town. I had a male friend come over to the house. It was around Christmas time. He wasn't into the Christmas kind of stuff. I am. My half of the living room had a Christmas tree. My friend came over with his two kids. My son was there. They know each other but he hadn't met my boyfriend. He came over during the time my boyfriend was out of town. I didn't say anything about it. It didn't even cross my mind to mention it. I didn't think anything of it. My son mentions it to him. He says, "Oh, I hear you had company while I was gone." "Yeah. He and the boys came over and we put up the Christmas tree." "What do you think the neighbors may have thought about some man coming to my house while I'm out of town?" "I don't care what the neighbors think. This guy's a friend of mine. What did you think happened with the kids being there and all?"

He felt I betrayed him. Then he said, "I've never met him." I said, "Wait a second. You travel cross-country and stay with female friends I've never talked to on the phone, have never seen. You don't really share their names. I have to trust that you're doing the right thing when you're away with your other female friends. You're saying I betrayed you because I had a male friend of mine come over with his kids while you were out of town. I don't get it. Where is the betrayal in that?

"If I had fucked him, pardon my French, then that would be betrayal in your house. That would really be a bad thing to do." I'd say, "Yeah brother, I betrayed you. A friend comes over, helps me put up a Christmas tree and leaves with the kids. Betrayal? You travel and stay with whatever female friend you want, and it's okay with me because I trust you. We're in a relationship. I can't be worrying about what you're doing and who you're doing it to, and all that kind of stuff when you're away from me. I don't have that kind of energy. I've got other things to worry about. I've got my son, my job. You're the last thing I want to be worried about, because you love me. I love you. We're partners. We're in this together. So we're going to do the right thing for each other."

That was one of his issues, that I had betrayed him by having this guy over. I'm like, I don't get it. I'm just totally out of the mix. I don't understand it anymore. The dynamics of a relationship are eluding me now. I don't know what kind of small talk to make with a brother anymore, what kind of things to bring up. Do I talk about my kids? Do I talk about my age? They say the chances of me getting married; I'd be kidnapped by terrorists first. I'm hopeful, but I still don't understand it.

If I had my way in a relationship, I would first like to see a good solid friendship. I would like for there to be a comfort level where I don't want to sound like a cliché, but that *Waiting To Exhale* premise where you can just go (deep sigh). "This is the man I am with. I know who he is. I don't have to like everything about him. He's doesn't have to like everything about me. We intrinsically respect each other. We trust each other." The genuine affection that is there supersedes "when you get angry with each other." Things are going to happen in a relationship where you are going to get pissed off. There's got to be a common ground or a safe space that you establish beforehand. "Yeah, I'm pissed off at your butt, but that doesn't mean I don't like you. It doesn't mean the relationship is on the line. This is causing a problem in the relationship? I don't think we should stay together. This is upsetting me." It should never get to that point.

"We're going be upset, but we're going to stay together and work this out because we want to be together. That is the bottom line. If you decide to be with me, I will commit to be with you. What can we do when these things come up that may cause discordance? In the final analysis, I'm with you, you're with me. The rest of the world be damned. It's like you and me against the world. You're my partner. You're the one I'm going to be with. The issues, we'll deal with here." Everybody on the outside can see this united front.

In terms of child rearing, one of the other issues he would say is, "That's not my son." I would say, "But you're the primary male in his life. Why keep separating? You knew it was a package deal when we met. You knew I had a son. You knew he was not your child. Why is that an issue now?"

I put everything up front. I hate to say, "Love me, love my child. It's a package deal. If you want to accept the responsibility, if you want the job, fine. If you don't, don't take me and try to not be involved with my son."

Things change in relationships. People change as they age. Some things we might like. Some things we might not like. "If I still love you, I have that genuine affection no matter what, you're my guy whatever it is. Whatever comes up, I'm willing to say, 'let's just work this out.' Let everything else fall by the wayside until we come to a resolution. If we have an issue or you have an issue, don't just let it start tainting the relationship by holding it in."

This brother was bringing up stuff that happened a year ago. "Remember when you didn't do this, or you didn't do that?" "Oh, you're keeping tabs? You're just waiting for the right moment to say, 'This is it, because all these things were happening.' I'm supposed to know by osmosis that these were your issues?"

Both of us being two intelligent articulate people, I figured we could work it out, whatever it is. There are times when you are going to run into brick walls. There are times when you have to say,

"Well, let it go. Is it that important where I have to hold it? Look, if it's making me not like you, I don't want to not like you. Let me let that go then. In the scheme of things is it a really big deal?"

I want to be the one they don't want to lose. I want to be the issue that stays, not the one that goes. I don't know how else to say it (tears of emotion). That's just it.

Right now, I do need the time to be more centered. If you're confused and not focused, for me, it's real easy to get hung up in somebody else's agenda. "You want to do that? I'll help you do that," and then forget what I want to do. The things that are important to me become second. I need to be focused and to become more centered prior to getting into another relationship.

I want a relationship by all means. I met a guy who wanted to get physical a little too fast. "You don't even know me. Why are you trying to put your hand under my blouse? We're not teenagers anymore. I need more time." By then, I'll know exactly what I want in a relationship. I'll know why I'm there.

I'm a romantic. I love being in love. I love the affection, the attention, all that kind of stuff that comes with it. At the same time, I want to be sure that it's what I want too, that the agenda includes things on my list of things to do. I don't think that is necessarily a man's fault. For me, a lot of times, I will put my stuff on the back burner. "You like to do this? I can get you this and I can do that. My time's flexible and I can fit it in." Then forget what I may have wanted to do.

In this last relationship, when my issues came up it was like, "Oh no. You didn't ask me that before." When the whole focus has been on the other person, why all of a sudden when I have needs, wants, and desires, then I become too needy. I become too demanding.

Next time, I want to be sure that they know me up front, "This is who I am. Instead of me trying to fit in your space. You fit into mine." I don't mean that from a negative kind of thing. It's simply that, "This is where I am. This is who I am. If you think you can fit into my afternoon, then I'll fit into yours one day. We'll trade off." At least see me where I am. Know where I am, what I want, and acknowledge that. Then I'll see where you are and we'll work on that too. Just let it be a give and take.

I think in my past relationships I gave too much. I subjugated what I wanted. I'm not a martyr by any means. Don't get me wrong. I gave to the point that I was trying to fit all of my stuff into theirs. I would like for someone to try and fit their stuff into mine. I was definitely into denial of my needs, thinking that if I give you what you need, you'll give me what I need. "I did that for you. Now it's my turn." Then when it became my turn, it was, "You weren't doing this before." It becomes a surprise. It becomes a demand.

I need to get centered, focus more on what I really want. You can't give to somebody if you're not real centered or focused yourself. Things get a little twisted or changed. I know people don't know each other in the beginning and it takes time to develop the relationship. You can see which way it is going to go. I hope to be able to recognize if I'm sitting too much of my stuff in one place. It's never going to be equal ground, but let me have my day too. I don't believe 50/50 ever happens, but one day it just might. One of those months might be a 50/50 month. It might even get 60/40. I might get a little more here (laughs). I would just like for that to happen. I'd like to be able to be clear on what the important issues are. I think I am an important issue. There were times when I didn't. I used to think that the problems were my fault. "If I do this, they'll like me. If they like me they'll want to be with me." It turns out that it doesn't always work that way. It doesn't always turn out to my benefit.

℘

My son has observed just about all that has gone on with me during my relationships. He has his emotional ups and downs. He went through his own separation anxiety from this last relationship.

He's bounced back. He's a good kid. He knows that he's loved. His thing with his dad is already established. He knows that. When I broke up with this last guy, his comment to me was, "First my dad, now this person."

I don't think he was blaming me. I just think he was acknowledging the situation. He was like, "I wish it didn't happen that way. Couldn't you just separate and try to work it out rather than not be together?"

He was trying to think of, "Couldn't you have done something else rather than break up?" He was comfortable. He was okay. Here we go again. Then he asked, "Was he mad at me?" "No." We tried to establish that when we initially broke up. He said, "I still want to spend time with your son." My thing is, "Fine." John has no other male influence in his life on a regular basis, nobody who can come take him out, to go even to the barbershop, which is a traditional guy thing.

I said, "Great. If you want to do that, I'll put my shit aside, my emotional stuff with you aside so you can deal with him. But you are going to have to take him out of the house. You can't be doing it in the house. I still have to work out my stuff with you. I'll be glad to let you have access and spend time with him." There was genuine affection between them. There was a genuine relationship there. I'd rather him have that than nothing.

Unfortunately, as it turned out, the man didn't follow through. He said there were certain things he wanted to do. I made it clear to him, "I am not going to make my son responsible for maintaining a relationship with you. You're the adult here. You asked us to leave. As such, it is your responsibility to maintain that relationship. You say you want to do that, I'm saying okay. But do it." It didn't happen.

Initially, he made the grand gesture. He bought him a set of junior golf clubs because he liked to golf. He told me all these glowing reports that my son has "a natural acumen for the game." Took him one time. That was almost a year ago. The only other times he's come over or called, it would be like a two or three month interval. Then he'll call and ask, "Why haven't you called me, man? When are you going to call me so we can do something?" The one time my son does call to do something, "No man, I can't do it. I don't have the time."

My son was in a play at school. He looks at me and says, "I want him to come to the play." I called and told him what time the play was. He came to the play. We sat together and watched the play. My son's eyes lit up. He was glad to see him. It just hurts my heart to see that. It was not that this man didn't like him, it's just that he's not ready to assume the responsibility. Number one, it's not his child. That was an issue during the course of our relationship. He never treated him badly. The man's remarried. He wants to start a new life. He wants to start a family with this younger woman who will supposedly be his hope for the future.

I told him, "I don't know how my son is going to fit in this new situation." His thing was, "I've made it very clear to her that I love John. He is like my son. I'm going to be spending time with him. She said it was okay." I said, "If it's okay with her, I guess it's okay with everybody. Just as long as he is okay." He's old enough to tell me if something isn't right. If he was younger, I wouldn't let him. Now he's old enough. He can communicate.

There was never that consistent time that was talked about. I'm not sure if I wanted it to be anyway. Initially, I'm thinking this is best for John. He needs a male role model. He's not a bad man. So, maybe they could maintain a genuine friendship without me being directly involved, or mostly involved with it. I kept trying to rationalize it that way. As I see it not happening, I'm becoming bitterer about it, in terms of the unfairness of it. The man couldn't commit to me, why in the hell would I expect him to commit to my son? This is kind of par for the course in terms of his behavior. It's just that my son is dealing with his own separation anxiety.

One night, about a month ago, we're sitting in the den watching TV. He says, "Mom, you know I miss my dad and I miss

John. But it's okay. I'm all right." Those were his exact words. I looked at him, "Really. I'm glad to hear that." "I miss 'em and everything. I know I get lonely for them sometimes, but it's okay." He looks at me and says, "I just want to know if you're okay. Do you still miss them?" "Yeah." "Do you ever wish you were with my dad?" "Sometimes I wish that things would have worked out between me and your dad." "Yeah. Me too."

They've both gone on and married different women – in the last relationship, in a really short span of time. We broke up and six months later he's married.

I'm wondering what lesson I am giving my son by these successive failed relationships with these men. I don't want to teach him that people are so easily replaceable, that partners are so easy to find. Men are going to grow up knowing that women are going to be 5-to-1, 10-to-1, whatever the ratio might be, that they can have their pick. I also want him to know that it is important that you keep one person, that you commit to the relationship, though I don't have anything to show for it.

I was with this last guy four years. Before him, seven years. There haven't been a lot of men in my life. The two relationships in his lifetime that he's been involved with have failed. I don't want to put him in that position again. I do want to be careful. I do want to make sure that I am centered and focused, that it will be the right person – someone who is willing to accept the fact that he is there and the responsibility that he is there, to be able to say that "Yes, this is my son. Yes, we're a family."

It takes, to me, a big person to do that. It really does. I know it's difficult. I'm thinking, "Maybe I'll meet a man that already has kids, so he'll know that part is out of the way. They'll know what goes into childrearing, parenting, how to fit things in together. The juggling that somebody has to do to accommodate dating. Then we can have a nice friendship and maybe a nice permanent relationship. This next one, I do want it to be for keeps. I don't want to go into old age with one successive relationship after another. I think I would rather be by myself and just date. Let it be a matter of convenience as opposed to a long-term relationship.

Loneliness is something I deal with a lot. I read a lot of books. It depends on my mood. Sometimes I'm struck with inertia, I can't do anything. I just sit and mope or space out. That happens more often than not. Other times, I find something to do. During the course of the day it doesn't bother me because I'm busy. I have other things to do. When my son is in bed, I'm sitting here channel surfing. A romantic movie might come on, or I'm listening to music with an old song that I like, then I start feeling nostalgic. I start feeling like I want somebody to love and all that good stuff. I just kind of sit down and stare out the window, fantasize about what is going to happen next time, or what I used to do with the person I used to be with. "I remember when so-and-so and I used to do this. I went down there with so-and-so," things like that.

I call myself using the time as a constructive, getting focused and centered kind of time. When I'm sitting here in these quiet moments, I'm really doing this self-examination. "These were the things that worked the most. What was I doing to make them work? These are the things that didn't work. What happened so that it didn't work?" That kind of thinking. Of course, being the perfect person that I am in all of these relationships (laughs), it's always their fault.

There are times when something goes wrong that it is definitely my fault. Sometimes I am not too tolerant. I can be real acerbic, real sarcastic. I think my mouth gets me in real trouble. Rather than try to sugar coat something, I'll just say what I'm feeling sometimes.

My worst enemy is this accommodating thing. I acquiesce too much. Sometimes I say, "We'll do that," when I really don't want to do it. Then I might not like myself or I feel bad that I didn't follow through with what I wanted to do in the first place for fear of being rejected, for fear of not being accepted in terms of this person who's in full support of whoever my partner might be, or not be.

That's where I am my own worst enemy.

This neediness to be liked or to be wanted, I sometimes put myself in a position where I do too much. I don't know anymore what doing too much could be. I guess it differs. I'm the kind of person if I'm in the store and I'm shopping for something for me and my son, I see a T-shirt or a polo shirt that I think my partner might like, I'll get it. It's no big deal, no special thing. "Here, Hon, I was in the store today and I picked this up for you." I'll write a little card or something if you're going out of town. I'll stick a card in your suitcase, just a little love note or something like that. I put it under the pillow, a flower, stuff like that. I enjoy that kind of stuff. I think sometimes it could be misinterpreted.

Sometimes the other person will feel, "Now I have to get you something." It becomes a "What's the occasion? Why'd you buy this? What'd you get me this for? I don't need it." "Just because."

If they don't do the same, that's never been a bone of contention for me. First, it doesn't happen that often. I see it for what it is. It's something that I wanted to do. It's something that makes me feel good. It might not necessarily be that person's thing to do those kinds of things. I provide it because I like it. Ultimately, it's not a bad thing. The other person gets enjoyment out of it. It was primarily for me. I never bring it up in terms of, "I got you this and you didn't get me this."

I do know that sometimes that becomes a problem, particularly with finances in a relationship. Part of the issue was, I didn't own the house but I paid half the mortgage. I did that because I was going to be there. We were going to get married. These were things that weren't issues for me. "I'm going to be your wife anyway." That was my thinking. When it came time for me to move, I stopped paying on the mortgage.

In the last situation I was in, ownership was a big deal. "This is mine. This is yours. This is what you pay on this. This is what we do here. We split this and we do that."

It became an issue when I wouldn't offer funds at one time.

He had a car wreck. He needed to get a new car. I wasn't paying on the mortgage at this time because this was when we were on the outs. He said, "You didn't even offer me money when I crashed my car. You knew that I hadn't worked in a while." I said, "I also knew that you had money. You went out and bought a new car. You didn't ask for money from me. I figured if you needed it, you could ask." "You should have offered." He had no trouble asking me for money before, if he needed it. When we did the groceries he'd say, "Go on and give me the 50 bucks." We'd split whatever we'd spend. I guess finances could be a bone of contention.

Another thing I may have done wrong, I don't know if it's wrong or not, because it was my son and I in the relationship, I tried to not make my son his responsibility in terms of finances. Buying him new clothes and, "I need this for John. I need that for John." I got everything John needed. I paid the tuition. I took care of the childcare.

If we were going out, he would arrange for a sitter. He would do things like that and pay for the sitter. In terms of the everyday, when he did buy things for him, it was by choice. It wasn't like, "I got to get this, or I got to do that." It would be, "I picked this up at so-and-so for John."

We would decide jointly if it was a birthday what to get. The main responsibility was on me. He was my son. Those were issues he didn't really have to deal with. I'm thinking, I don't know if that was a mistake or not, but it was part of my way of accommodating. Like, "Yes, this is my son, but I can take care of him. I was taking care of him when we met, so why should I stop taking care of him?"

When I think about all that I have gone through in my life and if I had to sit and talk with some teenage girls about relationships, I'd try to tell them to respect themselves, to know who they are, what they want in a relationship. To be as clear as they can about commitment from that person. If they're going to decide that this is the person that they want to share their life with, to get the commitment, for them to be in a married relationship as opposed to a live-in relationship.

As old fashioned as it may seem, I would advise being married and hold off on having kids if they could, let them experience some things first in their lives, educational and career goals prior to committing to a family. They could be married but wait to have kids. It's kind of rough. Get to know themselves and their partner.

I'm not saying that living-in can't work. The thing about living together, you always have in the back of your mind you can walk whenever you want to without having to worry about alimony, child support, or whatever. I think it kind of undermines the sense of security. That's why it became an issue for me in the last relationship. I wanted a commitment. I wanted this person to stand before God, the world, and everything else and say, "This is my wife," as opposed to saying, "This is my lady."

Makeda Shareem

Ms. Shareem is a 21-year-old single university student. She is very intelligent, aware, and more confident about herself and her future than many young women her age. She represents the typical trials and tribulations that a young female college student goes through. Her early life has had a great influence on how she relates to men. Tragedies she has had to face with father figures in her life have had an astounding sway in how she has shaped her attitudes towards people. Even equally, is the importance colorism has played in her life. The issue of light skin/dark skin has infiltrated her normal behavior. She is unique in how this plays out in her everyday reality and the way she makes friendships and relationship choices based on her internal beliefs about color. She is living proof that some of the remnants of slavery still haunt us, even with a very young intelligent woman. There is no doubt that she will be successful in whatever occupation she chooses in her life. She is a very strong-willed individual with a competitive nature that drives her to be the best.

I was born in Los Angeles, California. My childhood was very stressful at times. It was my mother and I at first; my biological father was not there. She remarried around 1981, then I had a father. That was good. He accepted me, I accepted him. It was like he was there from the beginning. He was murdered when I was nine years old. He was killed the day before my birthday. First, I didn't believe it. I didn't understand it at first. I was turning nine. Two detectives came to the door. I was home by myself because my mom was at work. It was me and my brother. I knew not to let anyone in, and when they said they were police officers, I called my mom, and she called my grandmother. My grandmother just got home from work, so it was made to seem that she ran to her house to get something. It was the law at that time that you couldn't leave underage children alone.

I was just, like, shocked. They didn't tell me at first. My grandmother called my mom to tell her over the phone that she needed to come home. He was missing for about a week. When she came home, they told her, the two detectives. Two white guys. When they told her, she just screamed. Then is when I realized that something happened. Later, she told me he died. I didn't find out that he was murdered until last year. It was always something that wasn't discussed. It was that he died but we never got into how. It was funny, my brother was the one who told me. He asks more questions than I do. If I see that it is a delicate subject with Mom, I don't pursue it. My brother's like, "What happened? You have to tell me." He found out. He told me. That's how I found out a year ago.

It affected me a lot because I was real close with him. I used to go everywhere with him. He was a carpenter. After school I would go with him to his projects. I was just always around him. Every birthday we went to the House of Pancakes. That was my favorite place to go. I knew that was not happening anymore. That kind of hurt me. It played a significant part.

I kind of grew to where I got a little meaner. I kind of built up a wall. I did it because it was like someone leaving you, which people are going to have to leave, sooner or later. To not feel that emptiness, I would not let anyone get too close so that when they leave, I'm not in shambles, crying and upset. I really never took anyone seriously, relationship-wise, because I knew they were going to have to go, sooner or later.

Now my mom was back into being a single parent and now with my brother being born, she went back to school, and that's how I got stressed. That's when the stress came about. I was left in charge a lot because with her going back to school, trying to make more money and maintain the house, I had to watch my brother. I couldn't just leave the house like I used to, to go outside and play. I had to make sure my brother was okay, maintain the house until she got home from work and school. She started school while I was in the sixth grade and finished when I was probably a junior in high school. She went to three different colleges. She completed everything. She did what she had to do to reach the level that she felt she needed to reach.

The only role models I had regarding relationships that I could reference back to was my mom and my stepfather. It was a very loving relationship. They used to always throw Halloween parties. They were very active, always smiling. I reference back to that. It was short, because they were married in 1981. I was four and he died when I was nine, so that was five years that they were married. I saw the arguments, but it was never physical. It was basically regular marriage arguments. They always patched things up. It was never kicking him out of the house or him sleeping on the couch. It was usually discussed and they came to agreement by night.

Based on their example, I do want to get married. I do want to have the two little children, the husband, the wife, the house, and two working parents. I think their example has some input on now. It's kind of vague. As I get older, I seem to forget. It didn't fade away, but it is not as bright as it used to be. Then with other influences and how I feel relationships should be kind of contradicts some of the values that they had.

I had my first relationship when I was 14. When someone showed interest in me, that's when I actually started being interested in boys. I was always interested but I never pursued anyone. Usually, I would say that I would maintain a friendship. I figured a friendship would last longer than a relationship, until someone showed interest in me. That's when I would return, I guess, affection towards that person.

My first real serious relationship was my last one. It was my first real relationship where it crossed his mind and it crossed my mind that this is a person I don't mind being with. I didn't see any flaws that would prevent me from being with this person. Right now, we are a little apart, but still together, if you understand what I mean. We had irritations, but you can live with irritations. That's simply your values, what you believe in your behavior as opposed to theirs.

We met at a food stand where he worked with some friends. I was going to school for a loan entrance interview. I was riding the bus then. He was in the food stand and it was burning hot. He tapped on the window and said, "Come here." I was like, "Okay," there was nothing he could do because he's in the food stand. It had glass and everything, so he can't do anything to me, so I said to myself, "Okay." He had a big old tall glass of lemonade. I was burning up hot. I was just sweatin'. He wrote a little note. It said, "I hope this quenches your thirst. Maybe you could call sometime," and left his number, and left it as that.

Then I wrote, "Thank you for the drink, maybe you could call me," and I returned his number. He left it to where I didn't have to give him my number, or felt threatened that, "Well, I gave you this drink. You have to give me your number." From there, he called me. I called him. It was nothing really serious.

That was the one time I went to school for an entrance interview. That was during the summer. I just needed to complete the process for my loan. Until then, I started working two weeks before school started. That's when I started getting serious with him. Not physically, but kind of like, I'll give him some of my time instead of just talking with him on the phone. I would see him.

Overall, it's progressing. He's maintained the same way since I met him. For myself, I'm starting to trust him more, letting down the walls, like barriers, letting my feelings show. If I feel a certain way, instead of waiting for him to tell me, I say it. For a long time he would say, "I really care about you." And I was like, "Okay. I hear you" I wouldn't return it. Even if I was feeling it, I wouldn't return it for fear that he would see how much I cared about him, turn it around and try to use it against me. Now, slowly, I guess I'm letting down these little barriers and walls I have.

I've been hurt in the past. I didn't want him to use that

against me, knowing how I felt about him, to see if he could try to take advantage of me, just to determine if he was playing games or not. From what I've seen, some guys just like to say all the right things, not actually having the actions to support it, but just feel that is the thing to say. They will just say anything.

All the little hurts I have gone through do not compare with the one I just went through. When I used to attend a college in another city, I met this guy during the summer. We got along. It progressed real slowly. I was supposed to move in with some of my friends, but that didn't happen because of some misunderstanding, they said it was. So, I moved in with him. By that time we had already established that we were seeing each other, that we were going to see each other exclusively.

My mom approved of it, that's why I continued to stay with him. With me living with him, I saw him in a different light. He abused drugs. With the abusing of drugs, his whole mental state of mind was different every day. He wasn't the same person every day. I was in school and I was working. I was paying half the rent, trying to contribute as much I could. Him, on the other hand, I guess he considered himself a hustler. The streets were his office. His clients were the other abusers. It was like an abuser selling to another abuser. He was doing that.

His whole attitude would change to where it would affect my schoolwork. I'm not understanding what's wrong with him until later. "Oh, he's doing this." I didn't know this until after I moved in and at that time I had no other option. I've been around people who have done marijuana. It's just a high. They get hungry, they get sleepy, plain and simple. They act the same way each time they do that. What he was doing, I guess they call it "sherm," I've never been around that. I've heard about it. I've never been around a person like that. He was paranoid all the time. He wouldn't eat. He lied. He did everything. I started noticing that. He wouldn't come home for about two days. I wouldn't talk to him. That whole situation was just terrible.

I moved out once. He said he was going to change. Of course, just like everybody, you go back, "Oh, he's going to change." He tried to, I guess, act right. That only lasted for about a month-and-a-half. We got into an argument concerning money. I was the one working. I was the one going to school. Where he got his money I didn't even ask. He took that as if I was going into his business. Long as it went to pay the rent and put some food into the house, that's all I was worried about. All I was concerned about was finishing school. That was my whole thing, and just having a place to sleep. It stopped me caring about him, trying to maintain this household, put something in my stomach and have a roof over my head. That's all I cared about. So, if I had to put up with his stuff, I just had to.

Then it got to the point of him not coming home all of the time, and women calling and harassing me, saying they were going to kill me. I was, "Oh, I can't deal with this." I asked him, "Do you want me out?" He would say, "No, no, no." I made several attempts where I told him I was going to leave. "We can still be friends. But I'm going to leave." That's when he got possessive, "You are not going to go. I'm going to track you down." I'm like, "Oh, okay. Let me just stay here."

One night we got into a big old argument, I said, "Okay, fine. I'm making enough to split rent with somebody, but I'm not making enough to hold an apartment on my own. I'll just stay here until the end of the fall semester and I will move back home." He agreed upon it, but when his moods changed, he wouldn't remember what he had told me.

Another argument came to where he told me, "You have to leave." At that point, I am fed up with his moods. Everything else in my life was going decent. I was getting good grades, I enjoyed my work. Work was sometimes stressful but I could deal with it. It had not become a pain. He was the only thing in my life that was upsetting it. He left, called my mom, who was at home in another city, and told her everything that he said to me. She said she's coming down.

The difference from where she was added up to about three hours. I swear she came in about an hour-and-a-half, two hours. She came and got me, got all of my stuff, and I came back to her house. I had to explain to her that I cannot risk getting "W" (withdrawals) or incompletes this semester. It wouldn't be fair to me, and then transferring to another school, they would want to know what all these W's are. I would have to send an appeal, satisfactory progress appeal, and do all this stuff, so I told her, "Let me just stay there for now. I need to at least finish this semester. Let me finish this semester and I will come back home and transfer to a college closer to home."

She allowed me to go back to school. On going back, I moved in with a friend who was familiar with the situation I was going through with him. She let me stay there. I had to stop work because by missing those two days, they didn't fire me, but they laid me off. I was without money, I was without food. I had only a certain amount of clothes. I had probably the last two checks to last me so I could wash my clothes and eat. I stayed there for about a month-and-a-half. I passed all my classes. During that time, I think I did better in my classes than I did when I was living with him, because that stress in my life was gone.

Staying with him though, I was not doing well in my classes. I wasn't grasping the concepts of my classes. One particular class, social statistics, I had to re-teach myself the whole course in two weeks so I could take the final. I was going from a D to an F, but having to re-teach myself, I passed that class with a B+. I had to re-take tests, all in a matter of two weeks, and then take the final. I got the same kind of grades with my other classes. After that, that last week after school, I just went home.

During that time he knew where I was so he stayed in contact. My fault was staying in contact with him, not really severing ties. Eventually I did. Even when I came back home, it was hard for me to sever the ties, but gradually it was easier. He still kept calling, which kind of messed everything up, lying to my mom, saying I was doing this and that during the time I was supposed to be over my friend's house, which I was. He told her I was over his house spending time with him, that I lived with him, that I really didn't live with the girl that I said I did. That started a whole little argument between my mom and me, trying to make it seem like I was lying. He called me one time and I asked him, "Why did you do that?" He said, "I don't know." He did it on purpose.

Out of all my relationships, that was the worst. All the other stuff I could handle, the little breakups, little stuff, little high school stuff. That was the biggest thing I have had to deal with.

It was unusual for a mother to give her daughter permission to stay with another person of the opposite sex, but she said that I am strong-willed and I am going to do what I want, regardless. She let me do it, but she has always said, "We're going to help you find another place." She knew that I was there, but she knew, deep down, that's not where I wanted to be. I was there because there was no other way for me to find another place to stay. She was constantly trying to help me find another place. She would constantly say, "Come down here. Come down here." So, I had that, "Come down here," and I had him, along with trying to go to school and go to work.

She never really approved of it, even now she references back to it, "I never wanted you to do that." So, I knew she never wanted me to do it, but she knew that I was gonna do what I want. Her being in another city, I was kind of out of her reach. Another factor is, the year before, she paid for me to live on campus to prevent me from doing something like that. When this academic year came up, she lost her job. She knew she couldn't help me as she had done in the past, the two years that I attended, so she kind of didn't know what to do. She didn't really know anybody there. We didn't have family in the city I was in so there was nothing she could do. She just kept telling me to come back home, but I was so set in my mind that I didn't want to come back home. That was another problem, to where she couldn't stress that while also trying to find another job. She still had my brother, the house, and the car to worry about.

I played sports before and I always wanted to be first in everything. This probably shows in my personality and relationships because I feel I should always be right. What I say goes. If you don't think so then you should leave me alone. That's in the relationship I am somewhat involved in, but I'm trying to not feel that way, to where now I accept his opinions and his thoughts. I try to take that into consideration before I just up and say something. Usually, it's me disagreeing with him. He will just say, "Okay." He doesn't argue with me. He just sits there and looks at me.

Our last discussion was regarding his work schedule. I'm upset about it. He works for a transportation company. Before, he was part time. He's transferring to full time. With transferring to full time, I guess to see how determined he is to going to full time, his company puts him on any old route or time to see if he would take them. If you do not take them, it counts against you in transferring to full time. He really wants to be a full time employee. They will give him a 3:00 am schedule and he just came off of work a few hours ago. He will take it. Now with that, I don't know his schedule. "I'm upset because you're not available to me. I don't know your schedule. You're just gone all of the time. It's not right that your job wants you to come back and you just got off." To me, it's not right. They're just using him. He's like a little Guinea pig. "Since he wants to be full time, we'll going to make him pay." I don't appreciate that. That was the basis of our argument.

He says, "By me turning full time, that's going to help us." He's more us, us, us. "I'll have more money and I can do more things for you. I can help you." He always includes me. I'm like, "Okay." That was basically my argument. He just gives me the benefits of him being full time. I give him all the reasons why I don't like it. I'm not saying full time is not right. I'm just saying the way they are going about it is not right. "I don't have a schedule. You're

not there for me. You don't pick me up from school anymore."
That's my whole argument.

I have no disagreement with him personally. It's just that he's concentrating all of his energy into his job, whereas when he was part time, most of his energy was all into me. That was like the beginning of the relationship, where I guess he had to win me. I figure now that I am at the point where he wants me to be, he's like not ignoring me, but not spending enough time with me.

Sometimes I use my energy towards being on top with school and my friends. If I wasn't as pretty as them at least I was going to be smarter than them. It's really concentrated more with my friendships with different girls.

ℓ

When it comes to the issue of skin color, I chose my mate based on this color complex that I have. I usually talk to dark-complexioned guys. I will not approach a lighter-complexioned Black guy for the simple fact that, perhaps he doesn't feel that I am as attractive as a light-skinned Black woman, so I don't approach them. I usually go towards the darker-skinned guys. Though some light-complexioned guys have approached me, I really don't take what they say seriously. I figure it is a game. 'Cause I feel, "How could you be interested in me when two guys before you thought I wasn't attractive, so what is your reason now for talking to me? Are you playing games with me?"

Dark-skinned guys are more sincere. Though I have met some who are not, out of the majority they are more sincere than not, so that determines how I pick my mate. The guy I am seeing now is dark-skinned. That's the one thing I noticed about him. That was the first thing I noticed about him. I didn't even notice that he was working in this food stand when he first approached me. "Is that what he does?" I didn't even think about that because a job's a job. It was an honest job to me so I didn't even pay attention to that. The first thing I said was, "Oh, he's dark-skinned. Okay, check, I'll talk to him. Or, I will approach him." That was the first thing.

As far as my friends, all of my friends have been light-complexioned. Not because I choose it, it just happened that way. We had something in common. I really do not have a preference for what color my friends have to be. I just know whatever it is, I have to be better than them in something. I guess to feel validated.

I guess this started when I was small. I lived on a block where there were all girls on one side. There were all boys on the block behind us. We ranged in colors. There were two lighter-complexioned girls who were sisters. Then another girl who was light. They all had long hair. Then there was another girl who was a little darker, a little lighter than me who had long hair. Then there was me.

We were friends, but out of all of those girls they didn't see the difference between us. I did. I never brought it up to them. I never really understood it, being as small as I was. I bring it more to their attention now. I always knew it was a problem. When the boys from the back used to come they would regard me, "Oh, she's just a friend. We can run. We can fight. We can flip. We can play and all that stuff." But the other girls, they were girls. I was a girl, but I wasn't like them. They would tell me, "Oh, I really like your friend." They would treat me more as a homegirl, and treat the other girls as, "They're delicate. They're girls." That's where it came from. It all started from there.

Then there was school. We all went to the same elementary school. We all went to the same junior high, though I was the oldest, only by two years. It started in junior high. As I got older it started to get more severe. Until that time, until the boys from the block came to distinguish what was different about us, I never really paid attention. They were my friends. But when someone else came and told me, "You're different," that's when I said, "Well, maybe I am." That's when I started noticing that I was different.

I remember in the second grade this guy used to make fun of me. I never knew why. I would never see him. I used to sit and wait for my stepfather on this cement bench. This boy came by and saw me and all of a sudden started making fun of me. I think he was in about the fifth or sixth grade. I never understood why. Each day after school, because that was what happened every day, I would hide from him. He would always find me. Not like he was personally looking for me, but we would always run into each other. Every day he used to bother me. I never knew why.

I mean he wasn't ugly, but he wasn't nothing special to me. I just remember that boy always bothering me. I never found out why. I think he graduated. I remember asking my mom, "Mom, I want to walk home." I didn't live far from my school. I started walking home; therefore I could avoid him. "Hurry up and leave," so I used to hurry up and go right after school.

My color complex has made me feel inferior, has made me doubt myself. I kind of ask myself sometimes, "If I looked this way, how would things be?" I daydream that if I was to look a certain way how would my life be? Usually in these daydreams I have more things because I am like this. I don't do it as much as I used to when I was smaller, now it's, "If I had this much money, how would I be different?"

Before, it was if my hair was longer, if my eyes were lighter, if my skin was lighter, I would probably have more things. I would have been introduced to more things. I probably would have more friends. Certain little things like that.

Today, because of this, and being aware of it, I don't approach people. I am never the first one to try and open up to someone and become friends with them. They have to come to me. I kind of stay more to myself. I can't wait to get home.

To a certain extent, the inferiority thing is there. Then I will say, "This is what I have. Try to improve it. Just work with what I have. Dress up with what I have." When I do decide to get all dressed up, I tend to put more emphasis on "Well, I have to fix my hair this way. I have to look a certain way as far as my clothes." I wear makeup. That seems to make me feel better, in a sense. Then after a while, I get tired of the primping and stuff. I usually just want to, I guess, be me.

I have not discussed this with the guy I am seeing. It's funny, he told me of a situation because he's dark. He's a little bit darker than I am. He told me about things he went through when he was little. He tells me things he goes through now. One time, just recent, when he used to live with his parents, he had a family with a father, a mother, grandparents, and their children. The parents of the children used to tell them that because they were light, they were better than his mother, him, and his nieces and nephews. They were all dark. His mother is dark. He is dark. His nieces and nephews are dark. He was telling me that he was having a conflict with them. I was like, "For real?" We never really discussed it because that hurt him.

A lot of times he makes reference to himself like, "Oh, I'm dark." It makes me mad. I'll be like, "Shut up. Don't say that." When he does that, when he talks down on himself, it makes it seem like I picked an ugly guy. He says it like he's deformed, like no one would want him. That kind of makes me feel like, "You're with me, so what are you saying about me?" When he talks about that or degrades himself, I don't approve of that. I say, "Don't do that. Shut up. Why would you say something like that?"

I don't see anything wrong with it. I particularly like his dark complexion. He's dark and he's clear. His face is clear. It's just pretty to me. We usually don't talk about it because I know he's dealt with that in his past, and I've dealt with it in my past. I usually don't try to discuss that.

I just now told him the topic for my research paper (light skin, dark skin) which he was surprised. He was, "Oh, for real? Why would you write something like that?" He asked me, "Does that really go on?" I said, "Well, you just explained it to me two weeks ago a problem you had when you were living with your mom. You know that problem goes on. What are you asking me?" "It really goes on? It's really a big topic?" I say, "Yes. It hurts people's feelings. It's wrong."

When talking with my friends, they're like, "That's how you feel?" They don't see me as that. They just see me as their friend, plain and simple. They never paid attention to my complexion. They never ever mentioned it to me, until I started talking about it. They would say, "Why would you think that way? Why wouldn't you talk to us? If I didn't talk to you, you weren't going to talk to me about it? That's not right." They go on with that.

℘

When I get together with my girlfriends, probably one of the main issues we talk about is how Black women are portrayed in music videos, how a lot of Black men feel like they can't have a relationship with a Black woman because she's too strong-willed. She's demanding. She always wants and never gives. Those are the biggest problems I see between the Black woman and the Black man – that a woman of another race is more compatible to them than their own race. That affects the Black woman because it's like you're saying, "You came from a Black woman, so you're saying your mother is not good enough?" It's like they're down-talking their mother. "Your mother's Black, and you're with a White woman? You don't like your mother?"

I started noticing that in college. Every now and then, as you go further out into the city of Los Angeles, you see interracial couples. You never really see it in urban areas, as what they call South Central. You don't really see that. I guess they know not to come down here because it's less accepted. But the further you go out, the more you see it.

In college, you experience different things, different people. So of course, you are kind of like, "Hey, she's interesting. Let me see what's up with her." Women do the same thing. But I feel more Black men do it than Black women. You rarely see an interracial couple with a Black woman and a White man, or a Black woman with another race. You hardly see that on a campus. If you do, it's one couple. It's one noticeable couple. There might be other couples, but they don't do it on campus.

You will see Black men on campus parading their little White girlfriend for that period of time, or their Asian girlfriend, or even a Hispanic girlfriend. They parade them around sort of saying to the Black women, "She's better than you. I find everything I need in her. She understands me. Though we are of the same race, you don't understand me. She does. She accepts me. She takes care of me. You want me to take care of you, but she takes care of me."

I don't know how other Black women feel when they see a Black man with a White woman. When I see it, it kind of makes me mad. Like, "What do you see in her? What does she have that you couldn't find in a Black woman?" That's how I see it. Some Black women I talk with, it doesn't bother them. They say, "He's probably worthless anyway so it doesn't matter." That's how most Black women I've talked to see it. Others I've talked to feel that it's like degrading to the Black woman - seeing a Black man with a woman of another race.

As a 21-year-old woman, when I look for a man, I feel he should be doing something with his life, as far as working, going to school, or both. He can do both. I don't like laziness. I don't feel that he should always be at home. There's always something you should be doing as far as work. You should have some kind of activity going. That's my biggest thing. I don't feel he has to support me. I can go out and work. We are in a day and age where a woman can go out and work. She may not make as much as he would, but she can work and take care of herself. I expect him to be able to take care of himself, being responsible if he has children from the previous relationship, taking care of them. In this day and age, there are a lot of men who have children from other relationships. They should maintain that household, keep your children taken care of, even if you are not with them. Even keep the lines of communication open between the mother of the children, because you are dealing with your children. Just take care of your responsibilities. Be active. Go to work. Go to school. Do something that you can be proud of.

My goals are basically no matter what I do, I want to be able to take care of myself. I do not want to have a man to take care of me. I can be married, but if I wasn't married, I still want to be able to take care of myself. I don't want to have to be married to have to survive. "That's the sole reason I am with this man, then I will love him. And then we have children" I don't want that. If we were to separate and I have children, I could take care of them.

Whether I get into the desired career that I want, I just want to be able to take care of myself. That's my biggest thing. No matter what I do, whether I am a police officer, an engineer, or whether I work at McDonald's. If I can pay my bills, that's all that matters.

I know that in the old days the woman was totally dependent on the man. I'm not saying there are no good men or there isn't a man available or a man that meets your criteria. You are going to be forced to take care of yourself no matter what. You cannot depend on him. I know that I cannot always depend on a man to always be there, to take care of me. I'm stuck with myself. He's not stuck with me. He can divorce me. He can leave me. He can die. He doesn't have to be with me if he doesn't want to. Because I know that, I know that I have to take care of myself.

As far as my mom and my stepfather, though there were two incomes, all of the money that they made went into the family. When he died, it was one income. I know things are going to happen where a man is not going to be there. Whether he dies, whether he leaves you, whether he divorces you, or even goes to jail. My mom couldn't let the house or her children all go into shambles because he died. She had responsibilities whether he's there or not. She wasn't always married to him. It was me and her before. She was taking care of me and her then, now she has to take care of me, my brother, the house, and other things. I know that a man is not going to always be there.

I am not planning to be with a man temporarily, but it's about being prepared. I don't like surprises. Someone dying or divorcing you just out of the blue, it's like a surprise. You know how they put Black men in jail for nothing. I don't like surprises. I like to know everything. My mom says I'm nosy, but I like to know where I'm about to go. I want to know why I have to go there and when I am going to come back. I want to know. I don't like surprises.

As far as a man and woman staying together, it is in hopes of getting married. I figure that's your goal. When I stayed with that guy, before I knew about the other things, I knew that we would eventually get married or remain together and have children, you know, do all of that. I see living together as trying to reach the goal of getting married. It's leading up to that. You may have skipped over a couple of steps. Instead of marrying, you lived together then you are going to get married. I see it all linked to that.

I am aware of the moral violation people feel. It seems that more people accept it now. As each generation goes on they tend to accept it more and more. It's just the norm.

Now that I have lived with somebody else, I don't choose to live with anyone else. I'd rather live by myself, just to have my own space. I am not ever going to be put in that predicament where I can have someone tell me to go. I'd rather be the one to say, "Oh, you can leave my house," or, "You can go." If we both agree, he's going to go to his place and I will go to mine. I would never, without carefully thinking about it, move in with another person.

I would have to think about could I really deal with his habits? How he is? It's different from being together when he lives at one place and you live at another. When you live with each other, it's like everything is in your face. You see how he is day in and day out. I don't disagree with it, but right now, I am not for it. I was never for it when I had to do that. I just figured that was something I had to do to stay at that school. I wanted to stay at the school I was in at the time. There were no other options that I felt I had. It was something I had to do. It was not something I really wanted to do.

If I was talking to a group of girls about relationships, I would tell them not to rush relationships. They will happen. Feel good about yourself. Respect yourself before you go into a relationship. Don't expect him to give you the respect you should have for yourself. Don't expect him to always be there. Being in a relationship, make sure that he respects you and treats you right. If he doesn't, don't be afraid to leave him. Don't always be concerned with what he might feel. It all depends on you. Are you happy? Don't stay in a relationship just because you are worried about him. It's your life and if you are not happy, what's the point?

Shanté Lewis

Ms. Lewis is 42 years old and single. She works as an administrator in the health industry. Her ability to overcome devastating circumstances and lead a normal life is astonishing. If there is any result of things she has endured, it may be that she is content in not having a man. This may be partially due to the absurdities of her young life. What she went through could have had more devastating effects than they did. And then later to experience having to terminate a life could have put her in a negative mental state of no return. The fact that she was able to survive and make something meaningful of herself is a testament to the fortitude of her spirit. She is an example of a person developing options for herself that enabled her to grow and evolve as an independent and conscious human being. What is amazing, that despite her past, she is still voluntarily helping others.

I was born in Los Angeles, California. My childhood was very interesting and not unlike a lot of what children are going through. I didn't realize that I was part of the terms describing some kids today: being a latchkey kid, or being abused in some ways. My abuse came in being with a dysfunctional family and sexual abuse. I experienced sexual abuse from family members when I was about five or six years old until I was 11 or 12 years old.

I didn't realize that I was being sexually abused until I got older. Around five or six I didn't know. I was too young to perceive what was happening to me. Because I was not hit or physically injured, other than sexual, I didn't perceive it as being harmful. When I did become aware of what was happening, it affected me in terms of my self-esteem. It affected my growth as a child, a teenager, and as a young adult. As I got older and learned more about what took place, which was actually sexual abuse, I felt like damaged goods.

Growing up, I just dealt with it. I became more of a cautious person in my dealings with people. I think I am more standoffish, more distant, in terms of being with people. I didn't really trust people. I didn't really trust relatives, which is a hard way for a child to grow up. It hurt me in that way.

Male cousins in my family were the ones initiating the sexual abuse. My mother dropped us off to her cousin's house because she had to go to work. We would play, but play would turn into something else. It would turn into sexual abuse encounters. When I became aware of what was happening, I didn't tell anybody. Unfortunately, I don't know why. I guess it's the same thing that I see other young children go through now on television, documentaries, or who are interviewed. They are afraid or they fear that they have done something to bring it on. I believe I had the same feelings. I didn't inform my mother. My mother raised me. She was a single parent early on. She got divorced when I was very young.

What brought it in the open, when I was around 11 years old, a girlfriend of mine who happened to be spending the night informed my mother because I wouldn't tell her. I was too afraid to tell my mother, so she did. The sexual abuse was with my younger cousins. It also happened with a cousin that was more my mother's age. He was left to take care of me and my younger brother and sister.

My recollection of how my mother reacted when she found out is real vague. I know she was concerned, but I don't remember her being terrified by it. I remember her keeping me from those relatives after it was told to her. She did not follow up with any legal proceedings.

In my adult life, it has made me apprehensive. In some ways, it's kind of unusual. I feel like I've been blessed in a way because of how I grew up and what I've experienced as a child, as a teenager, as a young adult. I've had relatively normal relationships with the opposite sex, nothing too abnormal that I know of. I know I'm a bit more cautious because I had low self-esteem. I'm pretty sure that hampered a number of relationships that I've had.

Going through the sexual abuse was just part of my early negative experiences. The rest of it was the non-support that I had within my family. My family was basically dysfunctional. My relationship with my mother was not very close. She was the head of the household because she divorced early. My perception was that she did what she was supposed to do as far as being a mother. In terms of being nurturing and having the affection that a child needs when they're an infant all the way up through life that was absent. Because of that, I sought it from other people. Hence, I do have what you call "play mothers." As I grew I found them. They became my extended family who in times of need became my base of support. They helped by nurturing me or giving me what I needed that my mother could not give. They supported me emotionally.

Things that I could not discuss with my mother that I could not speak to her about, I could speak to them. My eyes were opened up to a bigger world through them. I could live beyond my block. I could see further than my neighborhood through these people. I was given what I needed to feel that I was a worthwhile person, that I wasn't all that bad, and that I wasn't damaged goods. They made me feel that I was good enough. That's what I received from my extended family.

℮

I became interested in boys early on because of my peers. I remember having affection for a boy in grammar school. I was, like, imitating other kids. You do what they do. I had pretty much a normal childhood. I know it sounds weird, but it was kind of like Dr. Jekyll, Mr. Hyde. There were two lives going on. I experienced normal childhood, but at the same time, I dealt with a lot of problems once I got home.

My mother was one of those types where she had to "keep up

with the Joneses," not so much in terms of financial, because we didn't have the money to do that. But giving a facade that everything was okay with the family, even though it wasn't. I perpetuated the same thing in my growing up, unconsciously, just following the same pattern.

It's hard for me to explain because I have good memories of my childhood. I can remember my school days. I can remember somewhat having good interactions or relationships with boys, being interested in boys. All throughout that time, from being a child to my mid-20s, I was still not feeling good enough, that I was not right or something was wrong with me. If I didn't get the attention like some of my girlfriends did, it was okay. I perceived myself as not being totally 100% like they were. That was always in the back of my mind. I still feel, especially in conversation with others, like I had a pretty normal childhood, though.

I got involved in my first serious relationship when I was in high school. I was in about the 11th grade. What attracted me to him was not so much something meaningful. When I was a teenager, I had some of the same attractions that some of my other girlfriends did. The boy had to have a certain build. They had to be physically attractive in certain ways. Besides that, I liked a gentleman. The boy I met happened to be a real gentleman. We went on events. He was involved in a lot of things. With him, there was no sex. When I was a younger teenager, throughout my late teens, I didn't experience sex too early, or too frequent, I should say. Being a gentleman was my first attraction to him.

We were friends before we were actual boyfriend and girlfriend. He was a very caring person. We maintained a friendship for as long as we possibly could, but I believe I was too young and he was too mature for me. He needed more from me than I could give or was willing to give at the time. Our relationship lasted almost six months.

After that, I would be involved with what you might call normal relationships. For me and some of my girlfriends, we had maybe two or three boyfriends at the same time. None of them were really serious, in terms of being sexual.

Now that I think of it, there was one relationship that was serious, prior to the boy who was a gentleman. I was going to Catholic school. That was my first sexual experience. I think I was 15 or 16 years old. It took a while for that to happen. Eventually, it did. We kept a serious relationship on and off. It started when I was 15. It kind of maintained in that status for years, until I was around 21.

The third relationship was at a religious school that I am currently involved with. I met someone in that organization and we became serious – serious to the point where I was going to get married, but I wanted to wait until I graduated from high school. I met him while I was in high school. I met him in the 11th grade. We maintained a relationship throughout my last year of high school.

When I graduated, we planned on getting married. For some reason he became very possessive. I don't know if it is something innate, or because of what I experienced, or part of my personality. It is hard for me to kind of distinguish. But I am not one to, quote/unquote, be dominated. I believe in coming into maybe a compromise. If you're right, then you are. If I am, that's fine. Someone who feels like they need to control me because I am a woman, or because we're together as a couple, that has never sunk in to be right with me, even when I was younger. This person, after a while, became kind of possessive. That led to the downfall of our relationship.

Unfortunately, in that relationship, I became pregnant. I became pregnant towards the end of it. We were together for about a year-and-a-half to two years. At first, I had decided to have the child. I was still living with my mother. I was not going to tell her until it was too late. I was going to wait until the third month. I was about 17 or 18 years old at this time.

A friend of my mother's happened to notice my body changing. Certain parts of my body were more accentuated than the others and it was developing very fast. He brought it to my mother's attention that, "It was a possibility that she could be pregnant." He stopped me to ask me. I said, "Yes."

My mother's reaction was about 180 degrees different than what I thought it would be. Because of my relationship with her, I felt that she would throw me out of the house. She didn't do that. Instead, she came to me 180 degrees to the left, or to the right, whichever, and says, "Well, you don't want to make the same mistake that I did, or go through what I had to go through." My mother had me young. She had me when she was 17 or 18. "I want you to be able to go to school, go to college."

Because she approached me that way, and I had never experienced that with her, I took to heart what she was trying to convey to me. Someone had offered to pay for an abortion. With some time and thinking about it, I made the decision without discussing it with the father. I decided to have the abortion. That really led to the demise of our relationship.

I had asked him to wait on marriage. He asked my mother for my hand in marriage. He could tell that she didn't like that, because she wanted me to go on to school. I told her that I was going to go to school anyway. She approached me when he asked for my hand and asked if I was pregnant. I was not at that time. We just planned on getting married. I understood where she was coming from. I was just getting out of high school. I knew nothing but part time jobs. He had a full time job, but I didn't think it was all that secure. I figured maybe we should wait and allow ourselves to get more organized and stable, get more financially together. He didn't like that. That was one of the things that led to the demise of the relationship, besides the fact that I decided to terminate the pregnancy.

When I was going through the procedure of having the abortion, I was very scared, afraid, not knowing exactly what I was doing after waiting so long to make up my mind to do it. Like I said at first, I was determined to have the child. Because my mother found out about it, that was one of the main reasons why I decided to have the abortion.

Something else comes to mind. I've had experiences of fainting spells when I was a child, as young as the fourth or fifth grade. The last one ended up being an epileptic seizure. The reason I bring that up, the doctor said that could be a factor in my pregnancy. I don't know if that was done to help deter my decision to have the child or what. It seemed to be a concern with the doctor. The fact that I had seizures and I had to take medication for seizures that could be a potential problem. Given that, the other circumstances, and talking with my mother, I decided to terminate the pregnancy.

The significance of what I did, terminating a life, not too long after doing it, I thought about it. At the same time, I don't know if it is a mechanism within your brain, but it kind of helps you get over certain things. It is filed in the back of my mind, though. I found myself, either consciously or subconsciously, thinking about how old my child would be. Feeling that I should know or not know what the sex of the child would have been. Knowing how old my child would be now. That, I believe, will forever stay with me. I've never had to worry about safe sex, in terms of preventing pregnancy after that. I never want to go through that experience ever again. I always make sure that I have the appropriate contraceptives, regardless of who I am with. If they did or didn't, I made sure that I was appropriately protected, so that I would not have to endure or go through the experience of an abortion again.

My last serious relationship lasted for about three years. That was another close call, as I call it – close to being married. It started off being okay. It was sort of like playing house, you know, when a couple gets together and they're really idealistic about getting their lives together. You meet someone who you feel is serious enough to be with, to marry and start a life with. It started off like that, really good. It had its rocky periods because we discovered that our personalities started clashing. I know that I discovered that perhaps this wasn't a good thing for us, getting married, even though I was approached about it and had desires for it. I know I didn't give an answer right away. I waited.

Because of my experiences in relationships, I've been alone for about twelve years now. Also, I do not want to compromise. In life, you go through different stages that help you grow, despite some of the negative experiences that you go through, if you're blessed enough you survive them. You learn from them and gain some type of wisdom. I think I've done a lot of different things related to relationships with the opposite sex, either compromising too much or giving more of myself then maybe the other person was doing. I would overcompensate for the other person. Maybe I was getting into relationships that were not so serious, but not giving enough of myself for them to work. I would reveal to a person what I wanted and then do just the opposite, having it reciprocated almost 50%.

I've done the gamut when it comes to relationships, as far as I am concerned. I think I know what I'm looking for, but I know what I don't want. I'm not willing to compromise. Because of age and experience, you're not going to deal with certain circumstances as you did when you were younger. Then, I was naïve and didn't know. But now that I know, I approach things differently. I really haven't found what I feel I want or need in a man.

With some of my girlfriends, I kind of have three different descriptions of the male gender: there are young boys, there are guys or males, and then there are men. Many of those who think they are men really aren't. I seem to observe more young males who think that they are men or have a perverse definition of what a man should be.

I don't know if it is this region. I know I have actively gone out to seek a mate, which is not what I want to do. I'm the type of person who believes that if it happens, it happens despite if I'm going out partying or going to a bar, what have you. I believe it will happen in a place I don't expect for it to happen. It's not something that I actively seek. In my description of different categories of the male gender, I run into too many of the other characters, other than men. A male, who is a man, is a person who is his own man. He can think for himself. He's not trying to impress me just for the sake of impressing me. We can just talk, communicate, and have fun that way. That's something that is innate within him. That's part of his personality. He would do that with any woman or me whether she is an older woman, younger woman, or what have you. He's still a gentleman.

When it comes to loneliness, I primarily deal with it through friends. Friends are an active support. I get involved in different activities such as concerts, or getting together with those that have the same compatibility or outlook on life helps.

After my last relationship, I gave myself a vacation for about a year before I thought I'd get involved with anyone. I got involved in an Afrikan organization that did me a lot of good. It helped me heal and helped me grow in terms of being a whole person. I sought and seek things that help me as a person.

Being in the organization had a definite effect in increasing my consciousness as an Afrikan person. It made me think about things I never thought of before. It helped me think for myself, gain knowledge, process that knowledge, and get an understanding on my own. Sometimes with different Afrikan organizations, it's trial and error. If you're involved long enough, depending on how intelligent you are, because I was a very naïve person when I was younger. For me, I eventually saw some of the mistakes, downfalls, or pitfalls of certain organizations. You learn to kind of table, put things on the shelf, and use what's good for you. You know what to assimilate, what can help build you as a person. You learn how to put certain things on the side that do not enhance you as a human being. It can aid your consciousness in telling you what is right or wrong.

The organizations I was involved with helped me a great deal in being a person. Even to the extent that had I continued with my last relationship and had gotten married, I don't think I would know as much as I do now, or be the person that I am today. I think it would have hampered my growth. Our personalities were different, even though I was kind of attracted to him. I thought he was somewhat Afrocentric. But as time went on, I found out that he wasn't as serious a brother as I thought he was. He was more materialistic, putting it lightly. He was more involved in his business ventures than he was anything else. This helped lead to the demise of that relationship. I didn't mind his focus and hard work, but I was sort of like a sideshow in his life.

Knowing what I know now, if I was to meet a man with no Afrikan consciousness, I think it's possible that we could get together, if that person shows willingness or is open-minded enough to discover or investigate. That's what I needed, using myself as an example. Unless I was open enough to investigate and check out things for myself, I wouldn't have continued with the organizations that I did. If that person has the same openness or willingness to investigate or check things out or at least give it a chance, there could be some hope. If he's open to grow, in terms of knowing who he is, knowing the history of his people in order to not make similar mistakes in the future, I think it's possible we could get together.

Although I have friends and I am involved in different activities that counter the loneliness, there are times when I do fantasize about being with someone and sharing myself. That happens frequently. I'm a normal, healthy person and I'm not a eunuch. I think over the years I've dealt with it. I'm presently involved in a religious school that helps me greatly. I've been involved with it since high school. I've gone through my growth period, in stages, with that too. Being young, there are a lot of things you cannot appreciate because you're going through that stage. If you stick with something, in my case not so much me sticking with it, I think it stuck with me, you learn.

I am not going to say that there are not times when, yes, I

fantasize with either having a family or being with someone. Even if my convictions were different and we weren't suffering from so many diseases, I said this to some of my girlfriends, that maybe I could be casual with someone. But in all honesty, I really can't see myself having a casual relationship. There doesn't seem to be anything fulfilling about that.

Dealing or getting to know yourself, or trying to be your own best friend, especially because of what I have had to deal with, is a common practice with me. When I was a child, I had to be my own best friend. I've had to deal with certain situations alone. I don't know, but I think it's an automatic mechanism. I believe definitely that the Creator is the one who has put that for me to do. It's like a mechanism that comes in and helps me when I need it.

Like I said, because of my convictions and because of how I perceive what's out there for me, I'm not in a big hurry to be involved with someone. I see a lot of everything that's out there. I see men who are confused maybe as much as I am sometimes and probably groping trying to find themselves. I see a lot of things that say that I would have to conform or be a certain way in order to be attracted to a man, which I am not willing to do. I don't want to say that I've gotten lazy with my approach to men, but if it's meant to happen it will happen.

I don't really see myself seriously getting together with someone that I don't know ahead of time. We would have to establish some type of relationship, other than intimate. Establishing a relationship of being friends first. I know that sounds kind of clichéish nowadays, but for me, it's very apropos. I would definitely want to know the person. If that were to happen and my attraction went further than just friendship, nature would just take its course. But that hasn't happened.

I really can't explain other than what I've experienced in my past, why being with someone is not a priority in my life. All I know is, it's not. I'm not saying that I will never be serious with someone of the opposite sex. I have reconciled within myself just as there are people who are married, or not married, or people who get together and have children, that's not for everybody. There are single people in life, single people who are not gay, which I am definitely heterosexual. I am not willing to compromise on standards that I have for myself. I am not going to force myself into a relationship that doesn't feel comfortable. I feel that eventually it will happen if it's meant to be. If it's not, it won't. I have been able to deal with being alone since my last serious relationship. I'm dealing with it fine now. I can deal with it in the future.

I have gotten to a point where I am kind of comfortable with being to myself. Maybe I should say, since that relationship in 1986, I have had an off-and-on semi-relationship with someone I dealt with in the past. I feel like that is normal too. But within both our minds, we knew that nothing serious was going to come of it, even though I believe he wanted it to be a little more serious than I did. Somewhere in between that period of 1986 and now, closer to the past though, there was a semi-relationship, but not really serious. All it did was confirm the fact that he wasn't it either. But after all that, I am pretty comfortable with being to myself.

℘

As I observe male/female relationships today, I really admire the ones that last, especially here in Los Angeles, and what they're faced with, year by year, season by season. It's very hard to maintain a relationship here. It's not like I've lived anywhere else. I think I'm mainly going by hearsay and what I've seen from other states that I've visited. In other states, where they maybe experience all four seasons, people depend on each other a little bit more. They seem to be closer in terms of a community. There seems to be more seriousness related to commitment. Here, which is known as "La La Land," there's more distractions, more distractions that take you away from what should be a priority to you, in terms of your family.

I really admire the couples who do stay together and who are committed to each other. I feel like it is a struggle out here. To me, that means that they are both strong people. You see a lot of couples who get together and break up frequently like they did in high school.

A lot of our children watch television. It seems like they study what's on television. They go to the movies and tend to imitate what they see. They grow up thinking or socialized to think that commitment is this, or they have a perverse definition of what commitment is. When you don't have a strong family background or unit, your definition of what a commitment is could be vastly different of what someone else's is.

I see a little bit of everything out here. I think, if anything, diversity is not just limited to a person's ethnic group or nationality. Diversity is also how a person is socialized, or their perception of things. You see it played out every day. It amazes me what relationships actually do last. You see some relationships you just know they will not last. They start off being shallow, but through some effort on their own, they get stronger. For whatever reasons, they stay together.

When I look at my case and reflect on any models for relationships that I may have had when I was growing up, other than the religious organization I have been involved with, there were no models for me. My mother was divorced early. The person she was divorced from was my stepfather. I never knew who my real father was. I really don't have any strong male examples in my family. The uncles that I had, that are decent, those that I didn't feel were a threat in terms of trying to approach me sexually or abuse me, were in different states. I could respect them for being just that, a relative who was in different states, and we never got together that often. As I said earlier, the sexual abuse that I experienced was from relatives and they were cousins from my mother's side, so I don't think I really had a healthy or very good male example, people to look up to.

I think that not having a strong male model has affected me in relationships. I've had advantages and disadvantages with that. It has helped me because I have survived what I've gone through. It has made me more of a dominant figure, I guess, compared to other women. In a way, that has made me a little bit more intimidating. I will stand up for myself. I will not compromise on certain things.

It's hard to really evaluate that because I haven't had any strong or positive male figures in my relationships or in my life. I've always had to fend for myself. I tend not to depend on men to help or support me, even when they're trying to be gentlemen. It's obvious that I don't encounter men that often. If they're trying to be a gentleman, I feel kind of awkward in situations, until I can see with him that this is normal procedure. Once I see that this is part of his personality, I eventually acclimate to it. I guess I kind of have a schism when it comes to that. It's kind of weird for me at times.

The only couples that I know of, that I could feel good about who were strong and I could relate to, were people involved in the religious school that I am involved in now.

Probably one of the most intimidating factors to men that women have today is being assertive. After that, being self-sufficient, self-supportive, having a mind of your own. To me, that should not be intimidating or threatening to anybody. I won't say especially to men. I would think that, especially these days, that some men perceive women or ladies being money grabbers or what have you. When you run into something that you're looking for, then you're afraid of it, well then that's a problem they have to deal with. Maybe there's some type of insecurity there. I find those to be certain factors that define intimidating, and things I have observed.

Other female intimidating behaviors I see that affect men are women being professional persons, having a higher education, handling things on their own either because they had to or they set off to do so on their own, regardless. It doesn't diminish the fact that they are still women and want to have a man with them. It seems like that would be an asset to a relationship. For me, it would be an asset.

Financially, I am not anywhere close to where I want to be, but at the same time, I can support myself. I'm not looking for a relationship with a man to support me. I believe that certain things are automatic.

We both know that you need to work or find some kind of way to make money. You have to do certain things in order to make it in this world or this society. That should be an automatic thing that you would go and do, because you're going to do that on your own anyway. To me, that's a given. What I'm looking for is support, emotionally. Important to me than anything, that would be the greatest thing to find. Along with that comes who I am, who I had to be. Not to say that I want to lay all this heavy weight on a man, but at the same time I want him to know who I am. I've done that. I tried to let somebody know certain things in my past so they would know what they were getting into. If I seemed to be a certain way, or maybe my self-esteem was low a little bit, and they couldn't deal with that, maybe I laid too much on him. I've been with people who could deal with it.

Men have to realize that women do not just automatically appear and not have a previous life. They've experienced different things that make them who they are today. If this person has experienced life and has survived certain things in their lives and still came out smelling halfway like a rose, still have all their faculties together, then they should appreciate that. To me, that's something to appreciate, not let that be threatening or something to fear. You have to observe the person, but observe the person and see that what they have is something that could enhance your life also.

When my girlfriends sit around and we talk about men, when it is all said and done, it basically comes down to commitment. Being able to find someone you feel comfortable with, someone you can trust and be yourself with, someone you can be honest with, someone you don't have to hide be apprehensive or inhibited with, it all comes down to that.

I can only imagine what took place with women who gave up on men or who are led to same-sex relationships. Even though I can't condone same-sex relationships, not only because of religious convictions, maybe I shouldn't bring that up. I just don't see it. I don't understand it for me. But at the same time, and I don't know if this is part of a schism, I can understand it with some women. I am a woman and I have suffered at the hands of men. I've seen the abuse some women go through. If it wasn't with me, within my family unit that it took place. I can see how it would lead to lesbianism.

For some reason, homosexuality between two men, to me, and I don't know why I bring this up, it is more horrifying than it is with two women. I don't know if that is because I am a woman and I can understand and sympathize with why women are doing what they are doing. I am not of the mind that you're born that way. If I'm wrong about that, that's something the Creator is going to have to show me, clarify in my mind.

From what I've seen, and women who I've known who have gone that way, it has been due to the abuses that they suffered from men. I sympathize with them. I understand. But for me, if I had to go outside of my particular ethnic group to find someone, if that was what I needed to do, then I think I would do that before I would get involved with someone of the same sex.

That's been a topic within the circle of girlfriends that I have. That's been discussed also, dating or marrying someone outside of your particular ethnic group. Some can see it and can do it. I see them do it and I can understand that, just like I understand the thing about women who become lesbians. At the same time, I know it's not for me. Something within me tells me that I couldn't do that.

I went to a high school that was basically almost half-and-half, it was still more White. It was all around me. It's not like I was naïve or ignorant of that. I've seen some of my girlfriends or schoolmates date people of other ethnic groups. It was something that was prevalent and could be done. I've had a friend who was male and he was White or European. We got real close. I could tell that he wanted us to be more than just friends. I wouldn't allow it because I felt uncomfortable. Even though I think I really did try. He wanted me to kiss him one day like he was my boyfriend. I just couldn't do it. Why I couldn't do it, I couldn't tell you. I wasn't that conscious at that time when I was a kid. My consciousness, as far as knowing about my people and myself came very late, compared to some of my friends, early to mid-20s. It's not like being conscious, or being Afrocentric was an obstacle at that time. It was something other than me. It was something that was within me that would not allow that to happen, so it just didn't happen.

As I observe relationships among young people, unfortunately, I don't see healthy relationships developing. Part of the reason stems from what they have as role models and what they perceive as being typical boyfriend/girlfriend relationships. The lack of love or attention that they get is not adequate among many of them.

I am in a position to see quite a few young relationships. I see more interracial relationships coming about because of a lack of self-esteem or a lack of knowledge of self. Fortunately, with those who have a strong mind or a strong family background, I do see some successes. It's hopeful for some. I don't see a majority. I feel that some of them will develop good healthy relationships because they've risen above what they've had to deal with in this society. I don't see that being a high percentage, though.

When I see the results of some of these relationships, that is, young girls having babies, that varies too. I've had a chance to encounter some who are either late high school or first or second year of college. I've run into a lot of young women who had their children in their mid to late teens, for whatever reason have decided to continue their education and raise their children at the same time. I really admire them for doing that. I try to encourage them. Even though they've had children young, that's something that's already taken place. I do not believe in discouraging them or putting them down because of them having children at that age. I encourage them and make them look at what they've accomplished so far.

I also know young women of the same age group or younger

who are having children just because it's the thing to do. They get involved with the negative elements in the hip hop environment or whatever their peers are in, and they're just doing it. It's almost like they're going to a store and buying a baby doll and not really realizing the seriousness of circumstances of being responsible for another human being.

Unfortunately, I also see, and this is strictly from my eyes, that though there are young women having babies, it's still one of the ways of repopulating ourselves. I really don't see a lot of older adults my age, or women of mid-20s having children, at least not having more than one. Unfortunately, I see the young women repopulating our particular ethnic group by cause and effect, because we need it.

The downside of this, women must have a level of maturity and good parenting skills to raise healthy children. Most of them do not have this, so they are probably not going to raise healthy children, emotionally. They themselves are children. They themselves have too many complexes. The only way I can see these children surviving or coming up healthy is only by the blessing of the Creator, and the Afrikan saying, "It takes a village to raise a child." Unless there is an extended family, I really don't foresee the future of those children being very good, or even their mortality lasting that long. Their options are very limited.

If I were talking to several young people about relationships, the first thing that comes to mind, and I don't know if this is the right thing to say, but I would say to, "Respect yourselves. Respect who you are as a person. Get to know who you are individually first before you decide to deal with someone else seriously." Depending on the age group, it's okay to be curious about the opposite sex. Curiosity is healthy. That's a stage in life. Along with curiosity, going even further, comes responsibilities. I would especially emphasize with the young ladies that they really need to respect themselves, because they are the conduit for the future. Without women, there is no future.

In the same breath, I would tell the young men, "If you see that there is no future without women, because all young men came from a woman, why can't you give them respect? The mother's egg was fertilized. She carried you for nine months. She gave birth to you. She's the first person that will nurture you. She's the first person that you see. So what kind of respect should you be giving young women? Especially for those who you see yourself raising your children with. You really need to think about that.

Have more respect for yourself and the opposite sex, whether it is your mother, your girlfriend, or your grandmother. You should see, at some point, all of them in the same light." That is the best I can offer them for now.

About the Author

Kwaku Person-Lynn is a native of Los Angeles, a husband, father of five sons, and grandfather of two. Professionally he is a historian, musicologist, educator, author, filmmaker, and radio producer. He has published two books: *First Word: Black Scholars, Thinkers, Warriors, Knowledge, Wisdom, Mental Liberation* (Harlem River Press, New York, 1996) and *On My Journey Now – The Narrative and Works of Dr. John Henrik Clarke* (California State University, Northridge, Department of Pan African Studies special edition of *The Journal of Pan African Studies*, Northridge, California, 2001). He is currently working on other works, including some 200 articles, essays, and book chapters. In the early 1980s, his dissertation chapter "Rap Music – Afrikan Music Renaissance" was the first scholarly publication on rap/hip-hop and has been published in several books and on the Internet.

In the early 1970s, he was a record producer for A&M Records, the first Black recording engineer at the company, and only one of four Black record executives in the country. He was also founder of the Malcolm X Center in Los Angeles. He received his bachelor's degree from California State University, Dominguez Hills, his master's and doctorate from UCLA, being the first person of Afrikan descent in the history of UCLA to graduate from the Individual PhD Program, requiring two majors (Afrikan World History and African World Music, and a minor in Anthropology). Dr. Kwaku has also produced two films: *Afrikan World Civilizations*, covering the history, culture, and accomplishments of Afrikan people around the world, the first of its kind, and *Afrikan World Masters*, featuring John Henrik Clarke, Ivan Van Sertima, Frances Cress Welsing, and Fela Anikulapo-Kuti. He also teaches adult and youth history classes in the Los Angeles community.

BRASS KNUCKLE FINANCE

THE ULTIMATE GUIDE FOR BEATING
DEBT, MASTERING YOUR MONEY AND
RECLAIMING YOUR LIFE!

BRASS KNUCKLE
FINANCE

JARIM
PERSON-LYNN

www.ingramcontent.com/pod-product-compliance
Lightning Source LLC
Chambersburg PA
CBHW072115270326
41931CB00010B/1568